TRUSTS

TRUSTS

Kenneth McK. Norrie, LL.B., D.L.P., Ph.D.
Lecturer in Law, University of Strathclyde

and

Eilidh M. Scobbie, M.A. LL.B.
Lecturer in Law, University of Aberdeen, Solicitor

with

Andrew M.C. Dalgleish, LL.B., N.P.
Solicitor, Edinburgh

W. GREEN/Sweet & Maxwell
Edinburgh
1991

First published in 1991
Reprinted 1993
Reprinted 1996

© 1991
W. GREEN & SON LTD.

ISBN 0 414 00965 7

A catalogue record for this book
is available from the British Library

Typeset by LBJ Enterprises Ltd, of Chilcompton and Tadley.
Printed and bound in Great Britain by
print in black, Midsomer Norton, Bath

To
Allison Margaret Hoskins
who was born on the day this book was conceived

PREFACE

For many years now Scotland has lacked an up-to-date textbook on the law of trusts which is short and is aimed at the needs of those coming fresh to the subject. The works on the Scots law of trusts that are currently available are either extremely detailed, entering the interstices and examining the intricacies of the subject; or part of a much larger work and not available as an independent entity. The present work is designed to fill this gap. It is hoped that this book will attract a readership both amongst those who have not examined the subject of trusts before, and those who have done so but for whom the relevant rules and principles are no longer as fresh as they once were.

The aim of the book is to present, in readable form, the rules and principles of the Scots law of trusts in a fashion that is easily understandable both to the student and the practitioner. We have attempted to present these rules and principles in a practical context, hoping that the reader will discover not only how trusts work, but also the various and sometimes unexpected uses to which the concept can be put.

The practice of trust law today is very closely linked to revenue law, for the consequences of dealing with property through the medium of a trust invariably involve taxation. We have therefore added 'Tax Points' throughout the book at those places in the text where the most significant tax consequences follow. The taxation of trusts is a whole subject in itself and would need a book many times larger than this to be comprehensive. Consequently the Tax Points are merely to put the practitioner on notice of matters that must be taken into consideration. For the tax lawyer dealing with trusts, it is hoped that this book will prove of some use beyond the Tax Points themselves: it is only by having a basic grounding and thorough understanding of the principles of trust law that a tax practitioner can argue successfully with the revenue authorities any tax point that he or she may be faced with in dealing with trusts in practice (see for example *Esdaile* v. *Inland Revenue* (1936) 20 T.C. 700, in which the issue was one of liability to income tax and it was resolved by analysing the powers and duties of the trustees in that case). This book attempts to provide that basic grounding. It should perhaps be remembered that tax law changes much more quickly than most areas of law, certainly trust law; and it follows that the precise rules given in the Tax Points are likely to become out of date sooner than the other rules contained in this book. However the points at which tax matters should be taken into consideration will change much less quickly, and consequently the notice given by the Tax Points ought to remain relevant.

As this book goes to press, Chancellor Lamont announced in the 1991 Budget Speech the beefing-up of the CGT rules (designed to counter the long-standing tax attractions of off-shore trusts for U.K. trusters). At the same time, the Inland Revenue issued a consultative document on the taxation of U.K. resident trusts, which, if implemented, would radically alter the computation of income tax and CGT for many trusts.

The writing of the basic text of this book was primarily undertaken by Kenneth Norrie. The Tax Points were primarily the responsibility of Eilidh Scobbie, though she added considerably to the way the whole text was finally presented. The third collaborator was Andrew Dalgleish, of Messrs. Brodies, W.S., Edinburgh, whose task was to read the completed text and to add such thoughts as would be appropriate for the trust practitioner, as well as any other thoughts he considered relevant. Together we hope that the text as finally presented in this book will prove useful for the student, the tax practitioner and the trust practitioner.

A number of individuals were kind enough to read various sections of this book in draft, and provided us with many helpful comments. We are accordingly grateful to the following people: Professor A. E. Anton, Professor D. J. Cusine, Professor M. C. Meston and Mrs J. H. Pearson, all of the University of Aberdeen, and (in particular, for reading the whole text) Professor R. A. Burgess of the University of Strathclyde.

Kenneth McK. Norrie
Eilidh M. Scobbie

CONTENTS

CHAPTER 13: VARIATION OF PUBLIC TRUSTS ..

CHAPTER 14: REVOCATION AND TERMINATION OF TRUSTS ....

TABLE OF CASES

TABLE OF STATUTES

xxiii

ABBREVIATIONS AND AUTHORITIES

A.C.	Law Reports, Appeal Cases (England)
App. Cas.	Appeal Cases (House of Lords)
All E.R.	All England Law Reports
Am. J. Comp. L.	American Journal of Comparative Law
Beav.	Beavan (English Reports, vols 48–55)
Brit. Tax Rev.	British Tax Review
CGT	Capital Gains Tax
CGTA 1979	Capital Gains Tax Act 1979
Ch.	Law Reports, Chancery Division (England)
Conv. Rev.	Conveyancing Review
Crim. L.R.	Criminal Law Review
D.	Dunlop (Session Cases)
D.L.R.	Dominion Law Reports (Canada)
Enc.	*Stair Memorial Encyclopaedia of the Laws of Scotland,* Law Society of Scotland/Butterworths, Edinburgh 1989
F.	Fraser (Session Cases)
FA	Finance Act
Green's Enc.	Encyclopaedia of the Laws of Scotland (1933 ed.), W. Green, Edinburgh
Halliday	Halliday, *Conveyancing Law and Practice,* W. Green, Edinburgh 1985–1990
Harv. L.R.	Harvard Law Review
I.C.L.Q.	International and Comparative Law Quarterly
ICTA 1988	Income and Corporation Taxes Act 1988
IHT	Inheritance Tax
IHTA 1984	Inheritance Taxes Act 1984
Int. Enc. Comp. L.	International Encyclopaedia of Comparative Law
J.L.S.S.	Journal of the Law Society of Scotland
J.R.	Juridical Review
Leg. Stud.	Legal Studies
M.	Macpherson (Session Cases)
Mackenzie Stuart	Mackenzie Stuart, *The Law of Trusts,* W. Green, Edinburgh 1932
McLaren	McLaren, *Wills & Succession,* 3rd Ed., Bell & Bradfute, Edinburgh 1894

Macl. & Rob.	Maclean and Robinson (English Reports, vol 9)
Macq.	Macqueen (House of Lords, Scotland)
Menzies	Menzies, *The Law of Scotland Affecting Trustees*, 2nd Ed., W. Green, Edinburgh 1913
Moffat & Chesterman	Moffat & Chesterman, *Trusts Law: Text and Materials*, Weidenfeld & Nicholson, London 1988
N.E.	North Eastern Law Reporter (U.S.A.)
New L.J.	New Law Journal
N.S.W.R.	New South Wales Reports
N.Z.L.R.	New Zealand Law Reports
Ockelton	Ockelton, *Trusts for Accountants*, Butterworths, London 1987
P.	Law Reports, Probate Division (England)
R.	Rettie (Session Cases)
Riddall	Riddall, *The Law of Trusts*, 3rd Ed., Butterworths, London 1987
S.	Shaw (Session Cases)
S.C.	Session Cases
S.C.L.R.	Scottish Civil Law Reports
S.L.R.	Scottish Law Reporter
S.L.T.	Scots Law Times
S.T.C.	Simon's Tax Cases
Stair	*Institutions of the Law of Scotland*
T.C.	Tax Cases
Todd	Todd, *Equity & Trusts: Text, Cases and Materials*, Blackstone Press, London 1989
W.L.R.	Weekly Law Reports
Walker	Walker, *Civil Remedies*, W. Green, Edinburgh 1974
Wilson & Duncan	Wilson & Duncan, *Trusts, Trustees and Executors*, W. Green, Edinburgh 1975

CHAPTER 1

INTRODUCTORY MATTERS

DEFINITION OF TRUST

A TRUST is a tripartite relationship, involving a truster, trustees and beneficiaries, which involves the passing of property for purposes. Though there may be other legal, particularly fiduciary, relationships which do not precisely fall within this definition but which are commonly dealt with under the law of trusts in a wide sense,[1] this definition does cover all forms of trust (in the narrow but more correct sense) that are recognised by the law of Scotland today, and it contains all the elements necessary to the concept of the trust. There must be three parties, the transfer of property and the laying down of trust purposes. McLaren brought out these elements when he defined the trust in the following way:

> "A trust may properly be defined as an interest created by the transfer of property to a trustee, in order that he may carry out the truster's directions respecting its management and disposal. This definition includes the two essentials of a trust, viz., the conveyance or transfer of the legal estate to a trustee, and the constitution of a trust purpose."[2]

McLaren's definition was cited with approval by Lord Reid in the House of Lords in the case of *Allan's Trs.* v. *I.R.C.*,[3] and it will be the one used as the basis for much of this book.

1. Three parties

A trust is the conglomerate of rights and obligations regulating the relationship between three categories of person.[4] First, there

[1] *e.g.* some forms of what are called "constructive trusts": see Chap. 4.
[2] At para. 1510.
[3] 1971 S.L.T. 62 at p. 63.
[4] McLaren at para. 1508.

is the truster who creates the trust by giving property to another person or persons to be used for the benefit of a third party. Secondly, there are the trustees, who take legal title to the property, but who are under a legal obligation to use the property for the achievement of the aims of the truster. Thirdly, there are the beneficiaries, who are the persons for whose benefit the property is to be used. In any given trust a single individual can fall into more than one of these categories. The truster may at the same time be the beneficiary or one of the beneficiaries; a trustee may be a beneficiary, or indeed may be the truster. The only combination that is legally impossible, for reasons to be discussed shortly, is that a sole trustee cannot be a sole beneficiary.

2. The passing of property

A trust is a proprietorial relationship, whereby title to property is held by the trustees to be used for the benefit of another person. If there is no property involved then any obligation the trustee has to the beneficiary is not really a trust obligation and, if legally enforceable, will more properly come under some other heading in law. Not only must there be property, but there must be a passing of ownership in that property, in the sense that the person who becomes the trustee must obtain some proprietorial right from the truster. Without such a passing of property there can be no trust (except in relation to trusts for administration,[5] where the truster is not divested of the property). A person who finds money in the street may be legally obliged to hand this in to the police,[6] but that is not a trust obligation since the finder does not take title to the money. Trustees on the other hand must take legal title to the property.[7] This title will give the trustees a real right in the property, which is enforceable even against the truster.

3. The laying down of purposes

A trust is a means whereby the property which has passed to the trustees will be used by them in a particular way which is legally

---

[5] See Chap. 2.
[6] Civic Government (Scotland) Act 1982, s.67(1).
[7] Though the trust may come into existence before title is completed in the names of the trustees (see Chap. 4), it is essential that this is the intention of the parties, and that the transfer of property is legally competent.

enforceable. The essence of a trust is its purposes. It is for the truster to lay down what the purposes are, that is what aims the trustees must achieve with the property. While the trustees have a real right in the trust property, the laying down of trust purposes confers on the beneficiaries a personal right against the trustees to insist that they carry out the purposes. The trust purposes therefore complete the legal relationship between the parties.

THE TRUST CONCEPT AND ITS CHARACTERISTICS

A trust constitutes a separate and independent category in law and will not fit neatly into any other legal relationship. It is clearly not a contract, for the remedies for breach of trust are of a different nature from the remedies for breach of contract,[8] and are more nearly delictual than contractual.[9] Nor is it analogous to the relationships of mandate or deposit[10] or principal and agent. In these, property does not vest in the mandatory, the depositary or the agent as it does in the trustee; and the relationship does not end on the death of the truster as it does on the death of the mandant, the depositee or the principal. The trust is a legal institution separate from and independent of all others. It is not itself a legal person, but the trustees acquire a new legal personality, separate from their own.

A trust has many characteristics, each of which can exist on its own in other legal relationships, but which together will make the relationship one of trust.

A trust is a strongly fiduciary relationship, indeed is the typical example of a fiduciary relationship. It is based on good faith, or trust, and this has a number of significant consequences, which will be mentioned throughout this book.

In Scots law the fundamental characteristic of the trust is that a real right to the trust property vests in the trustees, while a personal right vests in the beneficiaries which they can enforce against the trustees to ensure that the purposes are carried out. As Lord Moncreiff put it in *Inland Revenue* v. *Clark's Trs.*:

"The right of property in the estate of the trust is vested in the trustees to the exclusion of any competing right of property, and the right of the

---

[8] See Chap. 10.

[9] *Croskery* v. *Gilmour's Trs.* (1890) 17 R. 697.

[10] Though there are some similarities with these contracts: see Lord President Inglis in *Croskery* v. *Gilmour's Trs.*, *supra*, at p. 700.

> beneficiary . . . is merely a right *in personam* against the trustees to enforce their performance of the trust."[11]

This is however a very peculiar personal right since it is one that can, in some circumstances, defeat a real right. The trustee's right to the property is strictly constrained by the law of trusts, and by the right which that law confers upon the beneficiaries. So the right of the trustee does not transmit on his death to his successors, nor is it available for the satisfaction of the trustee's personal debts.[12]

If a single individual with the real right in the property (a sole trustee) becomes the person who alone has a personal right against the trustee (a sole beneficiary) the trust relationship is extinguished *confusione* as the legal and beneficial titles are thereby rejoined.[13]

THE DEVELOPMENT OF TRUSTS

According to the English legal historian Maitland, the development of the trust concept was "the greatest and most distinctive achievement performed by Englishmen in the field of jurisprudence."[14] It is frequently claimed that the trust is peculiarly English in concept and in origin, having been created solely by English legal thought, or, more correctly, by English legal procedure. While it is certainly true that the peculiar procedure adopted for the administration of justice in England did provide the background which allowed the trust as we know it today to take root and flower, it is as well to remember that the law of Rome contained institutions that could perform much the same functions.[15] However it cannot be denied that the English influence in this area of Scots law has been strong, though the trust in English law remains conceptually very different from the trust in Scots law.

The English idea of trust arose almost accidentally from the procedural intricacies of English law, whereby a dual system of jurisprudence had arisen as early as the fourteenth century.

---

[11] 1939 S.C. 11 at p. 26. It should be noted that the nature of the beneficiary's right may alter when the trust comes to an end: see *Johnston* v. *MacFarlane*, 1987 S.L.T. 593, and further, Chap. 14.

[12] *Heritable Reversionary Co. Ltd.* v. *Millar* (1891) 18 R. 1166.

[13] McLaren at para. 1512.

[14] Maitland, *Selected Historical Essays*, (1936), at p. 129.

[15] See Johnston *The Roman Law of Trusts*, Clarendon Press, Oxford (1988).

There were two judicial structures in England, consisting of the common law courts which administered law, and the Chancery courts which provided equitable relief when the application of strict law in the common law courts either gave no remedy or gave an unjust one. Equity was basically the application of the King's conscience to petitions brought before him. His confessor was the Chancellor and it was through the Chancellor's office, the Chancery, that such petitions were brought. As these petitions became more and more frequent the Chancery inevitably took on the characteristics of a court: thus evolved the Court of Chancery. The granting or rejecting of the petitions inevitably came to be decided upon by the application of rules which, to all but the English lawyer, were rules of law: thus evolved the Rules of Equity.

One of the most common types of case brought before the Court of Chancery was that involving the *Use*, which was a form of landholding particularly common in the early centuries after the Norman Conquest. Though originally designed as a means of avoiding the feudal burdens of landownership, it proved its usefulness and flexibility at the time when many of the great landowners of England went off on those reiving parties that history now refers to as the Crusades. These landowners would be unsure when, if ever, they would return, and so frequently transferred their lands to trusted companions, known as *feoffees to uses*, who would undertake in honour to give the land back when the landowner returned, or pass it on to the landowner's successor if his foray into the East resulted in his death. Many of these feoffees to uses proved themselves unworthy of the trust reposed in them, ignored what their honour demanded, and, founding on their legal title to the land, attempted to keep it themselves. The common law courts would recognise only the legal title and it was left to the Court of Chancery to impose an equitable obligation on the persons with legal title to fulfil their trust. It did so by evolving the theory of legal and equitable *estates* in land whereby one person (the trustee) could have the estate of legal ownership, while another person (the beneficiary)[16] had at the same time the estate of beneficial ownership. Both trustee and beneficiary had real though different rights in the property.

In Scotland early precursors of the trust tended to be public rather than private which was the norm in England. In Scotland

---

[16] Even today the beneficiary in England is often referred to in the Norman French as the *cestui que trust*.

land was often passed over for ecclesiastical uses or other public purposes. The *fideicommissum* of Roman law played a large part in the development of trust-like obligations in relation to land in Scotland, though that civilian institution is clearly part of the law of inheritance rather than any other category, which is probably why it assisted the development in Scotland of entails[17]. Similarly, the *familiae emptor* was an institution not far removed from what we now call a trust for administration. Canon law, as well as Roman law, influenced Scots law. Mortifications of land for ecclesiastical uses were recognised in Scotland through the influence of Canon law. By the Reformation it seems to have been established that the legal title to trust property rested with the trustee. This took Scots law well away from the contemporaneous development of *fideicommissum* in the civilian legal systems,[18] and put it much more on a par with English law. However, probably because Scotland has always had a unified system of law and equity, Scots law never adopted the theory of legal and equitable estates, with the result that Scots law never recognised that the beneficiary could have real rights in trust property. This is probably the single most important difference between Scots law and English law in relation to trusts.

Because the trust splits the legal ownership of property from the person who is to benefit from it, the trust was found to have great utility in Scotland. It proved a very efficacious means of ensuring that family property, in particular land, remained in a single family for generations, with the head of the family being effectively barred from disposing of the land outwith the family. The perception of land ownership in Scotland reflected a clan *more* that was very different from that pertaining in England.[19] The trust also proved particularly attractive to Scottish landowners during the dynastic struggles between the Stuarts and the Hanovers in the eighteenth century. The fear of forfeiture if one supported the wrong side could be obviated by having one's land held by a trustee, for the beneficial owner would then own nothing that could be forfeited. Again in the nineteenth century the private trust became common in Scotland owing to the dynastic aspirations of private individuals during that era; while the public trust became common owing to the rise of Victorian philanthropy. Many of the principles that are applied today

---

[17] Enc. 24:4.

[18] In, for example, German law the *fideicommissum* developed into the institution of *nacherbfolge*, which is similar to the Scottish idea of liferent and fee.

[19] See Kolbert & MacKay, *History of Scots and English Land Law* at pp. 177–182.

evolved during this period, independently of course of Roman law, but also independently of English law.[20]

The greatest English influence today in the Scots law of trusts is probably in the terminology used. It is not always the same, (for example the truster tends to be referred to as the settlor in England, and the trust itself as the settlement) but the phrases *constructive trust*, *resulting trust* and *cy près*, which originally came from England, are used in Scotland today. However, the substantive rules for each of these concepts differ somewhat in Scots law and in English law; indeed much of the English law of trusts appears to have a superficial similarity with Scots law, but is in its fundamentals very different. English law is today not always suitable to give an answer to a problem arising in the Scots law of trusts, except in relation to the taxation of charitable trusts where the English concept of charity is applied in Scotland.

MODERN FUNCTIONS OF THE TRUST CONCEPT

Throughout the centuries the trust has proved a remarkably resilient and flexible concept. Uses have been found for it that reflected the needs of the times. Its use in the eighteenth century as a means of avoiding forfeiture has already been mentioned. In the Victorian period it was often used as a means of controlling one's family, even after one's own death. Today, as well as retaining its old uses, the trust has been put to many new ones.[21] It is impossible here to be comprehensive, but the following paragraphs indicate most of the uses common in Scotland today.

1. Protection of the incompetent

One of the longest established uses to which the trust can be put is to protect the incompetent. Legally, property may be held by any person, but this would be unsatisfactory if the person were in some way legally incompetent and therefore unable to deal with the property. For example, a pupil child can own property but cannot deal with it himself. This is also the case with the mentally incompetent. If a person wishes to pass on property to such a

---

[20] See further, Burgess, "Thoughts on the Origins of the Trust in Scots Law" (1974) J.R. 196.

[21] The *International Encyclopaedia of Comparative Law* lists 26 different uses to which the trust can be put: see Vol. VI, Chap. 2, para. 1.

person, a sensible way of doing so is to set up a trust whereby competent persons are appointed trustees with the full complement of powers to deal with and administer the property, but with an obligation being imposed on the trustees to do so for the benefit of the incompetent.

A parent will frequently make provision for his death during his offspring's childhood by setting up a trust. Alternatively a regular income can be provided for someone not capable of managing his own affairs, by setting up a trust with competent trustees being appointed to administer the property. The trust may also be used in other circumstances in which a child comes to own significant amounts of money.[22]

2. Charitable or public uses

Another function of the trust concept that has been common for many centuries is its utilisation for charitable purposes or for the public good. If, for example, a landowner wishes to set aside land for use as a public park, or a person wishes to leave his money for educational purposes, either can be done efficaciously by means of a trust. Likewise historic buildings and areas of scenic beauty or scientific value can be protected by means of a trust and such properties are today often maintained from the income of a trust expressly set up for that purpose.[23] The achievement of public or charitable purposes is often easier and cheaper when a trust is used as opposed to administration by a local authority or use of a charitable corporation. Many established charities are in fact trusts, and indeed charitable trusts are extremely common in Scotland. Disaster funds that are set up in the wake of great public disasters normally utilise the trust concept by accepting donations from members of the public (the trusters) for equitable distribution amongst the victims, survivors and dependents of victims, of the disaster. Public trusts and charitable trusts are examined more fully in Chapter 2.

---

[22] Though it should be pointed out that the Scottish Law Commission sees objections to the use of the trust in administering children's property, and would prefer the court itself to take on the administration of funds, or to appoint a judicial factor: see S.L.C. Discussion Paper 88, *Parental Responsibilities and Rights, Guardianship and the Administration of Children's Property* October 1990 at paras. 4.1–4.12. See also *Scott* v. *Occidental Petroleum (Caledonia) Ltd.* 1990 S.L.T. 882.

[23] Indeed the tax legislation encourages such trusts: IHTA 1984, s.77 & Sched. 4; CGTA 1979, s.147A(2)(*b*) (iii); ICTA 1988, ss.690–694.

3. Protection of the improvident

It has been seen that the trust can be used to protect the incompetent (see 1 above); it can also be used to protect the improvident. A property owner may consider that his intended heir is likely to dissipate any property left to him, or is under the doleful influence of others; and a means of preventing the harmful consequences of this would be to create a trust with sensible provident trustees taking the legal title to the property, but with the beneficial interest resting with the improvident successor. A liferent is a common means by which this can be achieved and is discussed more fully in Chapter 2.

This use of the trust might prove particularly attractive if the property consists, for example, in a controlling shareholding of a family company, and the original owner, though intending his son to benefit financially, does not trust the son's business acumen sufficiently to look after the business properly. The shareholding might therefore be given to trustees, the purpose being to run the company in a sound commercial fashion, and to pay over the dividends to the son.

4. Manipulating control of companies

Following on from the above, the same process could be followed not to protect the improvident son, but simply to avoid any single person acquiring a controlling shareholding of a company. If for some commercial or other reason the original owner does not want another person or body to acquire a controlling shareholding in a company, a sufficient number of shares could be taken out of commercial circulation and put in trust. This might be a method of protecting the company from a hostile takeover. It should be recognised however that this procedure might well have the effect of limiting the company's freedom of manoeuvre, as the trust holding would be subject both to trust considerations and to commercial ones, and company decisions would be tightly bound into the welfare of the trust.[24]

5. Unincorporated bodies

In general, in Scots law, property can be held by institutions so long as they are recognised as having the status in law of a legal

---

[24] See a discussion of this in the English case of *Bartlett* v. *Barclay's Bank* (*No. 1*) [1980] 1 All E.R. 139. In the USA in the late 19th Century the trust was used as a means of gaining and maintaining control of a number of companies, to the detriment of competition. Thus today anti-monopoly legislation in that country is referred to as "anti-trust legislation."

person. Companies, Royal Corporations and chartered bodies are legal persons and can therefore hold property. Bodies that are unincorporated associations and lack legal personality cannot, in their own name, hold property. For example sports clubs, social clubs, many student organisations and societies, have no legal personality. Partnerships have legal personality in Scots law, but only in a limited sense, and they can hold moveable property in their own name, but not heritable property.

A way of allowing bodies that cannot hold property the benefits of doing so is to create a trust whereby the trustees will hold legal title to the property, with the purpose of the trust being to further the aims of the club, society or whatever. This is in fact a very ancient use of the trust, for before the Reformation many religious orders, such as the Franciscans, were forbidden to hold property, but could benefit from property held in trust on their behalf. Today it is very common for clubs and societies to hold money, with the treasurer and other office bearers being trustees of the fund. Trade unions normally have their funds vested in trustees. With partnerships heritable property is commonly held on the firm's behalf by some or all of the partners as trustees for the firm.

6. Sequestration

A rather more specialised use of the trust concept is on an individual's sequestration. When a person becomes insolvent, the court may be asked to award sequestration of his estate under the terms of the Bankruptcy (Scotland) Act 1985. The debtor's property will vest through this procedure in a trustee in sequestration who will administer it for the benefit of creditors and distribute it in accordance with the statutory rules. Apart from the special rules in the 1985 Act, the principles governing ownership of the property, and the rights and liabilities of the trustees and beneficiaries, are similar to those appropriate in any other sort of trust.

7. Marriage trusts

Formerly, a common use of the trust concept was in relation to the ante-nuptial marriage contract, whereby a woman would give her property to a trustee just before her marriage, she retaining the beneficial right. This was a means of protecting the woman's assets at a time when one of the legal consequences of marriage was the transfer of control of the woman's property to her husband. This rule was finally abolished by the Married Women's Property (Scotland) Act 1920, and the ante-nuptial marriage contract became less common.

With the increasing incidence of divorce in modern society it is possible that something analogous to the ante-nuptial trust will again prove useful. If it is foreseeable that a marriage will not last a lifetime, a way of avoiding the financial arguments that frequently embitter the parties to a divorce would be to make provision for the holding of property in trust, with the aim of dividing it out equitably on the break-up of marriage. There may be a problem in relation to such a provision's validity. In the English case of *Re Johnston's Will Trusts*[25] a trust was set up which made provision by a father whereby his daughter was to receive certain sums in the event of her divorcing her husband. Clearly the father's intention was to provide for his daughter only if her husband stopped supporting her; but the court held that the provision was void as being contrary to public policy in that it amounted to an encouragement to the daughter to divorce her husband. It is submitted that such a provision may be a sensible one to deal with an event that is undesirable but foreseeable, so long as it does not encourage the undesirable event itself.

8. Tombstones and animals

It is very common for people to desire that after death their graves be marked with a tombstone, or that their pet animals be cared for. One way of achieving these aims which is legally enforceable is through the utilisation of the trust concept.

The general principle in relation to validity, which will be examined more fully in Chapter 4, is that a trust purpose is valid only when it confers some beneficial interest in property on another living person. However the law allows an exception to this by recognising as valid a trust purpose for the provision, on a customary and rational scale, of a burial place for a deceased, and a suitable memorial to his memory.[26] Lord Justice-Clerk Aitchison described this as a concession or indulgence shown by the law, which is based upon the "natural and human sentiments

---

[25] [1967] 1 All E.R. 553.
[26] *Per* Lord Kyllachy in *McCaig* v. *University of Glasgow*, 1907 S.C. 231 at p. 244.

of ordinary people who desire that there should be some memorial to themselves."[27] Likewise a person may wish to make provision for the continued comfort of a pet animal. The law of Scotland is likely to recognise this as a valid provision in law.[28]

While a provision for a tombstone or for an animal is likely to be considered valid, the issue of its enforceability has proved more awkward. If there is no person upon whom a beneficial interest is conferred, there will be no one with an interest to enforce the trust. The result of this it that while the trustees would be *entitled* to carry out the trust purpose because it is valid, they might not be *bound* to do so because there would be no one to challenge them if they decided not to carry it out, contrary to the wishes of the truster. One way around this difficulty would be to create an interest in favour of some person, and to make the taking of that interest conditional on that person ensuring that the trust purpose be carried out. It is perfectly competent for a trustee to be one of the beneficiaries, and it would therefore be possible to give a trustee some benefit on the condition that he ensures that a tombstone is put in place, or a pet animal is properly looked after. It is difficult to see how, apart from the medium of the trust, such a direction could otherwise be legally enforceable.[29]

9. Pension funds

An important modern use of the trust concept is to preserve and administer large funds such as pension schemes. Most employers now provide some form of retirement pension for their employees, with the employees and employer contributing funds during the working lives of the employees, which are used to provide pensions on the employees' retirement. Pension funds of this nature are now commonly vested in trustees who administer the funds; and nowadays these funds control vast amounts of money. In financial terms, this may well be the most significant use to which the trust concept is put today.

10. Unit trusts

Many small investors are unable to gain the protection of proper diversification because of the limited size of their funds.

---

[27] *Lindsay's Ex.* v. *Forsyth*, 1940 S.C. 568 at p. 572.

[28] For a fuller discussion, see Norrie, "Trusts for Animals" (1987) 32 J.L.S. 386. In *Re Thomson* [1934] Ch. 342 the English court held that a trust for the promotion of fox hunting was a valid (but not charitable) trust.

[29] Though during life this result can simply be achieved by contract (*e.g.* with an undertaker).

The unit trust gets round this problem and is consequently another highly significant modern use of the trust concept. A unit trust is a scheme whereby shares are held by trustees (normally corporate bodies like banks), and managed by professional managers for the benefit of investors who purchase units of the whole fund. Today these funds, like pension schemes, control vast sums of money.

11. The creation of remedies

The concept of the constructive trust is being used more and more by courts in other countries to provide proprietorial remedies in the absence of any other. This illustrates the flexible nature of the trust institution. One example of this approach comes from the United States of America, where the constructive trust is used to achieve the aims of the remedy of unjustified enrichment. If a person is enriched in an unjustified manner to the detriment of an innocent party, then the enriched person holds that enrichment on a constructive trust for the benefit of the innocent party. Another example comes from England where the constructive trust is used to get around the doctrine of privity of contract, which in that legal system prevents a third party to a contract from suing for benefits that the contract is designed to give him. If one of the contracting parties obtains the benefit designed for a third party, that contracting party may be held to be holding that benefit on trust for the third party.[30]

12. Statutory schemes

The trust is occasionally used by statute to achieve certain aims of the legislature. For example, in encouraging employees to obtain proprietorial interests in their employing companies, the Government has provided certain tax incentives for employers to establish employee share ownership trusts, as defined by and administered in accordance with the provisions of sections 67–73 and Sched. 5 of the Finance Act 1989. Likewise the medium of the trust has been used to transfer into public ownership educational endowments (see sections 105–122 of the Education (Scotland) Act 1980, as amended) and hospital trusts (see sections 11

---

[30] See the discussion in Cheshire, Fifoot and Furmston, *The Law of Contract*, (11th ed. 1986) Butterworths, London at p. 442–444.

and 12 of the National Health Service (Scotland) Act 1978). Though set up, and to a certain extent controlled, by statute these trusts are for all other intents and purposes normal trusts, and they do not, in Scots law, form a separate category to which special rules are applied.

13. The retention of family wealth

A common feature of those people who have wealth is that they generally want to keep it. More than that, they generally want to ensure that as much of it as possible remains in their family. For such people, the use of the trust is particularly efficacious, for the trust separates the legal ownership from the beneficial interest and at times the tax consequences of this split have provided encouragement for the use of the trust. Probably the most common motivation today behind the setting up of private trusts is that it provides a means of transmitting property down through the generations of a family in a way that is most efficient (that is, in a way that attracts the least taxation liability).

14. Protection during disputes

It can happen that during, for example, a conveyancing transaction, a dispute arises concerning a contractual term, which will not be resolved until after the purchaser has taken entry to the property. A way of protecting the parties is to place the purchase price on deposit receipt in the names of the respective solicitors, who then become trustees of the fund. Once the dispute is resolved, the trustees will pay the money out to the parties according to their entitlements.

15. Miscellaneous

The above are only some of the more common uses to which the trust concept can be put today. It is an exceedingly flexible institution and is capable of acquiring new and sometimes surprising functions: it is probably impossible to list all the potential uses to which it can be put. It can deal with unusual and unexpected situations. For example in 1979 the civil servants at Register House in Edinburgh went on strike. As a matter of conveyancing law, real rights in land do not vest in purchasers until such time as their titles have been registered or recorded, and the 1979 strike threatened to put the whole process of land transfer in Scotland into jeopardy. The problem was alleviated (though not completely solved) by sellers of land constituting themselves as trustees of the land for the benefit of the purchasers.

CONCLUSION

These then are a few of the uses to which the trust can be put. It can be protective, of person or property; it can achieve desirable aims, of a public or private nature; it can be remedial, for the benefit of those without any other remedy; or it can be distributive, in the sense of transferring wealth in a tax advantageous manner. There are innumerable other purposes of the trust, many of which will be mentioned in the following pages of this book.

Clearly the trust can not be dismissed as having outlived its usefulness. For the student its usefulness is possibly even greater, because the study of the law of trusts helps our understanding of the nature of property, of remedies, of equity, and of the legal system itself.

CHAPTER 2

TYPES OF TRUST

Introduction

THERE are many different forms of trust set up today, which reflect the various uses[1] to which the trust concept can be put. The law of Scotland classifies trusts in many ways that have no real legal consequence. The rules of validity, administration, investment, liability and distribution are in most cases the same, whatever is the nature or purpose of the trust. However it is possible to make certain factual classifications, which, in some respects, do carry legal consequences.

INTER VIVOS AND *MORTIS CAUSA* TRUSTS

Trusts may be classified according to whether they are *inter vivos* or *mortis causa*. An *inter vivos* trust is one that is designed to take effect during the life of the truster. A truster may establish a trust during his life for a variety of reasons, for example because the purpose of the trust requires to be carried out immediately, or because the truster wants to see the achievement of the purpose during his life, or because he foresees the possibility of losing his own competence to deal properly with his own property. One type of *inter vivos* provision is where the truster sets up

---

[1] See Chap. 1.

a trust for the benefit of those whom he wishes to succeed to his property on his death, but reserving a liferent to himself. This may be desirable because it will minimise the size of claims for legal rights by a widow(er) or children on the death of the truster: effectively the truster's estate for succession purposes is the accrued trust income rather than the trust fund itself.

Tax Point
This is only so for succession purposes, not for tax purposes. For the purposes of calculating IHT, the capital value of the liferented fund must be aggregated with the truster's own estate (IHTA 1984, s.49).

Ante-nuptial trusts were previously another common form of *inter vivos* trust.

Tax Point
Where the ante-nuptial trust funds derive from one spouse and the trust provides that the income from these funds will be paid to the other spouse, the truster-spouse will always be taxed on the trust income (ICTA 1988, s.685).

A *mortis causa* trust (otherwise known as a trust disposition and settlement) is one that the truster intends to take effect only from his death. This sort of trust allows the truster to retain full control over his own property during his life, thus permitting him to change his mind at any time. On his death the trust becomes effective: it is really a will that has on-going purposes. As a will, it has no legal effect before the death of the truster, and is consequently not really a trust until then.

The *mortis causa* trust and the *inter vivos* trust are treated by the law in exactly the same way, except for the practical point of when the trust becomes effective.

Tax Point
Whether a trust is *inter vivos* or *mortis causa* has practical tax consequences. As far as IHT is concerned the setting up of an *inter vivos* trust will either be a transfer of property that is potentially exempt from the tax (IHT will be payable only if the truster dies within seven years of the transfer) or IHT will be calculated at lifetime rates—one half of the rates applicable if the trust is *mortis causa* (and with an additional tax charge if the truster dies within seven years).

Likewise, transferring assets into an *inter vivos* trust will normally give rise to a CGT assessment for the truster, whereas assets pass into a *mortis causa* trust without CGT being payable.

PUBLIC TRUSTS AND PRIVATE TRUSTS

A distinction that has greater legal consequence is that between public trusts and private trusts. A private trust is a trust designed to benefit a specified individual or a specified group of individuals, and it is probably true to say that this is the typical type of trust in Scotland. So it is common for a truster to set up a trust for the benefit of his children, or his grandchildren, or for the benefit of named friends or acquaintances, or for the achievement of a purpose that benefits a particular individual or a restricted group of individuals. A public trust on the other hand is one that is set up for the benefit of the public in general, or of a specified class of the public in general. Public trusts benefit a potentially far wider group of people than do private trusts. For example a public trust might be set up for the benefit not of the truster's children but of all children living in a specified locality, or all children in a specified class, such as "orphans" or "native Gaelic speakers." Public trusts can be set up for a very large variety of purposes, and their determining feature is the fact that the benefit is conferred on the public or some specified portion thereof. The trust must confer some *benefit on* the public, and not simply be a trust within the public domain. The benefit conferred need not be a pecuniary one, but may for example be educational, environmental, or cultural. A public trust might be set up for the relief of poverty, or for the eradication of a disease, or for educational purposes, or for the establishment of a hospital or a school or an observatory, or for the protection of a species of animal or an historic building or a piece of land, or to provide income for a museum or a sports centre or some other public utility.

    "The primary distinction between a private and a public trust purpose lies in the truster's intention. In a public trust, the intention is not to confer benefit on any particular recipient, but upon the public. There may be a particular recipient or recipients; but they will take the benefit not as individual objects of the truster's bounty, but as vehicles for an intention which had a general and not a specific object, a public not a private end."[2] It may sometimes be difficult to distinguish between a large group of individuals and a limited section of the public. In *Salvesen's Trs.* v. *Wye*[3] a testator left a legacy to his "poor relatives, friends or acquaintances." This could potentially be a very wide class, and therefore possibly a public trust, but Lord President Cooper held that the "dominant determining factor" which defined the potential beneficiaries was the fact that they were connected with the truster, rather than the fact that they were poor: conse-

[2] Enc 24. 86.
[3] 1954 S.C. 440.

quently he held that this would be a private trust rather than a public trust.[4]

In most cases the distinction is easy to draw, but sometimes there are borderline cases in which drawing the distinction is more difficult. In *Glentanar* v. *Scottish Industrial Musical Association*[5] the truster gave a silver shield to a musical association, the purpose of the trust being to present the shield to the winners of an annual musical competition to be organised by the trustees. For reasons to be discussed shortly, it became important to know whether this was a public trust or a private trust, and the judges in the Second Division were rather equivocal in their reasoning. For practical reasons they clearly wanted to hold this to be a private trust, and in the end they did so. They held that because the trust was not a public trust "in the full and proper sense of the term,"[6] it should be considered a private trust. The result in this case has been criticised by Wilson and Duncan, who are of the view that the trust was clearly public.[7] However the decision can be defended on the ground that, if one accepts that the normal category in Scots law is the private trust, then one may properly start off with the presumption that a trust is private, and put the onus of proving otherwise on those who disagree. Such a presumption would be dislodged only if the trust clearly had the characteristics that would put it into the category of public trusts.

For most purposes of administration and validity, the public trust is treated in law in the same way as the private trust, but there are some circumstances in which it is of fundamental importance to know to which category the trust belongs.

First, in private trusts the truster has the right to appoint new trustees on the failure of the old[8]; this power does not inherently exist in public trusts, in which the truster retains far less interest. This was the cause of the problem in *Glentanar*, because on the failure of the original trustees the truster wished to make a new appointment: his power to do so depended upon the trust being private.

Secondly, who has title to sue the trustees in order to force them to carry out the trust purposes depends upon whether the trust is private or public. Private trusts can be enforced by any identifiable beneficiary, or by the truster. With public trusts on the other hand any identifiable or potential beneficiary may sue,

[4] In fact the gift was held to be void for uncertainty: see Chap. 6.
[5] 1925 S.C. 226.
[6] *Per* Lord Anderson, *ibid.* at p. 233.
[7] Wilson & Duncan at p. 170.
[8] See Chap. 5.

as may the Lord Advocate, representing the public interest. There is some doubt whether any member of the public can raise an action by way of *actio popularis* to enforce a public trust,[9] but the search for a precise answer is probably vain. With a public trust as with a private trust those who may benefit may sue to enforce it; with public trusts that class by definition will be large and will include any person who may receive benefit, of whatever nature, from the carrying out of the purposes. In *Andrews* v. *Ewart's Trs*,[10] which involved a trust for the establishment of a school, it was held that title to sue rested with "all members of the public who have, or may have, occasion to avail themselves of the means of education afforded by the High School."[11] This may amount in effect, if not in form, to an *actio popularis*.

Thirdly, public trusts are entitled to receive a benignant construction, that is the court will be rather more liberal in the interpretation of public trust deeds than of other deeds. There is again doubt about the extent to which the court can take this benignant construction, but it is probably true to say that the court will make a greater effort to save the validity of a trust that is designed for public benefit than to save the validity of a merely private trust. The court cannot ignore formal deficiencies in the deed, but it can try to avoid the truster's clear intentions from being defeated for technical reasons. For example, while trust purposes must be laid down with sufficient certainty before the law will give effect to them,[12] the court will accept as sufficient vaguer words in public trusts than in private trusts. A trust for "charities" with no other qualification is a valid public purpose,[13] notwithstanding the very many and diverse forms of charitable organisations that exist today.

Fourthly, the court can exercise a wider jurisdiction over the administration of public trusts than it can over private trusts. The Scottish court generally has very little power to involve itself in the administration of trusts, but in the case of a public trust if the

---

[9] See McLaren at para. 1691, Mackenzie Stuart at p. 110, Enc 24. 85 and Lord Jauncey in *Russell's Ex.* v. *Balden*, 1989 S.L.T. 177, who all think that this is competent in Scotland; but see Wilson & Duncan at p. 149, and Lord Cottenham L.C. in *Ewing* v. *Glasgow Commissioners of Police* (1839) MacL. & Rob. 847 at p. 860 to the contrary. Doubtless the English judge is less authoritative in Scotland than is Lord Jauncey. In *Andrews* v. *Ewart's Trs.* (1886) 13 R. (H.L.) 69, Lord Watson, at p. 73, assumed without comment that the action he was dealing with was an *actio popularis*.

[10] (1886) 13 R. (H.L.) 69.

[11] *Per* Lord Watson *ibid.* at p. 73.

[12] See Chap. 6.

[13] *Ibid.*

purposes fail or otherwise prove impossible, the court can step in and, in the exercise of its *nobile officium*, sanction a *cy près* settlement to vary the original public purposes. This is not available for private trusts, which have quite different rules for variation.[14]

TRUSTS FOR LIFERENT AND FEE

One of the most common types of trust found in Scotland today is one that provides for the income of property to be paid to one person (the liferenter) during a specified period (commonly the life of the liferenter), while the capital is given to another person (the fiar) at the termination of the period. The right to the income is known as a liferent, and the right to the capital is known as the fee. These can be set up in such a way that the liferenter actually acquires title to the property, subject to his not being able to dispose of it on his death except in the way in which the original truster laid down. This is called a proper liferent. In the trust situation there is what may be called an improper, or a beneficiary,[15] liferent whereby the property is passed on to trustees, who are then obliged to hold and administer the property, paying the income to the liferenter, and on his death transferring the property to the fiar.[16] Liferents are popular because of the flexibility that it is possible to build into them, for example by giving to trustees powers of advancement of capital to either liferenter or fiar, and indeed by giving the right to determine who will take the capital on the termination of the liferent.

A type of liferent that is very common in Scotland is the alimentary liferent, whereby property is given to trustees who are to use it to provide the liferenter with funds from which his maintenance and support is drawn, or his education paid. An alimentary liferent is designed to provide the liferenter with funds from which he draws his very living: it is a gift for the mainte-

---

[14] For the variation of private trusts, see Chap. 12; and for the variation of public trusts, see Chap. 13.

[15] This is the way these liferents are described by Dobie, in *Manual of the Law of Liferent and Fee in Scotland*, W. Green, Edinburgh 1941, (a book which remains of great use today).

[16] It is to be borne in mind that in the absence of anything in the trust deed the Apportionment Act 1870, c. 35 will govern the apportionment of trust funds between income and capital.

nance or the education, rather than for the enjoyment or the entertainment, of the liferent.

An alimentary liferent differs from the normal liferent in two main ways. First, insofar as it is not excessive for the liferenter's maintenance and support at the level to which he is accustomed, an alimentary liferent will be protected from the claims of his creditors.[17] Secondly, once the alimentary liferenter accepts the liferent, he cannot thereafter renounce it (though this rule is qualified by section 1(4) of the Trusts (Scotland) Act 1961,[18] which allows the court to authorise the variation or revocation of an alimentary liferent). A liferent may lose its alimentary nature if the reason why it was set up no longer exists. For example a liferent for the education of the beneficiary will become an ordinary (and therefore revocable) liferent when the beneficiary leaves full-time education.[19]

Tax Point

During the existence of the liferent (whether alimentary or not) the general rule is that basic rate income tax is payable by the trustees on all the trust income. The liferenter will therefore receive income which has already borne basic rate income tax and the trustees are under a duty in each tax year to issue to the liferenter a form R185E in which is disclosed the gross and the net income. If he is a basic rate taxpayer, the liferenter will pay no more; if he is a higher rate taxpayer he will have to pay the excess over the basic rate himself; if his income does not bring him within the tax net at all, he will be able to reclaim the tax paid by the trustees. This complicated process can be short-circuited by paying the income direct to the beneficiary, if that beneficiary undertakes to account to the Inland Revenue for the income.

The trustees are charged CGT at the basic rate on their aggregate chargeable gains, after deducting the annual exemption (CGTA 1979, sched. 1, paras 5 and 6). The termination of the liferent is treated for CGT purposes as a disposal of the appropriate trust assets at market value, and at the same time the trustees are treated as having reacquired these assets on behalf of the fiar at that valuation (CGTA 1979, ss.54 and 55). This will create a liability on the trustees to pay CGT, except that where the fee becomes available on the death of the liferenter, there is no CGT liability on this notional disposal (CGTA 1979, s.55).

For IHT purposes the liferenter is treated as if he owned all the trust property: this is because he is said to have an "interest in possession" (defined for Scotland somewhat unhelpfully in IHTA 1984, s.46). This English term is taken to mean "the present right to the present enjoyment" of the trust funds,[20] which clearly includes a liferenter in Scotland. If the liferent ends

[17] Any excess will be available to creditors; *Livingstone* v. *Livingstone* (1886) 14 R. 43.

[18] See Chap. 12.

[19] *McMurdo's Trs.* v. *McMurdo* (1897) 24 R. 458.

[20] *Per* Viscount Dilhorne in *Pearson* v. *Inland Revenue* [1981] A.C. 753 at p. 772, quoted with approval in the First Division by Lord Kincraig in *Robertson's Trs.* v. *Inland Revenue* 1987 S.L.T. 534 at p. 536.

during his life (*e.g.* on renunciation, or because it was for a period shorter than his life), this would be a transfer of assets that is potentially exempt from paying IHT (it being actually exempted on the beneficiary surviving seven years thereafter) (IHTA 1984, ss.3, 3A and 52). If however the liferent ends because of the death of the liferenter, the capital of the trust fund is to be aggregated with the liferenter's own estate, this in order to determine the total IHT payable on his death (IHTA 1984, s.94(1)). The trustees will be liable for a *pro rata* share of the IHT due on the total (IHTA 1984, s.200).

DISCRETIONARY TRUSTS

Though there is no special category of "discretionary trust" generally recognised by Scots law to which different rules apply, the term "discretion" does have some importance, for in nearly every trust the trustees will be empowered to exercise some element of discretion. In the course of administering a trust estate decisions will inevitably have to be made by the trustees, for example when to sell a trust asset, or in what to invest the trust funds. Though often referred to as a "power" of the trustee, the exercise of a discretion is more often a duty, in the sense that it must be exercised; the only power the trustees have being in choosing how to exercise it. This is the sense in which "discretion" will be used in the following discussion. The possibility of giving the trustees a discretion in the running of the trust, and in its distribution, gives the trust great flexibility since the trustees can thereby react to changing family and, importantly, tax circumstances without any extra authorisation; and can do as they think best for the beneficiaries without undue limitations imposed by the trust deed. They may be given discretion as to when and for how long to accumulate income; when and how to advance capital, or to allocate some or all of the capital to one or more beneficiaries to the exclusion of others; and they will usually have a discretion over how to administer the property, where to invest it, and when to realise it.

1. The exercise of a discretion

In exercising a discretionary power, the trustees must make their own decisions, and bear the consequences thereof themselves. The court in Scotland is loath to become involved in the administration of trusts and will not give the trustees directions as to how best to exercise their discretion. As Wilson and Duncan put it,

"In Scotland the cardinal principle is that the courts will not control the exercise of a discretion which has been conferred on trustees. 'The great principle in the administration of Scotch testamentary trusts is, to leave the administration where the testator himself has placed it, unless from fault or accident the trust has become unworkable.' "[21]

The law takes this view because it assumes that the trustees are in the best position to make judgments properly, being more cogniscant of the circumstances of the trust than the court ever can be.

Nor can the trustees' exercise of their discretion be challenged, unless the way it is exercised amounts to a breach of trust, or is clearly unreasonable. In *Chivas' Trs.* v. *Stewart*[22] the trustees were empowered to lay aside such sum as they thought fit for the payment of an annuity to a beneficiary. They were extremely generous in the amount they chose, but when this was challenged the Second Division held that it was not so extravagant an exercise of the trustees' power that the court could interfere. In *Brown* v. *Elder's Trs*,[23] the Lord Ordinary refused to interfere in the exercise of their discretion, on the ground that to do so would in effect amount to the court substituting its own judgment for that of those who were given the right to exercise judgment by the truster. On the other hand, in *Thomson* v. *Davidson's Trs.*,[24] in which trustees had been directed to grant relief to descendants of the truster, and they offered 12 shillings and sixpence a week to a widow with six children, the Second Division held that this was plainly unreasonable, and the trustees were directed to pay the widow £10 annually per child. It was however emphasised that this was an exceptional case. Lord Justice-Clerk Moncrieff said this:

"These questions in regard to the administration of trust-funds are of some delicacy, because they involve to a certain extent a supervision of the operations of the trustees. I am not of opinion that it is desirable in the ordinary case to interfere with the discretion of trustees acting reasonably in the discharge of their discretion. That is, I say, a delicate matter, and, generally speaking, the trustees may be said to be the better judges of such questions."[25]

If the trust deed allows the trustees to do nothing, they must make a positive decision to do nothing, but a failure to exercise

[21] At p. 334, quoting Lord President Inglis in *Orr Ewing* v. *Orr Ewing's Trs.* (1884) 11 R. 600 at p. 627. See also *Hall's Trs.* v. *McArthur* 1918 S.C. 646.
[22] 1907 S.C. 701.
[23] (1906) 13 S.L.T. 837.
[24] (1888) 15 R. 719.
[25] *Ibid.* at p. 722.

the discretion at all will render the trustees in breach of trust, and anyone who may potentially benefit has title to sue the trustees. In an action by a potential beneficiary asking the trustees to choose a beneficiary, the court can order the trustees to exercise their discretion, but cannot order them to exercise it in any particular individual's favour, not even that of the pursuer: the court has no right to say how the discretion is to be exercised, merely to say that it must be. This can be illustrated by *Ross* v. *Governors of Heriot's Hospital*.[26] Here a trust was set up to provide for the maintenance and education of certain classes of person, including, primarily, descendants of the truster, secondly, "poor fatherless children of freemasons and burgesses of the town of Edinburgh," and thirdly, other deserving applicants. The pursuer, who was a descendant of the truster and thus a member of a favoured class, raised an action to force the trustees to exercise their discretion in his favour. It was held that while the pursuer had title to raise the action to force the trustees to exercise their discretion, he could not force them to exercise it in his favour: all the court decree could do was to force the trustees to give the pursuer proper consideration, and they would be perfectly entitled, after that consideration, to decide to exercise the discretion in favour of someone else. The right to benefit from a discretionary trust is dependent not only on the applicant being a member of a specified class, but also on the trustees exercising a choice in the applicant's favour.[27] The court did however point out that as the pursuer was a member of a preferred class, the trustees would not be entitled to choose a member of a postponed class to benefit instead of the pursuer.

2. Administrative and dispositive discretions

Many discretions granted to trustees are of an administrative nature, concerning whether to sell, when to invest, and other matters in relation to the general day to day running of the trust. Sometimes however a grant of discretionary power is made in relation to the actual interests of the beneficiaries. Trustees are often empowered to exercise a discretion in such matters as who is actually to benefit from the trust, in what proportions and when they are to benefit, or in some other way concerning the nature and extent of the interests in the trust. The trustees have a

[26] (1843) 5 D. 589.
[27] *Ibid.*, *per* Lord Fullerton at p. 604.

dispositive rather than an administrative discretion, that is a discretion involving the very disposition of the trust estate rather than its mere administration. From the point of view of the beneficiaries, because it affects their entitlement under the trust, it is a dispositive discretion that is the more significant; and from the point of view of the law it is this form of discretion that is the more problematic.

A dispositive discretion can be granted in both private and public trusts. In private trusts the trustees may be empowered to choose from a specified class of individuals who is to take the trust estate. For example, a controlling shareholding in a family company may be left to whichever of the truster's children is, in the opinion of the trustees, most commercially competent. A farm business could be left to whichever of the truster's nephews has, in the opinion of the trustees, shown most interest in following a career in farming. The trustees would then have the power to choose from within the class of potential beneficiaries who is to become the actual beneficiary.[28] In public trusts, trustees may be directed to use the money for the achievement of some public purpose. The trustees would have to choose how best to achieve the purpose, or which organisation with the specified aim should receive the funds. A trust estate could be left for the furtherance of "charitable works," with the trustees being left to exercise a discretion by choosing to which particular charity from the whole field of charities to pay the money.

Tax Point

This distinction between administrative and dispositive discretions is, in private trusts, critical for IHT liability. Where the discretion is dispositive (in the sense described above) the IHT discretionary trust regime (described below) will apply. But if the discretion is administrative, although the trust can be described as containing discretionary clauses, it is not discretionary for IHT purposes. Instead the "interest in possession" regime (discussed under "Liferent and Fee" above) will apply. In the words of Viscount Dilhorne, "sometimes the line between an administrative and a dispositive power may be difficult to draw, but that does not mean that there is not a valid distinction".[29] In *Robertson's Trs* v. *Inland Revenue*[30] the Court of Session was called upon to make the distinction where the right of a liferentrix was subject to the trustees' power to appropriate part of the trust income to meet capital depreciation of trust assets. This power was held to be an administrative discretion, with the

---

[28] Though in fact it would be unusual for the truster to lay down the basis upon which the choice is to be made. Discretionary powers are usually granted fairly widely.

[29] In *Pearson* v. *Inland Revenue* [1981] A.C. 753 at p. 775.

[30] 1987 S.L.T. 534.

result that the liferentrix had an "interest in possession" in the trust fund and was therefore subject to the tax regime referable to that (described under "Liferent and Fee" above).

The distinction between administrative and dispositive discretions is important, not only for tax reasons, shortly to be further discussed, but also because there are consequences relating to who is entitled to exercise either form of discretion.

3. Who may exercise discretionary powers

Any person finding himself in the position of trustee is entitled to exercise discretionary powers, so long as these are administrative in nature.[31] However if the discretion is dispositive in that it concerns the nature or extent of the beneficiary's interest, then not everyone who comes to be in the position of trustee is entitled to exercise the discretion. For example, someone in the position of trustee but who takes his authority from the court rather than the truser may not be able to exercise a dispositive discretion. In *Robbie's J.F.* v. *Macrae*,[32] a testatrix directed her executors to pay the residue of her estate to such charitable purposes as they thought proper: the class of potential beneficiaries, all charities, was laid down, and the executors were appointed to choose which particular charity should receive the benefit. However, the executors died before they had the chance to make that choice, and a judicial factor was appointed to the estate by the court. It was held that the right to make the choice was personal to the executors nominated by the truser, and could not be exercised by anyone else. Thus the gift failed. This decision was later explained by Lord Jauncey[33] as being based on the rationale that the executors took their authority from the testatrix, while the judicial factor took his authority from the court: since the court cannot exercise a discretionary power, neither can the appointees of the court.

A rather different approach which achieved the same result was adopted in *Angus's Exx.* v. *Batchan's Trs.*[34] There a Will contained a provision to the effect, "all moneys after paying, please give to charities," but no trustee or executor was

[31] *Per* Lord President Cooper in *Angus's Exx.* v. *Batchan's Trs.*, 1949 S.C. 335 at p. 368.
[32] (1893) 20 R. 358.
[33] In *Russell's Ex.* v. *Balden* 1989 S.L.T. 177.
[34] 1949 S.C. 335.

appointed. A majority of a Court of Seven Judges held that the gift was void for uncertainty and that the court had no power to appoint a judicial factor who could exercise the dispositive discretion. The basis of the decision in this case was the concept of *delectus personae*: it was pointed out that the only justification for allowing the truster's nominees to choose the recipients of the truster's benevolence is the fact that specifically chosen individuals can be taken to be aware of the truster's preferences and prejudices, and will make a choice that reflects them. Thus if a truster indicates a wide class of potential beneficiaries, the truster must specifically choose the people who are to make the choice from within that class.

Various categories of trustees have no real connection with the truster. Assumed trustees for example are chosen by the existing trustees. Trustees appointed under section 22 of the Trusts (Scotland) Act 1921 are appointed by the court, as are judicial factors and executors dative: none is chosen by the truster. If the exercise of a dispositive discretion depends on *delectus personae*, then none of these would have the power to exercise such a discretion. However, illogically, that was not what was held in *Angus's Exx.*, for there it was expressly accepted that assumed trustees were entitled to exercise a dispositive discretion.[35] In contrast, the ground of decision in *Robbie's J.F.*, as analysed by Lord Jauncey, has no such logical flaw and is therefore more persuasive: those who represent the court, such as judicial factors, cannot exercise a discretion that the court could not exercise; and those who represent the truster can exercise the discretion that the truster conferred.[36] Assumed trustees represent the truster. Trustees appointed by the court, if they are appointed as trustees rather than as judicial factors, do not represent the court and are in the same position as the nominated trustees. It would follow (though there is no case expressly deciding this) that, at least where there is no element of *delectus personae* in the nomination of the original trustees,[37] court appointed trustees would be able to exercise the discretion that the original trustees had. Executors dative must be in the same position.

[35] But note that in *Ommanney, Petr.* 1966 S.L.T. (Notes) 13 the First Division disapproved of the assumption of a corporate trustee because the assumed trustee would have the power to exercise a discretion in family and personal matters, which was not an appropriate discretion for a corporate trustee to exercise.

[36] Indeed there is some support for this line of reasoning in *Angus's Exx* itself: see Lord Mackay at p. 352.

[37] *Miln's Trs.* v. *Drachenhauer* (1921) 1 S.L.T. 152.

The problem really only arises when the extent of the discretion is very wide. In *Angus's Exx.* it was held that the bequest was void *for uncertainty*. Lord President Cooper restricted the extent of his opinion in that case to "a case such as the present in which the class is so vast and amorphous as to include every institution and object capable of being covered by the comprehensive term 'charity.' "[38] If the choice were much more limited, for example between the truster's children, it would be hard to characterise a bequest to one of them as uncertain just because no one was specified to make the choice. In *Russell's Ex. v. Balden*[39] a trust to be used "in connection with sport" was held by Lord Jauncey to be much more specific than those in *Robbie's J.F.* and *Angus's Exx.*, and this justified him permitting a body other than that nominated by the truster from making the choice of how precisely to use the trust estate "in connection with sport." He gleaned from the authorities the proposition that "when the discretionary power conferred by a testator on his trustees is relatively narrow, it is easier to infer that he did not intend that the power, and hence the bequest, should lapse if nominated and assumed trustees failed."[40]

4. Taxation

Tax Point

The following applies to private discretionary trusts when the trustees' discretion concerns the individuals to benefit, the timing of the benefit, and/or its extent.

Under income tax, not only will the trustees pay basic rate tax but they will be assessed to "the additional rate" on the gross trust income under deduction of the grossed-up equivalent of any administrative expenses relating to income as opposed to capital (ICTA 1988, s.686).[41] Similarly any chargeable gains will be taxed not just at basic rate but at a rate equal to the aggregate of the basic rate and the additional rate (Finance Act 1988, s.100). Further, there is every 10 years a charge to IHT, with an "exit charge" applying when funds are paid out of the trust (IHTA 1984 ss.58–69). Where the capital distribution is of trust assets the trustees are deemed to have made a disposal of the assets at market value for CGT purposes and to have reacquired them on behalf of the beneficiary at that valuation. This creates a liability on the trustees to pay CGT.

[38] 1949 S.C. 335 at p. 367.
[39] 1989 S.L.T. 177.
[40] At p. 180.
[41] For a discussion on the distinction between capital and income expenses in this context, see the English case of *Carver* v. *Duncan* [1985] A.C. 1082. Note however that Lord Fraser points out (at p. 1113) that in a Scottish trust the matter would be determined by Scots law (which may well be the same in practice).

In practice there is a particular problem that must be considered in every discretionary trust from which an individual has received payment: is the discretionary payment "income" in the beneficiary's hands or is it "capital"? If it is income (and the fact that similar payments are made periodically or are used for the personal maintenance of the beneficiary does not necessarily make them income in his hands[42]) it is received by the beneficiary net of basic and also additional rate income tax. If on the other hand it is capital, there are no tax consequences for the individual recipient.

However, as far as the trustees are concerned, a payment of capital to the beneficiary will have IHT consequences. If the trust has been truly discretionary (in the sense of the trustees having a dispositive discretion) then the exit charge referred to above will apply. This contrasts with a trust in which the discretion is purely administrative, for then the "interest in possession" regime (discussed under "Liferent and Fee") would apply.

CHARITABLE TRUSTS

Though one frequently sees the phrase "charitable trust" in the Scottish law reports and textbooks, Scots law traditionally did not recognise any special category of charitable trust, for these were subsumed into the more general category of public trust. McLaren points out:

"the term 'charitable trust' is a convenient general name, but it must be kept in view that the law of Scotland . . . recognises no distinction either as to construction or principles of administration between gifts to charitable uses properly so called, and gifts to purposes which, though not charitable, are lawful and useful. The true distinction is between private trusts or bequests . . . and those which are intended for the benefit of a section of the public."[43]

The specialities that are sometimes said to attach to charitable trusts, such as the *cy près* jurisdiction and the benignant construction, are in fact attributes of public trusts: so in *Russell's Ex* v. *Balden*[44] Lord Jauncey expressly recognised that both of these attributes apply to public trusts in the sense defined earlier in this chapter.[45] "The prominence of charitable trusts in legal decisions results from nothing more than their being the most numerous class of public trusts."[46]

An important difference between Scots and English law should be noted here. In English law trusts are classified according to

---

[42] *Stevenson* v. *Wishart & Ors.*, 59 T.C. 740, *per* Fox L.J. at p. 764d.
[43] McLaren, at para. 1691.
[44] 1989 S.L.T. 177.
[45] *Ibid.* at p. 179.
[46] Wilson & Duncan at pp. 168/169.

whether they are private or charitable. "Charitable" in English law has a highly technical and somewhat artificial meaning, which derives from the meaning contained in the Statute of Charitable Uses 1601 (the Statute of Elizabeth). This meaning has been further rarified by extensive case law, because trusts that came within it were not subject to that most English of rules, the Rule Against Perpetuities. Scots law does not contain the Rule Against Perpetuities,[47] nor does it accept (apart from the qualifications about to be discussed) that charitable trusts constitute a separate category. It is suggested that, because the relevant category in Scots law is public trusts, and because the word "charity" today carries certain condescending connotations, it is probably better to avoid using the phrase "charitable trust," except in relation to the matters mentioned below.

1. Taxation of Charitable Trusts

One circumstance in which it is important to categorise a trust as "charitable" is in relation to revenue matters, and here the meaning to be given to the term is the technical meaning given to it, indeed created for it, by English law. Clearly there is sense in having revenue matters dealt with in the same way in both Scotland and England,[48] but it does mean that, for this purpose, one must be aware of the peculiar English meaning of the phrase "charitable trust." The concept of charitable trust in English law is complex and would require much time to examine it fully, and in a book such as this only the barest of outlines can be given. In order for a trust purpose to be considered charitable in English law (and therefore charitable in relation to taxation in Scotland) it must be designed for the relief of poverty, or for the advancement of education, or for the advancement of religion, or for some other benefit to the community. This last class is not nearly as wide as the Scottish concept of public benefit,[49] and it will be interpreted in a way that is coloured by the preceeding three classes.[50]

[47] See Burgess, *Perpetuities in Scots Law*, Edinburgh 1979, The Stair Society, at pp. 45–51.
[48] See *Inland Revenue* v. *Pemsel*, 3 T.C. 53; *Jackson's Trs.* v. *Lord Advocate*, 1926 S.L.T. 358, 10 T.C. 460; and *Inland Revenue* v. *City of Glasgow Police Athletic Association*, 1953 S.C.(H.L.) 13, interestingly discussed by Jones in "Border Issues" (1986) Brit. Tax Rev. 75 at pp. 92–94.
[49] Enc. 24. 92.
[50] See Moffat & Chesterman at pp. 650–653.

Tax Point

As a preliminary point it should be remembered that if a public trust is not "charitable" it merely loses the tax benefits given to a charitable trust: it does not for that reason alone lose its validity.

The tax advantages of charitable status are many when funds are put into a charitable trust (whether *inter vivos* or *mortis causa*). No IHT is payable (s.23 IHTA 1984). If on setting up an *inter vivos* charitable trust the truster transfers assets (rather than cash) into the trust, no CGT is payable, for the transaction is treated as taking place for such consideration that neither a gain nor a loss accrues to the truster (s.146 CGTA 1979). If charitable trustees purchase land or take a lease of premises, no stamp duty is payable, though the deed must bear a stamp denoting that no stamp duty is payable (s.129 FA 1982).

Insofar as it is applied to charitable purposes, all income is exempt from Income Tax on a claim being made to the Board of the Inland Revenue (s.505 ICTA 1988).

A chargeable gain applied to charitable purposes is similarly exempt from CGT (s.145 CGTA 1979).

Because of the tax advantages of charitable status, there are a number of anti-avoidance provisions in the tax legislation designed to prevent the abuse of the privileged tax status enjoyed by charitable trusts.

2. Administration and supervision of charitable trusts

Scottish public trusts that have chosen to attain charitable status for income tax purposes are subject to special rules in their administration, which rules were laid down for the first time in Part 1 of the Law Reform (Miscellaneous Provisions) (Scotland) Act 1990.[51] This Act provides certain rules for the administration of "recognised bodies," *i.e.* those bodies to which the Commissioners of Inland Revenue have given intimation that exemption from tax will be due under section 505 of the Income and Corporation Taxes Act 1988 in respect of the income of the body that is applied exclusively to charitable purposes.[52] The Act imposes duties on all those "concerned in the management or control" of any recognised body. In relation to trusts for charitable purposes, this will certainly include the trustees, and in appropriate circumstances will also include employees and professional advisers of the trust. Hereinafter these persons will be referred to as the "managers."

---

[51] Until the passing of this Act, Scotland was unusual in the freedom from state control that charitable trusts possessed. Charitable corporations in countries not recognising the trust have for long been subject to such control: see *Int. Enc. Comp. L.* Vol. VI, Chap. 2, s.124.

[52] s.1(7). The body must be established under the law of Scotland, or be managed or controlled wholly or mainly in or from Scotland. Religious bodies designated by the Secretary of State are exempt from many of the rules discussed in the text: s.3.

Charitable trusts are subject to special rules concerning the keeping of records and accounts. Section 4 of the 1990 Act provides that the managers of the trust have a duty to keep accounts that are sufficient to show the transactions of the trust, and its financial position. Section 5 provides that there must be prepared in each financial year a balance sheet, an income and expenditure account and a report of the activities of the trust. The accounts must be preserved for six years,[53] and must be made available to any member of the public on the payment of a reasonable charge in respect of copying and postage, or to the Lord Advocate free of charge.[54] If these accounts and reports are not prepared, then the Lord Advocate may appoint a suitably qualified person to prepare them, and that person will possess various powers to allow him to do so, the expense being borne jointly and severally by the managers personally.[55]

The 1990 Act also introduces into Scotland the concept of court supervision of charitable trusts. Under section 6, the Lord Advocate has an investigative function, and he also has the power to suspend any manager for not more than 28 days if it appears to him that there is or has been misconduct or mismanagement in the administration of the trust (hereinafter referred to as "present or past maladministration"), *or* that it is necessary or desirable to act to protect the trust property or to secure a proper application of the trust property to the trust purposes (hereinafter referred to as "anticipated maladministration").

The Court of Session also has various powers, which are exercisable on the application of the Lord Advocate. These differ according to three different situations.

First, under section 7(1), the court has certain powers if it appears to the court that there is present or past maladministration *or* there is anticipated maladministration. If this is established the court may interdict *ad interim* the body from representing itself, or holding itself out, as a charity, or, on the application of the Lord Advocate, from any such action as the court thinks fit; it may suspend any manager; it may appoint *ad interim* a judicial factor to manage the affairs of the trust; it may order any person not to part with any of the trust property without the court's approval; it may make an order restricting the transactions which that trust can enter into without the court's

---

[53] s.4(3).
[54] ss.5(6) and 5(7).
[55] s.5(10).

approval; and it may appoint a trustee as if under s.22 of the
Trusts (Scotland) Act 1921.[56]

Secondly, under section 7(2), the court has certain powers if it
appears to the court that there is present or past maladministration *and* there is anticipated maladministration. Here the court
may appoint a trustee as if under section 22 of the Trusts
(Scotland) Act 1921; it may interdict the body from representing
itself or holding itself out as a charity, or, on the application of
the Lord Advocate, from any such action as the court thinks fit; it
may remove any person concerned in the management or control
of the trust; or it may appoint a judicial factor to manage the
affairs of the trust.[57]

Thirdly, under section 7(5), the court has a final power if it
appears to the court that there has been past maladministration
and there is anticipated maladministration *and* it is not practicable nor in the best interests of the trust to retain its existing
administrative structure, *and* in the court's opinion the trust
purposes would be better achieved by transferring its assets to
another body. In these circumstances the court may approve a
scheme presented by the Lord Advocate for the transfer of any
assets of the trust to such other recognised body as the Lord
Advocate specifies.

The court may exercise any of the powers mentioned in the
preceding three paragraphs, on the application of the Lord
Advocate, if it is satisfied that a non-recognised body is representing itself or holding itself out as a charity *and* is established
under the law of Scotland or is managed or controlled wholly or
mainly in or from Scotland or has moveable or immoveable
property situated in Scotland.[58]

Section 8 of the 1990 Act provides that certain persons are
disqualified from being concerned with the management or
control of recognised bodies, and are therefore disqualified from
the trusteeship of a charitable trust. The persons disqualified are
(a), anyone convicted of an offence of dishonesty (unless the
conviction is spent under the Rehabilitation of Offenders Act
1974[59]), (b), any undischarged bankrupt[60] (c), anyone who has
been removed from office as trustee under section 6 of the 1990
Act, and (d), anyone subject to a disqualification order under the

---

[56] s.7(4)(a)–(f). (For a discussion of s.22 of the Trusts (Scotland) Act 1921, see
Chap. 5).
[57] s.7(4)(f)–(i).
[58] ss.7(3) and 7(5).
[59] s.8(2)(a).
[60] Defined in s.8(6).

Company Directors Disqualification Act 1986. The Lord Advocate may waive these disqualifications.[61] If a disqualified person does any act of management then he will be guilty of an offence[62] but the act itself will not be invalid by reason only of its being carried out by a disqualified person.[63]

It is to be emphasised that these special rules apply only to trusts that are charitable in the sense of having obtained entitlement to income tax relief under the Income and Corporation Taxes Act 1988. Other trusts with aims that would be regarded as charitable in the wide Scots law sense of the word will not be subject to the rules of administration and supervision in the Law Reform (Miscellaneous Provisions) (Scotland) Act 1990, and will be subject to the same rules of administration—and indeed taxation—as other public trusts.

ADMINISTRATIVE TRUSTS

An administrative trust is one in which the purpose of the trust is no more than to administer the trust estate on behalf of the truster or, as the case may be, someone else. There are no purposes other than the protection of the estate. The rules governing administrative trusts do not differ from those governing other trusts, except that a purely administrative trust for the benefit of the truster himself does not divest the truster of his property, and the estate may therefore be available to the truster's creditors. An administrative trust may be set up if for example the truster would prefer his private funds to be administered by a commercial organisation such as a bank because it is more experienced in financial matters than he is, or even because the truster has no confidence in his own ability to look after his own property. Alternatively a trust may be set up to administer property on behalf of someone who is incapable of looking after it himself, for example through mental incapacity, or because the truster does not trust the judgment of the beneficiary. A special type of administrative trust is one set up for the benefit of the truster's creditors. This may be set up in order to avoid the more formal process of sequestration. The purpose will be to distribute the estate, normally in accordance with the rules of distribution

---

[61] s.8(2)(b), but he would have no power to grant a waiver where to do so would prejudice the operation of the Company Directors Disqualification Act 1986.
[62] s.8(3).
[63] s.8(4).

laid down by the law of sequestration, as contained in the Bankruptcy (Scotland) Act 1985. This Act provides that such a trust deed will not be superseded by the truster's subsequent sequestration.

Tax Point
In administrative trusts the trust situation is ignored for CGT purposes, so that any disposal or acquisition by the trustees is taxed as if it had been made by the beneficiaries personally (CGTA 1979, s.46).

ACCUMULATION AND MAINTENANCE TRUSTS

Again, this form of trust is not a separate legal category, but it is fairly common in modern trust practice, because accumulation and maintenance trusts, as defined by section 71 of the Inheritance Taxes Act 1984, attract certain tax advantages. These trusts must be discretionary, in the dispositive sense discussed above, and they must provide for the trust income to be used for the maintenance, education or benefit of a beneficiary aged under 25, with any income surplus to that need being accumulated. The beneficiary must not initially be a liferenter, but must become entitled either to a liferent or to the trust capital on attaining a specified age, not greater than 25.

Tax Point
When a truster puts capital into an accumulation and maintenance trust, this is a potentially exempt transfer for IHT purposes (IHTA 1984, s.3A), and so IHT is payable only if the truster then dies within seven years. During the discretionary period, when income will be accumulated, the income tax and CGT rules for discretionary trusts (discussed above) will apply; but provided that the beneficiary receives the trust capital or the liferent thereof on attaining the age specified, the IHT discretionary trust regime will *not* apply: on the beneficiary attaining the specified age there will be no IHT payable on the trust capital (IHTA 1984, s.71).
It has been seen (see **Tax Point** under Discretionary Trusts) that generally where a beneficiary becomes entitled to a trust asset, the trustees will be liable to pay CGT on this disposal. In appropriate cases however the trustees of an accumulation and maintenance trust can postpone this liability by agreeing with the beneficiary that the chargeable gains will be held over until the beneficiary himself disposes of the asset (CGTA 1979, s.147A).
One other feature that makes an accumulation and maintenance trust attractive is that parents who set up such a trust for their children will not be taxed as they otherwise would be (under ICTA 1988, part 15, ch. II) on the trust income, provided that the trustees accumulate all the income while the child is under 18 and is unmarried.

TRUSTS FOR DISABLED PERSONS

Another useful form of trust (again not being a separate legal category) is a discretionary trust (not being for liferent and fee) set up for the benefit of disabled persons (whether physically or mentally disabled). The law encourages such trusts by granting them special tax benefits, where not less than half the trust fund or income paid out during the life of the disabled person is used for that person's benefit.[64]

---

[64] IHTA 1984, s.89. See also the slightly stricter CGT provision under CGTA 1979, sched. 1 para. 5(1).

CHAPTER 3

INTERNATIONAL ASPECTS OF TRUSTS

Introduction

THE rules of law considered in this book are the rules applicable to trusts governed by the law of Scotland, or applicable to those aspects of a trust governed by Scots law. In the modern age however it is becoming more and more common for the trust relationship to contain elements connected to more than one country. Some or all of the beneficiaries may be resident furth of Scotland (*i.e.* outwith Scotland), as may the trustees. Part or all of the trust property may be located outwith Scotland, as for example in relation to trust investments in companies registered in England or abroad. This raises two separate but related questions relevant to this book: in what circumstances will a trust be governed by the law of Scotland, and in what circumstances will a trust governed by a foreign legal system be recognised and thereafter given effect to in Scotland? Both questions are now answered by the Recognition of Trusts Act 1987. This Act was passed in order to allow the United Kingdom to ratify the Hague Convention on the Law Applicable to Trusts and Their Recognition,[1] which it did in November 1989.

The Convention itself is restricted to trusts "created voluntarily and evidenced in writing,"[2] but section 1(2) of the 1987 Act

---

[1] For a particularly useful examination of the Hague Convention, see the Explanatory Report, *Trusts—Applicable Law and Recognition*, in Proceedings of the Fifteenth Session of the Hague Conference, 1985, by von Overbeck, who was the Reporter.

[2] The reason for this restriction, according to Gaillard & Trautman, "Trusts in Non-Trust Countries: Conflict of Laws and the Hague Convention on Trusts" (1987) 35 Am.J. Comp.L. 307 at p. 317 is that the Convention aims to deal with the simple and straightforward trust, until such time as countries that do not themselves have trusts can easily understand the institution.

extends the application of the Convention rules in the U.K. to "any other trusts of property arising under the law of any part of the United Kingdom," and also to any other trust arising "by virtue of a judicial decision whether in the United Kingdom or elsewhere." Constructive trusts[3] arising under the law in any part of the U.K. will be covered,[4] and trusts judicially created anywhere will be covered.[5] The rules apply to judicially created trusts arising in any country, whether or not a signatory to the Hague Convention.[6]

WHEN IS A TRUST A SCOTTISH TRUST?

Though the position is now governed by the 1987 Act, it is helpful to be aware of what the common law situation was, because though the Act supersedes, it substantially reflects, the common law.[7]

At common law a trust was governed by Scots law whenever that system was chosen by the truster to govern[8] or alternatively, where the truster had made no choice, when Scotland was the "domicile of the trust."[9] An important qualification to this (which has not survived the 1987 Act)[10] was that trusts of immoveable property were governed by the *lex situs*[11]; it being determined by

---

[3] *i.e.* those that arise through the operation of law independently of the intention of the parties: see Chapter 4.

[4] So long as they are trusts "of property". Trusts imposed by the court simply as equitable remedies will not be covered, either by the Convention (Gaillard & Trautman at p. 318) or by the extension in the Act. See also Hayton, "The Hague Convention on the Law Applicable to Trusts and on their Recognition" (1987) 36 I.C.L.Q. 260, at p. 264.

[5] This last provision was necessary in order to satisfy the 1968 European Convention on Recognition and Enforcement of Judgments in Civil and Commercial Matters, which provides for European Community countries mutually to recognise each other's court judgments in civil and commercial matters (given effect to in the U.K. by the Civil Jurisdiction and Judgments Act 1982). See Anton, *Civil Jurisdiction in Scotland*, W. Green, Edinburgh 1984.

[6] Article 21 of the Convention allows states to restrict its application to contracting states, but the U.K. has not done so. Thus Art. 21 is not included in the schedule to the 1987 Act.

[7] See Anton, "The Recognition of Trusts Act 1987" 1987 S.L.T. (News) 377; Hayton, *op. cit.*; Gaillard & Trautman, *op. cit.*

[8] See, *e.g. Montgomery* v. *Zarifi* 1918 S.C. (H.L.) 128.

[9] See Anton, *Private International Law* (1st ed.) at pp. 469/470. The 2nd. edition, published in 1990, contains only the briefest of comments on the common law.

[10] Except to a very limited extent: see Anton, 1987 S.L.T. (News) 377 at p. 383, and Hayton *op. cit.*, n. 4, at pp. 273/274.

[11] See, *e.g. Brown's Trs.* v. *Gregson*, 1920 S.C. (H.L.) 87.

the law of the country where the property was actually situated whether that property was moveable or immoveable.

A trust was considered to be domiciled in Scotland when most of its elements were connected to Scotland, or when the trust had its most substantial connection with Scotland. In *Clarke's Trs. Petrs.* Lord President Clyde said this:

> "What constitutes a Scottish trust arises from a variety of circumstances which may or may not concur, thus (1) if the trust originates in the testamentary writings of a Scotsman; (2) if the truster declares that the powers and immunities of his trustees are to be ruled by the law of Scotland; (3) if some or all of the trustees are domiciled Scotsmen, and (4) if the greater part of the trust estate is in Scotland, then the trust is a Scottish trust."[12]

Other relevant considerations included the centre of the trust administration, the residence of the trustees and of the beneficiaries, and the place where the trust purposes were to be fulfilled.

These rules are now replaced by the Recognition of Trusts Act 1987. The Articles of the Convention, in which the rules are set out, are for the most part brought into U.K. law in the schedule to the 1987 Act. The Convention, unusually, has retrospective effect, and so applies to trusts which became effective both after and before the ratification of the Convention.[13] It is now provided that a trust can become a Scottish trust by one of two methods.

1. The subjectively chosen applicable law

First of all, Scots law may be chosen by the truster. Under Article 6 of the Hague Convention it is provided that if the truster chooses a particular legal system to apply to the trust he sets up, then this shall be the law to govern, whether or not that system has any connection with the trust other than the truster's wishes.[14] The choice can be either express or implied, and it should be of a legal system (*e.g.* of Scotland or of Quebec) rather than of a state or a country (such as the U.K. or Canada).[15] By

---

[12] 1966 S.L.T. 249 at p. 251. See also Lord Cameron in *Spencer's Trs.* v. *Ruggles*, 1982 S.L.T. 165 at p. 167.

[13] Article 22.

[14] Article 13 of the Convention allows countries not to recognise a choice where there is no other connection with the chosen system, but this has not been made part of U.K. law.

[15] 1987 Act, s.1(4).

Article 9 the truster can choose different legal systems to govern severable aspects of the trust. Theoretically it may be declared in the trust deed that the validity of the trust is to be determined by the law of Scotland, that the rights of the beneficiaries are to be governed by the law of England (which gives far more proprietorial rights to beneficiaries than does Scots law),[16] and that the powers of accumulation are to be governed by the law of the Isle of Man (which allows for unlimited accumulation[17]). This is known as *dépeçage* in European legal systems, and would normally prove administratively inconvenient, but might prove useful if for example some assets are held in Scotland and others are held abroad, for the law of the situs of each asset may be considered the most appropriate to govern their distribution.[18] It must however be established that the different laws govern "severable" aspects of the trust, and this might render different choices impracticable. In addition to *dépeçage* being provided for in Article 9, Article 10 allows the truster to provide that the chosen law can later be changed. This might be useful if, for example, certain contingencies occur, such as the removal of the beneficiaries to another jurisdiction (though this is only allowed if the law initially governing the validity of the trust allows it).

The choice need not be expressly laid down, and may be implied from the terms of the deed, interpreted, if necessary, in the light of the circumstances of the case. In order to establish an implied choice of a particular system, it would seem that initially only the terms of the deed creating or evidencing the trust should be looked at[19] and it would only be when the terms are ambiguous that the circumstances of the case could be called in aid. The sort of terms in a deed that will imply a choice of a specific legal system would be if the technical terms of one legal system were used throughout (*e.g.* using the Scottish "truster" rather that the Anglo-American "settlor") or expressly referring to the provisions of a particular legal system (*e.g.* "my trustees are to have all the general powers of administration laid down in section 4(1) of the Trusts (Scotland) Act 1921.") An ambiguity might arise from, say, a reference to a British trust statute, such as the

---

[16] See Chapter 10.

[17] See Chapter 6.

[18] *Dépeçage* is normally disliked by European lawyers, and its application here reflects a compromise between the European and the North American approach to conflict of laws, for the latter is often based on interest analysis and is happy to accept that different aspects of the same area of law can be dealt with by different legal systems.

[19] Art. 6.

Trustee Investments Act 1961, in which case the whole circumstances of the case will be used to determine whether this can be interpreted as an implied choice of either Scots law or English law. The matters mentioned in Article 7 (*infra*) will be among the relevant circumstances here.

2. The objectively determined applicable law

Many legal systems do not provide for the institution of the trust,[20] or a particular category of trust, and if the truster chooses such a legal system to govern his trust, that choice will be disregarded and the applicable law determined according to the rules in Article 7. That article will also be utilised when there is no choice made, express or implied, or the choice made is ineffective (such as for example a choice of "British law" or "Canadian law").

By Article 7 of the Hague Convention, "where no applicable law has been chosen, a trust shall be governed by the law with which it is most closely connected." There is a substantial identity between this and the common law concept of the domicile of the trust, and the cases on that concept will remain of use in determining the law with which the trust is most closely connected.[21] Article 7 lays down, though in no order of importance,[22] certain features that are particularly relevant to this determination, though the wording of the article makes it quite clear that this is not an exhaustive list. The features that are particularly relevant are, (a) the place of administration of the trust designated by the settlor, (b) the situs of the assets of the trust, (c) the place of residence or business of the trustees and, (d) the objects of the trust and the places where they are to be fulfilled. The current residence of the beneficiaries and the domicile of the truster will be other relevant factors, as will any terms of the trust deed which may provide an indication, though not in itself strong enough to amount to an express or implied choice under Article 6. The test is "closest connection" rather than a numerical superiority of contacts with a particular system.[23]

---

[20] The trust is, in essence, an Anglo-American institution, and is recognised in most common law countries. It also exists in a small number of civil law countries, such as Mexico, Venezuela, Liechtenstein and, for limited purposes, the Netherlands (see *Int. Enc. Comp. L.* Vol. VI, Ch. 2, ss. 111 – 123). The trust tends not to appear in systems of law that do not adhere to either of these legal families.

[21] Anton, 1987 S.L.T. (News) 377 at p. 380.

[22] Gaillard & Trautman at pp. 324/325.

[23] *Ibid.* at p. 325.

It is unclear from the terms of the Convention whether Article 9, which allows different aspects of the trust to be governed by different legal systems, can apply to trusts whose law is determined under Article 7 as well as those whose law is chosen under Article 6. The terms of Article 7 certainly assume that only one law will have the closest connection to the trust. But if one can accept the following as being "severable aspects," it is easy to imagine a situation in which, say, the distribution of assets would be most closely connected to one legal system, while the continuing administration of the trust is most closely connected to another legal system. Though this may be difficult to establish, it is suggested that the terms of Article 9 are wide enough to allow for different laws both to be chosen, and to be most closely connected to "severable aspects" of the trust.

Implicit in Article 7 is that the system with the closest connection to the trust will in fact provide for trusts in its domestic law. It may be assumed therefore that the courts will generally not hold a trust to be most closely connected to a legal system that does not contain that institution,[24] since to do so would amount to a frustration of the intention of the truster. However, if such a holding cannot be avoided, then, by Article 5, the Convention will have no effect over such a trust.

3. Matters governed by the applicable law

If, in applying either Article 6 or Article 7, it is determined that Scots law is the law applicable to a particular trust, then that will be the law to govern all aspects of that trust (unless the law governing a severable aspect is chosen or determined separately). The applicable law is the domestic law of the chosen or determined legal system, for Article 17 excludes the operation of *renvoi* (the application of the private international law rules of the applicable law). Article 8 lays down that the applicable law shall govern "the validity of the trust, its construction, its effects and the administration of the trust." The article also lays down a number of matters which, in particular, will be governed by that law. These are:

> "(a) the appointment, resignation and removal of trustees, the capacity to act as a trustee, and the devolution of the office of trustee;

[24] Hayton *op. cit.*, n. 4, at p. 272.

(b) the rights and duties of trustees among themselves;
(c) the right of trustees to delegate in whole or in part the discharge of their duties or the exercise of their powers;.
(d) the power of trustees to administer or to dispose of trust assets, to create security interests in the trust assets, or to acquire new assets;
(e) the powers of investment of trustees;
(f) restrictions upon the duration of the trust, and upon the power to accumulate the income of the trust;
(g) the relationships between the trustees and the beneficiaries including the personal liability of the trustees to the beneficiaries;
(h) the variation or termination of the trust;
(i) the distribution of the trust assets;
(j) the duty of trustees to account for their administration."

This effectively covers all trust issues once the trust is established. On the other hand, matters of trust law that concern issues *before* the trust is established are excluded from the Convention by Article 4. Preliminary issues relating to the validity of the trust deed (including such issues as delivery and intimation of the trust),[25] and capacity of the truster, will not be covered by the Convention. These will be governed by the legal system chosen through the forum's pre-existing conflict of law rules applicable to these issues. The difference is between issues relating to *whether* the trust is established (which are excluded) and issues arising *once* the trust has been established (which are included).

Another issue excluded from the terms of the Convention is that of taxation: a truster cannot escape the application of U.K. tax legislation simply by choosing a more advantageous system. Nor may a foreign truster obtain British tax advantages (attaching, for example, to charitable trusts) unless the trust is charitable according to the British tax definition. This follows from Article 19 of the Convention, which provides that nothing in the Convention shall prejudice the powers of the state in fiscal matters. This article has not been enacted in the Schedule to the 1987 Act, "presumably because it was thought that the matter went without saying."[26]

Tax point
Not only is taxation not governed by the applicable law, but the issue of whether the U.K. tax laws will govern a particular trust is determined in a very different way from the determination of the applicable law under the Hague Convention. The following is a brief outline of the circumstances in which U.K. tax law affects foreign trusts. The topic is complex and as far as Income Tax, Capital Gains Tax and Inheritance Tax are concerned, the matter is likely to be affected by Double Taxation Agreements.[27]

[25] See Chap. 4.
[26] Anton, 1987 S.L.T. (News) 377 at p. 380.
[27] *i.e.* agreements between the U.K. and other sovereign states which regulate the liability to U.K. and foreign taxation of a person who could potentially be taxed contemporaneously under the tax regimes of both contracting states.

Income Tax. Trustees' liability to U.K income tax depends primarily on the residence of the trustees: if the trustees are U.K resident, they are liable to U.K. income tax on the world-wide trust income, whereas if they are not U.K. resident, they are liable to U.K. income tax only on the U.K. trust income.

To be U.K resident, the trustees must all, individually, be resident in the U.K.; or alternatively, at least one of them must be so resident and the truster must have been resident, ordinarily resident, or domiciled in the U.K. when he put funds into the trust. (Finance Act 1989, s.110. See Simon's Taxes, Division C. 4.4).

Capital Gains Tax. For many years, trustees' liability to U.K. CGT has depended on the residence of the trustees and the place where the trust is administered. All trusts, including those with foreign connections, are presumed to be resident and ordinarily resident in the U.K. and consequently the trustees are assessed to U.K. CGT on their world-wide chargeable gains. However, exception is made for trusts where both (1) the trustees (or a majority of them) are, as individuals, neither resident nor ordinarily resident in the U.K.,[28] and (2) the general administration of the trust is ordinarily carried on outside the U.K.[29] (CGTA 1979, s.52(2). See Simon's Taxes, Division C. 4.4). Tax legislation has long contained a number of anti-avoidance provisions designed to charge U.K. CGT on some non-resident trusts. The proposals on non-resident trusts contained in the Finance Bill 1991 seek to reduce further the attractions for a U.K. truster of setting up a non-resident trust.

Inheritance Tax. Liability for U.K. Inheritance Tax depends exclusively on the domicile of the truster at the time the trust was set up. If he was then U.K. domiciled, the trustees are liable to IHT calculated on the world-wide trust funds. If he was not U.K. domiciled, the trustees are liable to IHT on the trust assets situated in the U.K., for any property situated outside the U.K. is excluded property and exempt from IHT. It should be noted that for the purposes of IHT, domicile has a wider meaning than it normally bears. (IHTA 1984, s.267 and s.48. See Foster's Capital Taxes Encyclopaedia, Part J.)

If IHT is payable on an *inter vivos* trust at a time when the trustees are not U.K. resident (*i.e.* a majority of the trustees are resident overseas *or* the administration is carried on overseas) then the truster may find himself personally liable for the IHT (IHTA 1984, s.201(1)–(5).)

Stamp Duty. Trustees' liability to U.K. stamp duty depends on the place of execution of the instrument or the situs of the property concerned, for if either the instrument is executed in the U.K. or the instrument relates to property situated in the U.K. or to any matter which is done or to be done in the U.K., U.K. stamp duty is payable (Stamp Act 1891, s.14(4).[30]

RECOGNITION OF FOREIGN TRUSTS

The main purpose of the Hague Convention, and the reason the United Kingdom suggested that trusts be considered at the

---

[28] A professional person who is a trustee will, even if himself U.K. resident, be treated for these purposes as non-resident if the truster was not resident, ordinarily resident or domiciled in the U.K. when he set up the trust: CGTA 1979, s.52(2).

[29] See CGTA 1979, s.52(2) for the tax residence of U.K. professional trustees.

[30] See Sergeant & Sims, *On Stamp Duties and Capital Duty and Stamp Duty Reserve Tax*, Butterworths, London & Edinburgh 1988 at pp. 82/83.

Hague Conference on Private International Law, was to provide for the recognition of trusts in countries that do not themselves have such an institution (*e.g.* most civil law countries). The Convention's rules therefore apply to all signatories, whether or not they recognise trusts in their own domestic systems.

1. What is to be recognised

Unlike most other legal institutions considered at the Hague Conference, the trust is an institution that simply does not exist in many countries, and therefore the drafters of the Trusts Convention felt obliged to attempt to give a definition of a trust. However, because the countries that do have trusts differ in their definitions, all the Convention could do was to lay down a number of common characteristics. This it has done in Article 2, which is in the following terms:

> "For the purposes of this Convention, the term 'trust' refers to the legal relationship created—inter vivos or on death—by a person, the settlor, when assets have been placed under the control of a trustee for the benefit of a beneficiary or for a specified purpose.
> A trust has the following characteristics—
> (a) the assets constitute a separate fund and are not a part of the trustee's own estate;
> (b) title to the trust assets stands in the name of the trustee or in the name of another person on behalf of the trustee;
> (c) the trustee has the power and the duty, in respect of which he is accountable, to manage, employ, or dispose of the assets in accordance with the terms of the trust and the special duties imposed upon him by the law.
> The reservation by the settlor of certain rights and powers, and the fact that the trustee may himself have rights as a beneficiary, are not necessarily inconsistent with the existence of a trust."

2. Consequences of recognition

If such an institution is valid according to the system of law chosen under Article 6 or determined under Article 7, then Article 11 provides that that institution will be recognised as a trust in all the countries that ratify the Hague Convention, whether or not these countries have trusts in their own domestic systems. Article 11 further lays down the consequences of recognising the trust: it provides that "such recognition shall imply, as a minimum, that the trust property constitutes a separate fund, that the trustee may sue and be sued in his capacity as trustee, and that he may appear or act in this capacity before a notary or any person acting in an official capacity." Further, *but only if the applicable law so provides*, other countries must also recognise and give effect to the following consequences:

> "(a) that the personal creditors of the trustee shall have no recourse against the trust assets;
> (b) that the trust assets shall not form part of the trustee's estate upon his insolvency or bankruptcy;
> (c) that the trust assets shall not form part of the matrimonial property of the trustee or his spouse nor part of the trustee's estate upon his death;
> (d) that the assets may be recovered when the trustee, in breach of trust, has mingled trust assets with his own property or has alienated trust assets. However, the rights and obligations of any third party holder of the assets shall remain subject to the law determined by the choice of law rules of the forum."

If the applicable law does not recognise one of these consequences, then no other country need do so either. For example if the applicable law is Scots law, consequence (d) need not be recognised in other countries, since the right to follow trust property is very limited in Scots domestic law.[31]

3. Exceptions to recognition

There are certain exceptions to the automatic recognition of the trust and its consequences, and these are to be found in Articles 15, 16 and 18. The former two deal with what are known as mandatory provisions (*i.e.* very basically, provisions that it would be against the policy of the court to allow a party to avoid), and Article 18 deals with public policy more generally.

By Article 15 if the recognition of the trust or any aspect of it would clash with a mandatory provision of the legal system governing the trust, according to the private international law rules of the forum (that is the choice of law rules that would have been applied had the Convention not been ratified), then the mandatory provision will be applied. This concerns in particular provisions designed for the protection of minors, creditors, or third parties acting in good faith, and indefeasible succession rights such as legitim. By Article 16, if the recognition of the trust or any aspect of it would clash with a mandatory provision of the

---

[31] See further, Chap. 10.

forum, the mandatory provision will be applied. This is intended to protect the interests of the state, by allowing the state to apply, for example, currency regulations or export restrictions which might otherwise be avoided by having a trust governed by a different legal system. The complicated matter of mandatory provisions is more fully examined in the von Overbeck Report.[32]

Article 18 allows the provisions of the Convention to be disregarded when their application would be "manifestly contrary to public policy." This is a common safety-net provision in the Hague Conventions. It may be used when Articles 15 or 16 would not prevent the recognition of something that the law of the forum abhors, such as (in English law) perpetuities.

[32] See n. 1 above.

CHAPTER 4

ESTABLISHMENT OF THE TRUST RELATIONSHIP

Introduction

A TRUST was defined in Chapter 1 as a tripartite relationship which involves the passing of property for purposes. The trust is in essence a proprietorial relationship, in which the intention to transfer property from the truster to the trustee is essential. It follows that capacity to be a truster depends upon capacity to transfer property. It may be stated as a general rule that any person who holds property on a title that allows him to dispose of it absolutely, and who has the personal capacity to do so, may create a trust by passing that property on to another person, with instructions as to how the property is to be used. Capacity to be a trustee similarly follows general contractual capacity.

It is important to be able to identify the moment in time when the trust relationship comes into existence, because it is at that moment that the various rights and obligations of the different parties to the trust come into being. The trustees acquire rights in the trust property as against the truster, and the beneficiaries acquire rights in the trust property as against the trustees. The trust relationship, because it involves many onerous duties, can normally be brought into existence only if the truster intends to create a trust and the trustees are willing to accept the responsibilities, but sometimes it is possible for a trust to be brought into existence independently of the intention of the parties. Different considerations apply to each situation, and consequently they will be dealt with separately.

VOLUNTARY CONSTITUTION

For trusts that are established voluntarily, with the truster intending to transfer his property to trustees for the achievement of certain purposes chosen by the truster, the trust will be constituted by the passing of property for purposes. This involves two distinct elements, both of which are necessary: there must be a declaration of trust by the truster, that is the imposition of an obligation to achieve certain purposes; and there must be a passing of property, that is a transfer from the truster to the trustees of the property to be used in achieving these aims.[1]

1. The declaration of trust

While the declaration of trust purposes may be made in the deed transferring the property, this is not necessary and the declaration is often made in a separate deed. It is usually more convenient to have both elements in the same deed, but this may not always be possible, for example, if the property is not such that a formal deed need be used to effect its transfer.

When property is transferred, it is a matter of interpretation whether or not the words used in the declaration amount to an obligation of trust, or alternatively constitute an outright gift. Each instance must be looked at individually—the aim is always to discover the intention of the granter. No particular words need be used, and the declaration need not even use the word 'trust,' if it can otherwise be established that this is in fact what is being created. Similarly the use of the word 'trust,' although highly persuasive, is not conclusive if it can be shown that the truster did not intend to create what the law understands by a trust. Proving intention from words and actions is never easy, and the number of decisions on this point should serve as a warning to drafters of trust deeds, who should always strive for clarity of expression, even if this results in the deed appearing verbose or sounding peremptory.

A failure to make it clear that definite instructions are being given can lead to many problems. In *Barclay's Ex.* v. *McLeod*[2] a testator expressed an "anxious desire" that a legacy to his widow be left on her death to certain other relatives. The Court held that this did not constitute a trust which imposed an obligation on the widow to follow her deceased husband's desires, because the words he used did not detract from the absolute nature of the gift. This case may be compared with that of *Reid's Trs.* v. *Dawson*,[3] in which the testator said "I would prefer" that the

---

[1] McLaren, at para. 1510.
[2] (1880) 7 R. 477.
[3] 1915 S.C. (H.L.) 47.

trustees pay over a sum of money to a beneficiary. The House of Lords held that this constituted a firm direction, since the words used were in essence simply a polite form of command. These precedents are interesting illustrations, but each case must be looked at on its own facts, because it is always a matter of determining the particular granter's intention. There is some authority in Scots law for the view that an instruction given to an executor will more readily be regarded as a trust instruction than will an instruction given to a beneficiary,[4] on the ground that one should presume that an executor takes the property in order to pass it on in accordance with instructions, while one should presume that a beneficiary takes absolutely unless the gift is in some way qualified.

It is more satisfactory to have an express declaration of trust, but the law will accept an implied declaration, if it can be established that this is a necessary consequence of the truster's intent, as evidenced by the language he uses.[5]

In principle, there is no requirement that the declaration of trust be in writing, but for a number of reasons writing is *always* preferable. First, proof of the existence of a trust will be restricted to the trustee's writ or oath if the trust comes within the terms of the Blank Bonds and Trusts Act 1696, *i.e.* if the deed transferring the property is on the face of it absolute and not in trust (though the courts are not keen to apply the rules in that Act unless they cannot avoid it). Whether or not that Act applies, proof of the declaration is much easier to establish when a formal deed sets up the trust. Secondly, certain types of property cannot be passed except by way of written deed, and while it is perfectly possible to have the trust purposes separately declared, it may well be tidier and more convenient to deal with when the purposes are laid down in the same document as that which passes the property (though this will not be possible for all types of property, *e.g.* shares). Thirdly, testamentary trusts must, like all wills, be in writing.[6]

2. The transfer of property

"A trust is . . . constituted when the owner of the property, who becomes the truster, transfers the legal ownership of the property

---

[4] See Wilson & Duncan at p. 23, quoting Lord President Dunedin in *Garden's Ex.* v. *More*, 1913 S.C. 285.

[5] See further, Mackenzie Stuart at pp. 18–36.

[6] English law has more scope for verbal trusts than Scots law, because it recognises the concept of 'secret trusts' (for which, see Riddall, at pp. 50–57; Moffat & Chesterman at pp. 158–168). These trusts have no place in the law of Scotland: see *Shaw's Trs.* v. *Greenock Medical Aid Society*, 1930 S.L.T. 39.

to trustees to hold it for defined purposes on behalf of the beneficiaries . . . The constitution of the trust is completed by delivery."[7] A trust being in essence a proprietorial relationship, its constitution is completed by delivery, because it is delivery or its equivalent that completes the transfer of property. However this does not mean to say that the trust does not exist until delivery: it simply means that the trustees' title to the property will not be complete until delivery. Trustees will invariably acquire a personal right to the trust estate at an earlier stage,[8] and the acquiring of this right will, it is submitted, be sufficient for the trust to come into existence, and therefore for the parties to have rights and obligations *inter se*. It is suggested that the personal right to the property acquired by the trustees is subject to their personal obligations to the beneficiaries.[9] On obtaining a personal right, the trustees will then be obliged to convert that into a real right, by completing the process in the way required for the particular types of property in the trust estate. As stated above, this will invariably require delivery or its equivalent.

It is a general rule of Scots law that ownership of property is not transferred until the property or the deed of conveyance has been delivered to the new owner (or his agent), or there has been the equivalent to delivery. The reason for this is that delivery puts it outwith the power of the granter to retract.[10] To transfer title in property that is to be subject to a trust, the property or deed of conveyance or declaration of trust must be delivered to the trustees or to the beneficiaries, or to one of their number.

Certain types of property cannot of their nature be delivered, and so the law will accept an equivalent to delivery, if this has the same effect of putting it beyond the power of the granter to retract from the transfer.[11] Registration in the Land Register or recording in the Register of Sasines may be the equivalent to delivery (though only if done with the intention of it being the equivalent to delivery),[12] as will intimation of the declaration of trust to the trustees or one of the beneficiaries.[13] In the context of *mortis causa* transfers, death is regarded as the equivalent to delivery.[14]

[7] Enc. 24 : 12. See also Mackenzie Stuart at p. 8.
[8] Wilson & Duncan, p. 248.
[9] *Cf.* Reid, "Constitution of Trust" 1986 S.L.T. (News) 177.
[10] Halliday, Vol. 1 at pp. 311 and 317.
[11] See Halliday, *op. cit.*, n. 10, at pp. 314–318 for the equivalents to delivery.
[12] *Cameron's Trs.* v. *Cameron*, 1907 S.C. 407.
[13] *Export Credits Guarantee Dept.* v. *Turner*, 1981 S.L.T. 286 (a decision criticised by Reid, *supra*, n. 9).
[14] Mackenzie Stuart at p. 8.

It is permissible in Scots law for a truster to appoint himself as sole trustee, and if this happens delivery of the property itself would be meaningless. In this situation there must always be an equivalent to delivery, and this will generally be constituted by intimation of the trust to the beneficiaries or one of their number.[15] It is essential in this case that the truster has, before intimation, identified property that he in future intends to hold in trust, and not for his own beneficial enjoyment.[16] Intimation before the trust property is identified would be no more than an expression of intention and would not therefore bring the trust into operation.[17] Likewise intimation before the declaration of trust has been executed would not bring the trust into operation, because the point of intimation is that it is the equivalent to delivery of the declaration of trust[18]: there cannot be delivery of a declaration until the declaration has been made. The First Division in *Clark Taylor & Co. Ltd.* v. *Quality Site Development (Edinburgh) Ltd.* summarised the position as follows:

"In order to bring about the successful constitution of a trust recognised as such by our law, where the truster and trustee are the same persons, there must be in existence an asset, be it corporeal or incorporeal or even a right relating to future *acquirenda*; there must be a dedication of the asset or right to defined trust purposes; there must be a beneficiary or beneficiaries with defined rights in the trust estate, and there must also be delivery of the trust deed or subject of the trust or a sufficient and satisfactory equivalent to delivery, so as to achieve irrevocable divestiture of the truster and investiture of the trustee in the trust estate."[19]

The court went on to point out that when the truster and trustee are the same person intimation is the normal equivalent to delivery, but it is not the only equivalent recognised by the law.

INVOLUNTARY CONSTITUTION

While the most obvious way in which the trust relationship will be constituted is by the truster expressly or impliedly setting up

[15] *Allan's Trs.* v. *Inland Revenue*, 1971 S.L.T. 62. See also *Stenhouse's Trs.* v. *Lord Advocate*, 1986 S.L.T. 73.
[16] *Clark Taylor & Co. Ltd.* v. *Quality Site Development (Edinburgh) Ltd.*, 1981 S.L.T. 308. In *Allan's Trs.*, *supra* n. 15, the trust was held to exist before the property was identified, but the point was not actually argued in that case and was not the basis of the judgment.
[17] *Kerr's Trs.* v. *Inland Revenue*, 1974 S.L.T. 193, *Export Credits Guarantee Dept.*, *supra* n. 13.
[18] Reid, *op. cit.* at p. 182.
[19] 1981 S.L.T. 308 at p. 312.

the trust and the trustees expressly or impliedly agreeing to undertake the duties flowing from that position, there are a number of situations in which the trust relationship can arise independently of the wishes of the parties. The law may impose a trust on parties owing to the factual circumstances they find themselves in, and if that happens, the person in the position of trustee will be subject to most of the duties (but will possess few of the powers) that a trustee in a voluntarily constituted trust would have.

There are three basic categories of trust arising from legal implication.

1. Constructive trusts

The broadest category of trust arising from legal implication is that known as the constructive trust, whereby a trust is construed by the law from the relationship in which the parties happen to be. The purpose of the constructive trust is, in general terms, no more than the accounting for assets. The limited nature of this trust purpose means that the trustee's powers are more restricted than with normal trusts: he is unlikely, for example, to be able to resign, or to appoint new trustees. However, the general duties of normal trustees apply to constructive trustees, such as the duty to look after the estate with prudence and diligence, and the duty not to become *auctor in rem suam.*[20]

In Scots law there is generally recognised to be two situations in which a constructive trust may arise: (1), where a third party to an existing trust comes to hold property, knowing that it belongs to the trust and (2), where a person owing a fiduciary duty to another person makes a profit or gains an advantage from his position in that fiduciary relationship.[21]

The first situation only arises when there is a previously existing trust, and when the third party knows of its existence and knows that the property he is holding belongs to that trust. It could be argued that this does not really constitute a trust except when the holder of the property in some way obtains title to the property, for trusteeship is essentially a proprietorial office. However the law does impose a trust-like obligation to restore the property to the trust in this sort of situation.

[20] *Black* v. *Brown*, 1982 S.L.T. (Sh.Ct.) 50 at p. 56.
[21] These are the two situations identified by Wilson & Duncan at p. 78. This classification has been accepted by the courts: see *Black* v. *Brown*, 1982 S.L.T. (Sh.Ct.) 50.

The second situation is rather broader, requiring neither a previously existing trust, nor the holding of property from such a trust. It does however clearly constitute a proper trust. Whenever one person is in a fiduciary relationship to another, that person may not make a profit or gain an advantage from that position, whether or not the profit is made at the expense of the other party, and whether it is made in good or bad faith. Any profit or gain made is held on constructive trust. This rule applies to all fiduciary relationships, such as agent and principal, partners, tutor and pupil, curator and minor, trustee and beneficiary, or government and spy.

For example, an agent is in a fiduciary relationship to his principal and if he makes any personal profit from that position he will be under a constructive trust to pay over that profit to the principal.[22] Similarly partners in a firm are in a fiduciary relationship to each other, and therefore will be under a constructive trust to share with the partnership any profit made or advantage gained from the position as partner. This may even extend beyond the life of the partnership, as is shown in the case of *McNiven* v. *Peffers*.[23] Here a partner obtained a lease of the partnership premises in his own name, and then terminated the partnership and carried on the business from the same premises on his own account. It was held that he was under a constructive trust to his ex-partner for the profits made after the termination of the partnership.

Trustees in an express trust are also in a fiduciary relationship to the beneficiaries, and it follows that they too will be under a constructive trust to account to the beneficiaries for any advantage they acquire from their position as trustees. So in *Cherry's Trs.* v. *Patrick*[24] a wholesale supplier of alcoholic liquor continued to supply certain public houses with his liquor even after he had become trustee of property which included these public houses. He had made no extra profit and had simply continued doing what he had done before, but the court held that he had made a personal profit from his position as trustee and that he was therefore under a constructive trust to pay over that profit to the trust estate.

An interesting example of a constructive trust, which arose incidentally to a fiduciary relationship is the English House of Lords case of *Attorney General* v. *Guardian Newspapers* (*No.*

---

[22] *Pender* v. *Henderson & Co.* (1864) 2 M. 1428.
[23] (1868) 7 M. 181.
[24] (1911) 2 S.L.T. 313.

2).[25] Here a man named Wright, who had worked for the British security services, wrote a book called *Spycatcher*, which the British Government claimed was in breach of his life-long obligation of secrecy. A Sunday newspaper published extracts from the book. The House of Lords refused to grant an injunction against future publication, because the facts revealed in the book were so well known; but it did hold that the newspaper was liable to account to the Government for the profit it had made through the original publication. This is an odd case because of the fact that it was Wright, not the defendants, who was in a fiduciary relationship to the Government. It may be explained by the fact that, as will be seen shortly, the English courts are rather more imaginative in their use of the constructive trust than the Scottish courts. It is suggested that without Scottish judicial sanction it would be unsafe to rely upon this case in Scotland.

In order for a constructive trust to arise in Scotland, the profit must be made from the fiduciary's position, and not simply incidentally to it. A solicitor in a legal partnership must pay in to the firm the profits he acquires from practising law, but he need not pay over royalties he makes from writing a legal text book researched and written in his own time.[26]

The necessary fiduciary relationship can arise even in the absence of a recognised pre-existing relationship (such as that between partners). It has sometimes been held to arise through a single transaction or a course of transactions. The mere existence of a commercial relationship does not automatically imply a fiduciary duty,[27] but it can arise if there are special circumstances. For example a fiduciary relationship (and thus a constructive trust) arose from a commercial transaction in the case of *Black* v. *Brown*[28] (in which the shrieval judgment contains an interesting and useful discussion of the concept of constructive trusts). Here a mother (owing to misunderstanding what she had succeeded to from her husband's estate) mistakenly believed herself to be the owner of a business. The business was in reality owned by her son, and she was merely a substantial creditor. She wished to make a gift of £5,000 to her daughter and, believing herself to be donating part of the business to the daughter, in fact assigned

[25] [1988] 3 All E.R. 545.

[26] The position might be different if the solicitor produced a style book, for which he had relied upon the firm's styles. The partnership agreement may well contain provisions to deal with such a situation.

[27] *Per* Lord Clyde in *Raymond Harrison & Co.'s Tr.* v. *North West Securities Ltd.*, 1989 S.L.T. 718.

[28] 1982 S.L.T. (Sh.Ct.) 50.

part of the debt to her. The son, who knew the real nature of the transaction, paid interest to the daughter at rates set by himself, but without ever explaining the true situation. The sheriff held that the son was in a fiduciary relationship to the daughter in relation to the debt, and thus owed to her not only interest but an obligation to account for all the profits he had made from the debt.[29] The extra element that turned this commercial relationship into a fiduciary one seems to have been the fact that the son was aware of the true nature of the transaction and was also aware that the daughter was not so aware.[30]

These are the two categories of constructive trust recognised by Scots law. It is a flexible concept and has been used rather more widely in other legal systems to achieve equitable ends that cannot otherwise be achieved.[31] For example in England the notion of constructive trust was used to achieve what is now covered by the forfeiture rule in succession. In *Re Crippen's Estate*[32] Crippen had murdered his wife and fled with his mistress. He was caught and hanged. His mistress benefited under his will, but she was held not entitled to that part of his property which had derived from Mrs Crippen, as Crippen was considered to have held it on a constructive trust for Mrs Crippen's heirs.[33]

The concept is also used in English law to achieve results that would not by any other means be achieved in Scots law. In *Grant v. Edwards*,[34] a man bought a house for the use of himself and the woman he lived with. The woman paid the household expenses, and bore and brought up his children. It was held that since both parties treated the house as if it were jointly owned, and since the man could not have kept up the mortgage payments unless he were relieved of the day to day household expenses by the woman, the title to the house was held by the man on a constructive trust for himself and the woman jointly.[35]

---

[29] In fact the sheriff also found that the interest paid to the pursuer covered any profit the defender had made, and so at the end of the day nothing was due to her.

[30] See also *Elias* v. *Black* (1856) 18 D. 1225.

[31] See generally, Oakley, *Constructive Trusts*, 2nd ed., London 1987, who gives examples from a number of jurisdictions.

[32] [1911] P. 108.

[33] This remains the solution adopted in some U.S. jurisdictions: see Bogert, *Trusts and Trustees*, 2nd ed. 1978, s.478. See also *Preston* v. *Chabot* (1980) 412 A2d 930.

[34] [1986] 2 All E.R. 426. See also the similar Canadian decision of *Novick Estate* v. *Lachuk Estate* (1989) 58 D.L.R. (4th) 185.

[35] In *Newton* v. *Newton*, 1923 S.C. 15, a similar claim failed in the Court of Session because the Blank Bonds and Trusts Act 1696 limited proof of the existence of the trust to writ or oath, neither of which was available.

The concept is taken even further in the U.S.A., where it is often used as an equitable remedy for unjust enrichment as well as in the proprietary sense used in Scotland.[36] There is no authority in Scots law for extending the concept beyond the categories already recognised: the principle of restitution and the concept of unjust enrichment are sufficiently developed in Scots law to render the use of the constructive trust to achieve these aims otiose. The trust is a flexible and developing institution, and its use in the future as an equitable remedy when the law provides no other cannot, and ought not, be ruled out.

2. Resulting trusts

Legal implication may create what is known as a resulting trust, the word "resulting" coming from *resultare*—"to spring back," or "to rebound." When a truster attempts to set up a trust for the benefit of a beneficiary, it may for some reason rebound back to him, in the sense that the trustees will thereafter hold the property, not for the achievement of the truster's purposes, but for the sole purpose of returning the trust estate back to the truster, or his heirs. Resulting trusts are designed to fill the gap if the beneficial interest in the trust estate is not effectually disposed of and it cannot go elsewhere. Resulting trusts arise on the failure of trusts that cannot be revived, for the truster will sometimes retain a reversionary right in the property he gives away in trust. There is no room for a resulting trust unless the truster retains some reversionary right in the trust property: so there is no room for a resulting trust if the nature of the transfer indicates that the truster intends to divest himself completely of all interest in the property, or if the trust is one to which the *cy près* jurisdiction can be applied, or an application under section 9 of the Law Reform (Miscellaneous Provisions) (Scotland) Act 1990 can be made.[37]

---

[36] As was famously said by Cardozo C.J. in *Beatty* v. *Guggenheim Exploration Co.* (1919) 122 N.E. 378 at p. 380, "A constructive trust is the formula through which the conscience of equity finds expression. When property has been acquired in such circumstances that the holder of the legal title may not in good conscience retain the beneficial interest, equity converts him into a trustee." See further, Bogert, *op. cit.* at ss.471–501.

[37] See Chap. 13.

Tax Point

Where the inheritance tax charitable exemption is claimed for a transfer into a trust it is necessary to establish that the trust funds may not be applicable for purposes other than charitable ones (IHTA 1984, s.23(5)). This provision means that if an individual could benefit under the trust provisions the exemption will not be granted. Similarly, if a resulting trust arises so that the funds come to be held for the truster or his heirs this exemption would be refused. However, provided that the trust is valid *ab initio* the *cy près* jurisdiction will prevent a resulting trust arising.

Resulting trusts may arise in a number of different circumstances. For example, the trust purposes may be invalid for one of the reasons discussed in Chapter 6, such as illegality or uncertainty. In that situation "there must be actual failure of the trust purposes, not a temporary uncertainty as to what these are or an indefinite postponement of their coming into operation."[38] In *Templeton* v. *Burgh of Ayr*[39] money was left to rebuild a bridge at Ayr. The bridge was repaired from other funds, but no resulting trust arose since the trust estate might be called upon sometime in the future for further repairs.

The trust might otherwise fail to take effect because the truster has failed to appoint trustees,[40] or because the trustees are not empowered to exercise a necessary discretion.[41] Likewise if the machinery of the trust is an essential part of the truster's scheme, the failure of the machinery will involve the failure of the trust, and a resulting trust will arise. The trust may also fail because no trust purposes at all are laid down, though there has been a declaration of trust (*i.e.* it is clear that the truster does not intend the trustees to take a beneficial interest).

The purposes may be achieved before the trust property is exhausted, as in *Anderson* v. *Smoke*.[42] Here a father passed property to his daughters for the benefit of his son, about whom there was some unexplained "peculiarity." The son died before the property was used up, and though the father had provided that in that event the daughters were to use the property as they thought proper, it was held that there was a resulting trust to the father and his heirs since it could not be said that there was an outright gift to the daughters (the destination over being void for uncertainty).

Another circumstance in which a resulting trust will arise is during sequestration, for if after paying off the debts and the

---

[38] Mackenzie Stuart at p. 43.
[39] (1910) 2 S.L.T. 12.
[40] *Angus's Exx.* v. *Batchan's Trs.*, 1949 S.C. 335.
[41] *Robbie's Judicial Factor* v. *Macrae* (1893) 20 R. 358.
[42] (1898) 25 R. 493.

expenses of sequestration there is property left over, the trustee in sequestration will normally hold this on a resulting trust for the debtor.[43]

It is sometimes considered that a resulting trust will arise when a public subscription fund has achieved its aims without using all the money collected.[44] However, the practical difficulties in trying to identify all the people who have donated small sums, often by putting coins in a collecting box in the street, are great and obvious, and the law ought to hold that such people intend to divest themselves completely of any reversionary right in their donations. In most cases a *cy près* scheme ought to be available to deal with such surpluses.[45]

Tax Point
A resulting trust can have tax consequences for the truster or his heirs. In the case of *Hannay's Exx.* v. *Commissioners of Inland Revenue*[46] the trust made provision for disposal of the capital, but for part of the administration period part of the income was not disposed of. The court held that there was a resulting trust of this income, in favour of the truster and this therefore fell to be taxed as part of the truster's income (s.673, ICTA 1988).

3. Fiduciary fees

The narrowest category of trust arising by implication of law is that known as the fiduciary fee, which in effect is a fiction designed to deal with a feudal problem.

When a liferent and fee are set up it is competent, indeed common, to confer the right to the fee on a person or persons not yet born. However it is considered to be a feudal impossibility for the fee of property to be in abeyance.[47] It cannot, it is said, float about on poised wing[48] waiting to alight at a suitable moment, nor be hidden in some crepuscular corner of the common law waiting

---

[43] Bankruptcy (Scotland) Act 1985, s.51(5). A very similar type of trust, though it is not strictly a resulting trust, is created by s.27(1) of the Conveyancing and Feudal Reform (Scotland) Act 1970, by which a creditor in a standard security who sells the security subjects holds the sale proceeds in trust to be applied to specified purposes, the last of which is payment of the residue to the debtor.

[44] This matter is more fully discussed in Wilson & Duncan at pp. 76/77, and Mackenzie Stuart at pp. 46/47.

[45] See Chap. 13.

[46] 37 T.C. 217.

[47] Though this is by no means a universally held view: see Wilson & Duncan at p. 62, and Mackenzie Stuart at p. 38.

[48] *Per* Lord Ardmillan, *Cumstie* v. *Cumstie's Trs.* (1876) 3 R. 921 at p. 927.

to spring out when the appropriate person comes along. In other words, the fee must always be attached to someone. The law gets around this problem by holding that the liferenter holds the fee in trust, that is holds it as a fiduciary fiar, until such time as the beneficial fiars are ascertained.[49] If there are more than one beneficial fiar, each takes as he comes into existence and his right to the fee is subject to partial defeasance if more fiars are later born.

Though there has been doubt expressed over the precise nature of the fiduciary fee, it is certainly more nearly a trust than anything else. The liferenter's right to the fee is of a very different nature from his right to the liferent. As Mackenzie Stuart points out[50] if the unborn children never do come into existence, the fiduciary fiar does not keep the estate: the estate reverts back to the granter. The fiduciary fee may therefore be considered to be a trust, though a very peculiar one.

Another doubt concerns the extent of the application of the fiduciary fee. There are dicta suggesting that a fiduciary fee can only arise when the beneficial fiars are the children or the heirs of the liferenter.[51] However Mackenzie Stuart suggests that the provisions of section 8 of the Trusts (Scotland) Act 1921, which is statutory recognition of the fiduciary fee, have rid the law of that restriction.[52] Wilson and Duncan suggest that the position is now that "while the fiduciary fiar cannot hold *only* for persons other than his own children or heirs he can hold for other persons if he is also holding for his own children or heirs."[53] This limitation seems rather illogical.

The powers of administration of such a trustee (that is of the liferenter) in this peculiar trust are very limited compared with a normal trust. By section 8(2) of the Trusts (Scotland) Act 1921 the fiduciary fiar does not have the usual powers of a trustee, but must apply to the court either for authority to exercise any power competent to a trustee, or for the appointment of an independent trustee who will act on behalf of both liferenter and fiar. He is however subject to the normal duties of a trustee, such as the obligation not to be *auctor in rem suam*.[54]

[49] See for example *Snell* v. *White* (1872) 10 M. 745.
[50] At p. 39.
[51] See particularly Lord President Dunedin in *Colvile's Trs.* v. *Marindin*, 1908 S.C. 911.
[52] At p. 40. Lord Kilbrandon in the Outer House case of *Napier* v. *Napiers*, 1963 S.L.T. 143 seems to be of the same view.
[53] Wilson & Duncan at p. 67.
[54] Mackenzie Stuart at p. 39.

CHAPTER 5

APPOINTMENT OF TRUSTEES

Introduction

A TRUST requires trustees, and cannot come into existence until trustees are, by some means or another, appointed. There is however no general requirement in Scots law for any set number of trustees, though, unless the trust is intended to exist for only a short time, it is advisable for practical reasons for there to be more than one trustee.

When the trust is first set up it is for the truster himself to choose who will hold and administer the trust estate. His choice is completely free, subject to the chosen person's legal capacity to accept the trust. "Anyone who has legal capacity for holding property and dealing with it may act as trustee in a trust regulated by the law of Scotland."[1] A pupil could not accept office as trustee. A minor may be appointed trustee,[2] though this is undesirable owing to the legal restrictions on minors' contractual capacity.[3] Juristic persons (such as corporations, local authorities, and, in Scotland, partnerships) can act as trustee, and, certainly in England, it has become very common indeed for a trust to be set up with a single corporate trustee rather than a group of natural persons.[4] In Scotland trust companies are not uncommon but the courts are not enthusiastic about them, particularly in relation to private family trusts. In *Ommanney, Petr.*[5] the First Division refused to grant a variation under section

---

[1] Wilson & Duncan at p. 227.

[2] See *Hill* v. *City of Glasgow Bank* (1879) 7 R. 68, a case which also illustrates the potential problems of having a minor as trustee.

[3] Wilson & Duncan at pp. 228–230.

[4] English law gives "gentle encouragement" to this movement, with a number of provisions allowing a single corporate trustee to act when English law would otherwise require more than one trustee: see Ockelton at p. 97. Scots law has no requirement for any particular number of trustees in particular circumstances.

[5] 1966 S.L.T. (Notes) 13.

1 of the Trusts (Scotland) Act 1961 insofar as it involved a bank being appointed trustee. The court said:

> "An impersonal body such as a bank or trust corporation is not a suitable party to exercise such a discretion involving personal and family considerations for its proper exercise."[6]

Certain types of trust, notably trusts for the maintenance of historic buildings and employee share ownership trusts, require a professional trustee, such as a solicitor or an accountant if they are to obtain the tax advantages accruing to such trusts.[7]

The duties and liabilities flowing from the office of trustee can potentially be very onerous, and they are not, therefore, to be imposed upon an unwilling party. With express trusts the office of trustee is always voluntary. Only in limited circumstances will a person become a trustee without his consent or against his own wishes. For example a person can become a trustee by operation of law,[8] where his wishes would be irrelevant. The holding of some other legal office may carry with it the imposition of trust duties for certain purposes (such as for example a judicial factor, executor, or tutor or curator).[9]

There are a number of different ways in which a person can come in to the office of trustee. However appointed, the rights and liabilities of all trustees are, generally speaking, the same.

THE ORIGINAL TRUSTEES

The original trustees are those whom the truster himself has nominated for that office, and who have accepted the office. Both nomination and acceptance are essential to establish the relationship of truster and trustee.

1. Nomination

The law assumes that the nomination of an individual to act as a person's trustee is based on *delectus personae*, that is, the truster

---

[6] The English courts seem to adopt a quite opposite approach and feel that because family members and family solicitors will be too close to the settlement to be objective, corporate trustees are to be preferred in family settlements: see Todd at pp. 20/21.

[7] IHTA 1984, Sched. 4, para. 2(ii) and Finance Act 1989, Sched. 5, para. 3(3)(c).

[8] See Chap. 4.

[9] All of which are included in the definition of "trustee" under s.2 of the Trusts (Scotland) Act 1921.

chooses a nominee because of the specific qualities that the nominee possesses, and because he can be trusted to carry out the trust in the way that the truster would have wished. The nomination of an individual to act as trustee can take many forms, and there is no legally required form. The clearest, and most common, type of nomination with express trusts is for the truster to have his wishes clearly set out in the document that sets up the trust. This can be done either by naming an individual ("Mr John Smith is to be trustee"), or by laying down a description ("the father of the beneficiary is to be trustee"). In the latter case it becomes a matter of fact and interpretation who actually fits the description.[10]

The nomination need not be in the trust deed itself, and it is open to the truster to nominate trustees in a separate and later deed, though in that case care must be taken to ensure that the nomination links in with the intended trust.

A nomination may be not of an identified individual but rather of the holder of a specified office, such as the minister of a certain parish, or the chairman of a certain company, or the holder of a specified chair at a certain university: if such a nomination is accepted the trustee will be termed an *ex officio* trustee. These are most common with public and charitable trusts. This nomination is, like all nominations, based on *delectus personae*, though with *ex officio* trustees the desired qualities flow from the office rather than from the individual holder for the time being of that office. It follows that if the individual and the office separate, the trusteeship follows the office and not the individual. Further, if the office changes character in some fundamental way, then the nomination will become invalid. This only happens however when the change is so fundamental that the office is no longer what the truster had in mind.[11]

2. Acceptance or declinature

The office of trustee being potentially onerous, an opportunity must be given to the nominee to accept or decline the office as he chooses. The choice is free, though the truster may give some incentive to acceptance, such as, in a testamentary trust, giving a

[10] With appointments by Will, affidavit evidence before the commissary clerk will be the way to establish identity. In practical terms appointment by description should be avoided for *inter vivos* trusts and for the assumption of trustees into existing trusts.

[11] *Vestry of St. Silas Church* v. *Trustees of St. Silas Church*, 1945 S.C. 110.

legacy that is dependent on the nominee accepting office as trustee.

"Whatever form the nomination of a trustee may take the appointment is not effective and the status of trustee is not attained until there has been acceptance on the part of the nominee. Only then does the relationship of trustee and beneficiary come into being and the nominee become vested in the rights and affected by the liabilities of the office."[12] On acceptance the trustees acquire a personal right to the trust property, and their first duty is to complete title in the required form, giving them a real right. A failure or delay in accepting office will impose no liability on the nominee, even when that causes loss to the trust estate.[13]

Acceptance will generally be express, and the most satisfactory form will be a written consent to act as trustee, which can be appended as a minute to the deed of trust. Verbal acceptance would appear to be competent, but is less satisfactory given the problems of proof. Acceptance may also be implied from the circumstances, though only when the nominee is aware of the nomination. If, for example, the nominee commences to act as if he were trustee, *e.g.* by gathering in the estate, taking title to it, or homologating trust transactions, he will be personally barred from later denying his acceptance. In *Ker* v. *City of Glasgow Bank*[14] a man allowed his name to be used as trustee in a stock transfer, and he also signed himself with the word "trustee" appearing after his name, even although he had never formally accepted the trust. It was held that he had impliedly accepted the trust.

Similarly a declinature may be express or implied. Again an express written declinature is the most satisfactory, but it would appear that a person who is nominated need not take any positive action to decline. He could ignore the nomination if he wants: "there is no presumption of acceptance."[15] Passivity on the part of the nominee is neutral in its effect. Circumstances may imply a declinature, such as if, in the knowledge of his nomination, the nominee refuses to take part in any trust meetings, or if he permits the other nominees to complete title in their names but not in his.

---

[12] Wilson & Duncan at p. 241. An exception to this could occur when property is transferred to a nominee before he accepts office, and he then declines to act as trustee—such a nominee would hold the property on resulting (non-voluntary) trust for the truster. On resulting trusts, see Chap. 4.

[13] Mackenzie Stuart at p. 153.

[14] (1879) 6 R. (H.L.) 52.

[15] Mackenzie Stuart at p. 155.

If the nomination is *ex officio* and that nominee declines to act, it remains open to a successor in office to accept the trusteeship.[16]

The nomination of trustees in Scots law is joint and several and it follows that each nominee can accept or decline without reference to the others or effect upon their nomination. Joint nomination (as opposed to joint and several) would result in the declinature of one nominee vitiating the nomination of the others. The truster may, if he so desires, provide for this in the trust deed. Such a provision is very unusual, but might be considered appropriate when for example the beneficiaries are children, and the truster wishes both parents to act as trustees.

NEW TRUSTEES

Trusts, of their nature, tend to continue in existence for extended periods of time. Public trusts especially can last for hundreds of years. The original trustees can continue in that office as long as they like, and if they resign or die, the title to the property, being joint and several, will automatically vest in the survivor or survivors. Eventually however in many trusts the time will come when new trustees have to be brought in to continue the administration. This can be done in a number of different ways.

1. Appointment of new trustees

After the trust has been established, with original appointees, new trustees may, exceptionally, be appointed (as opposed to the normal assumption: see *infra*). The truster may have reserved the right in the trust deed to himself, or to any named individual, whether a trustee, a beneficiary, or a stranger to the trust, to appoint new trustees in stated circumstances. Such a provision will be construed strictly. If a beneficiary is given such a power, this is one of the few circumstances in which any beneficiary will have a say about who is to be trustee.[17]

Even without such an express reservation of power, the truster of a private trust has a residual common law power to appoint

---

[16] *Ibid.* at pp. 155–156; *Magistrates of Edinburgh* v. *McLaren* (1881) 8 R. (H.L.) 140.

[17] Short of them exercising any power they may have to wind up the trust and resettle the estate: see Chap. 14. Another situation would be when the trust lapses due, say, to the deaths of all the trustees: the beneficiaries may petition the court to appoint new trustees, and they can suggest names.

new trustees to a trust, but only when the original trustees have failed, and the exercise of this power is necessary to prevent the trust lapsing. He cannot add to existing trustees, he can only replace them when this is necessary for the continuation of the trust.[18] Such a power only exists during the life of the truster, and does not pass on to his successors. It is restricted to private trusts, for the creators of public trusts retain much less interest in such trusts once they are established (unless the right of appointment is expressly reserved).

Under section 13 of the Law Reform (Miscellaneous Provisions) (Scotland) Act 1990 both the Lord Advocate and the existing trustees have the power, notwithstanding anything in the trust deed to the contrary, to appoint such new trustees as will bring the number of trustees up to three, but this applies only to public trusts that have charitable status for revenue purposes.

2. Assumption by existing trustees

Existing trustees, however they come into that office,[19] have the power to assume into the trust new trustees, either to act along with, or instead of, themselves. The power of assumption had, at common law, to be granted expressly, but now, by section 3(*b*) of the Trusts (Scotland) Act 1921, all trusts are held to include the power to assume new trustees, unless the contrary be expressed. This is by far the most common method by which new trustees come in to a trust. A sole trustee may exercise this power; if there are two trustees they must both agree; if there are more than two then the power of assumption may be exercised by a quorum, which is assumed[20] (unless the contrary be expressed) to be a majority. Less than the quorum can exercise the power of assumption, so long as the consent of the court is obtained to the deed of assumption and conveyance.[21] Though in all matters of administration, including assumption, there is a duty to consult all the trustees, this duty must be read in a reasonable and practicable light: it has been held that a quorum can exercise the power of assumption, even without consulting one of their number, if that one has gone abroad.[22]

[18] Wilson & Duncan at p. 263.
[19] Though doubt has been expressed about the right of *ex officio* trustees to exercise this power: see Lord President Cooper in *St. Silas Church, supra* n. 11, at p. 121.
[20] s.3(*c*) 1921.
[21] s.21.
[22] *Malcolm* v. *Goldie* (1895) 22 R. 968.

The exercise of the power of assumption is generally a matter solely in the discretion of the trustees (though as a matter of good practice—not law—trustees in private trusts will often endeavour to choose a person acceptable to the beneficiaries). It has been held in England that beneficiaries, even when they all concur, cannot force trustees to exercise the power of assumption, as this would be a limitation on the trustees' discretionary rights.[23] This seems sound and probably also reflects the position in Scots law.

There are however certain limited circumstances in which trustees would be forced to exercise their power of assumption. First, the trust deed may provide that there must be a certain number of trustees at any one time: if this is so then whenever the number falls below that stated, the trustees must follow the truster's instructions and assume new trustees. The trust deed may direct that certain persons be assumed at stated events, such as marriage of a beneficiary, or the attainment of majority. Secondly, the power of assumption must be exercised when a sole trustee wishes to resign. By section 3, proviso 1 of the 1921 Act a sole trustee (and, according to Wilson and Duncan[24] the existing trustees as a body) cannot resign unless he has assumed new trustees (and they have expressly accepted), or the court has appointed new trustees or a judicial factor.[25] Thirdly, there are certain statutory provisions providing for a minimum number of trustees in certain trusts subject to special taxation rules. For example in relation to public trusts with charitable purposes, the Lord Advocate and the trustees have the power to ensure that there are at least three trustees, notwithstanding anything to the contrary in the trust deed.[26] Similarly employee share ownership trusts require to have at least three trustees.[27] Apart from these exceptions, the existing trustees have the right to decide for themselves whether and when the power of assumption should be exercised. It is however advisable that the power be exercised when there is only one trustee left and the trust is still continuing, in order to avoid the risk of the expense and delay of having to go to court if the sole trustee unexpectedly dies.

By section 21 of the 1921 Act, trustees may exercise their power of assumption by utilising the style of a deed of assumption and conveyance in Schedule B of that Act, and such a deed

---

[23] *Re Brockbank* [1948] Ch. 206.
[24] At p. 256.
[25] For situations in which a judicial factor would be appropriate rather than new trustees, see Wilson & Duncan at pp. 272–276.
[26] Law Reform (Miscellaneous Provisions) (Scotland) Act 1990, s.13.
[27] Finance Act 1989, Sched. 5, para. 3(3)(*a*).

will have the effect of conferring title to all the trust property on the assumed and remaining trustees.

The statutory power of assumption is assumed into every trust deed "unless the contrary be expressed." It is often said that an implied exclusion will not be sufficient to supersede the statutory power,[28] but the cases do show that an express conferral of the power of assumption on named individuals or in specified circumstances will be taken to be an exclusion of that right from anyone else or in any other circumstance. In *Munro's Trs.* v. *Young*,[29] spouses had set up an ante-nuptial trust for their own benefit and reserved to themselves or the survivor the power to appoint new trustees. It was held that this excluded the trustees' statutory right to assume. And in *Thomson's Trs., Petr.*[30] a husband appointed his wife "and any others whom she may select to act along with her" as his testamentary trustees. The wife (now widow) assumed the dead husband's mother to act along with her, and then remarried and emigrated to Australia. The mother was left as *de facto* sole trustee, and she wished to assume new trustees. Lord Mackintosh held that so long as the wife remained a trustee, only she could assume new trustees, because the nomination in the trust deed was "equivalent to an express provision that so long as the wife is herself a trustee no other person shall be allowed to assume a trustee."[31] Good drafting would today suggest that no mention be made in the trust deed of the power of assumption, unless it is expressly desired to restrict it in some way.

The statutory power under section 3 provides that existing trustees may assume "new trustees"; the first proviso provides that a sole trustee may not resign until he has appointed "new trustees." The use of the plural here may be compared with section 22 of the same Act, which gives the court power to appoint "a trustee or trustees." The plural in section 3 has led some writers[32] to suggest that, certainly in relation to the proviso, it would be incompetent to assume only one trustee. The decision in *Kennedy, Petr.*,[33] however, buries this suggestion. Here a sole executrix (for this purpose in the same position as a trustee) tried

---

[28] See, *e.g.* the oft-quoted comments of Lord Gifford in *Allan's Trs.* v. *Hairstens* (1878) 5 R. 576 at p. 580.

[29] (1887) 14 R. 574.

[30] 1948 S.L.T. (Notes) 27.

[31] *Ibid.* at p. 28.

[32] Wilson & Duncan at p. 256, Burns' *Conveyancing Practice* 4th ed., W. Green, Edinburgh 1957 at p. 837.

[33] 1983 S.L.T. (Sh. Ct.) 10.

to resign having assumed a single new executrix to act in her place, and it was argued that it was incompetent for her to resign unless she had assumed at least two new executors, to satisfy the plural requirement in the Act. The sheriff held that the plural in the proviso could not be taken literally, as this would be the only example in the whole of the law of trusts which struck at administration by a sole trustee. He held rather that the plural in the proviso had been used simply to reflect its earlier use in the same section, which quite clearly included the singular. The difference between the phrases in section 3 and in section 22 was simply the result of sloppy draftsmanship. Consequently, he granted confirmation to the resignation of the sole executrix on the assumption of a new, single, executrix. Though a shrieval judgment has little precedential value, it is suggested that *Kennedy* will be followed because it accurately reflects the law.

On assuming a new trustee, the existing trustees are under an obligation to take reasonable care to see that they select a fit and proper person for the post. This is not a guarantee of the selected person's actions, but merely a duty not to select someone who is clearly unfit for the office. If the assumption is made with the express purpose of making it possible for a trustee to resign, he will be under a special duty to the beneficiaries to take care in the selection of new trustees.[34] Persons disqualified from acting as trustees cannot be assumed into trusts that have charitable purposes.[35]

An assumed trustee will have all the powers and duties that the assuming trustees have, neither more nor less, and if it is intended to bring in a trustee with more limited powers, this would have to be done by the court. However, all the rights of the original trustees may not necessarily pass to assumed trustees. It has been held that legacies left in the trust deed "to such of my trustees as shall accept and act" as trustee would be limited to the original trustees, and that assumed trustees could not claim a share of the legacies.[36]

3. Appointment by the court

At common law the Inner House of the Court of Session, in the exercise of its *nobile officium*, could appoint new trustees to a

[34] See Mackenzie Stuart at pp. 297/298.
[35] Law Reform (Miscellaneous Provisions) (Scotland) Act 1990, s.8.
[36] *Waddell's Trs.* v. *Bairnsfather*, 1926 S.L.T. 457.

trust whenever this was necessary for the administration of that trust. This power still exists, but statute now also provides a power to the court to appoint new trustees in certain circumstances; and if these circumstances exist, the statutory power must be used in preference to the common law power.

The statutory power is contained in section 22 of the 1921 Act, under which the court may appoint a trustee or trustees in certain situations. Any party having interest in the trust estate (which phrase covers the beneficiaries, the trustees—who both have interests, though of different natures—and the truster if he has some reversionary interest in the trust estate) may make the application. The court will be either the Court of Session, or[37] a sheriff court of the sheriffdom in which the truster or any of the trusters was domiciled at the time the trust came into operation. The circumstances in which the application may be made are as follows: (a) if trustees cannot be assumed under the trust deed, or (b) when a sole trustee becomes insane or is incapable of acting as trustee through physical or mental disability, or (c) when a sole trustee is incapable of acting as trustee by being absent continuously from the U.K. for a period of at least six months, or has disappeared for at least six months. An appointment under the first head will be either to act along with or instead of the existing trustees, but any such appointment under the latter two heads will have the effect of removing the existing trustee.[38]

In order to satisfy the first ground, it must be impossible or incompetent for the existing trustees to exercise their power of assumption, either because the trust deed expressly denies them that power, or because all the existing trustees have died. A failure to exercise the power, or an inability amongst trustees to agree about whether to exercise the power, will not satisfy the first condition. For example if a quorum of the trustees refuse to assume a new trustee, a minority trustee could not rely on section 22 to ask the court to appoint the new trustee instead. If an even number of trustees are equally split about whether or not to

---

[37] s.24A, added by s.13(D) of the Law Reform (Miscellaneous Provisions) (Scotland) Act 1980.

[38] Section 23 allows the court to remove a trustee for like reason, without making a new appointment. The court *must* remove the trustee on proof of incapacity, and it *may* remove the trustee on proof of absence or disappearance. The absence or disappearance does not *ipso facto* remove the trustee, and a court order under s.22 or s.23 is necessary: *Thomson's Trs.*, *Petr.*, 1948 S.L.T. (Notes) 27. It does however give the remaining trustees the right to act without regard to the missing trustees: *Malcolm* v. *Goldie* (1895) 22 R. 968.

assume a new trustee, section 22 will not be applicable, for that is more a case of failure than impossibility.[39]

However, in situations which do not come within the statutory provisions, the common law power of the Court of Session could be utilised. That power has been used in order to appoint a new trustee to resolve a deadlock amongst existing trustees,[40] and to appoint a new trustee when a sole trustee was removed for incompetence, and the trust would otherwise lapse.[41] In *Adamson's Trs.*,[42] where the trust deed provided that a spouse in an ante-nuptial trust, being only one of the trustees, had to consent to any assumption, the common law power was used when that spouse became insane and could not consent.[43]

The trustees appointed under section 22 will have "all powers incident to that office," and this means all the powers incident to the office of trustee in the particular trust in question. The appointee will be subject to all the restrictions the original trust deed imposed, and he cannot rely on the general legal powers that would otherwise be available. A trustee appointed under the common law power will have all the powers given by the court, which will normally be those given by the trust deed itself, but may, in certain circumstances, be more or less extensive. In *Glasgow Lock Hospital, Petrs.*[44] the court appointed trustees, but restricted their powers to the taking of title to a hospital and its endowments (the trust property). Likewise, a legacy to the original trustees may not, depending upon the terms of the trust, be claimable by the appointed trustees.[45]

The court has refused to appoint a trustee to carry out a discretionary right to choose beneficiaries from a wide class, on the rationale that there is no *delectus personae* between the truster and the appointee.[46] Nor is the court likely to appoint a corporate trustee to a family trust that involves a discretion concerning personal and family matters.[47] The Scottish court may, in appropriate circumstances, appoint persons resident abroad as

---

[39] The analogous English provision in s.41 of the Trustee Act 1925 uses very different wording, and is often used when the trustees cannot agree: see Moffat & Chesterman at pp. 422/423.

[40] *Aikman, Petr.* (1881) 9 R. 213. See also Menzies at pp. 44/45.

[41] *Lamont* v. *Lamont* 1908 S.C. 1033.

[42] 1917 S.C. 440.

[43] This might also have been a case of impossibility under the first head in s.22.

[44] 1949 S.L.T. (Notes) 26.

[45] Cf. *Waddell's Trs.* v. *Bairnsfather, supra.* n.36.

[46] See *Angus's Exx.* v. *Batchan's Trs.*, 1949 S.C. 335 (more fully discussed in Chap. 2).

[47] *Ommanney, Petr.* 1966 S.L.T. (Notes) 13.

trustees to Scottish trusts. The cases have involved situations in which all the beneficiaries have been resident in the foreign country, have all been able and willing to consent to the appointment of foreign trustees, and in which the appointees have given undertakings to the Court of Session that they will submit to that court's jurisdiction,[48] though the necessity for such undertakings has been doubted.[49]

Tax Point

The appointment of overseas trustees may put the trust outwith charges to U.K. income tax and CGT on overseas income and chargeable gains: see Chapter 2.

In the English case of *Chinn* v. *Collins*,[50] the U.K. resident trustees were replaced by the truster with trustees resident abroad (as part of a tax mitigation scheme). The Inland Revenue did not seek to argue that such an appointment was ineffective; and it seems safe to conclude that the appointment of overseas trustees can be countenanced even where the trust has no connection with the foreign country. There are certain cases where an overseas trustee cannot be assumed—for example in relation to trusts for the maintenance of historic buildings (IHTA 1984, Sched. 4, para. 2(1)(b)(iii)) and employee share ownership trusts (Finance Act 1989, Sched. 5, para. 3(3)(b)).

The Finance Bill 1991 contains provisions which will have the effect that, when trustees cease to be U.K. resident for tax purposes, CGT will be charged on the latent (but unrealised) chargeable gains on trust assets.

---

[48] *Simpson's Trs.*, *Petrs.* 1907 S.C. 87; *Coat's Trs.*, 1925 S.C. 104.
[49] Mackenzie Stuart at p. 305.
[50] [1981] 54 T.C. 311.

THE TRUST PURPOSES

Introduction

THE purposes of the trust constitute the very essence of the trust relationship, for it is the laying down of purposes that turns the passing of property into a trust. The purposes to be achieved by the trustees can be of a very specific nature, such as holding property for the benefit of a named individual; or of a much more general sort, such as "the furtherance of charity" or "educational purposes." Whatever their nature, the trust needs purposes. If property is passed to an individual but no purposes are laid down, there is nothing to qualify ownership, and the individual takes the property absolutely, that is, free from any trust. On the other hand if purposes are laid down but for some reason they are invalid, no initial trust is created, but the receiver will hold the property on a resulting trust for the original owner or his successors. A resulting trust like this will also occur if property is passed in a way evidencing the original owner's intent that the receiver is only to take as trustee, but he failed completely to lay down any purposes.

It is often said that for a trust to be valid there must be identifiable beneficiaries, either specified individuals (typically in a private trust) or a specified section of society in general (typically in a public trust). Very exceptionally however a trust may be set up for a purpose that benefits no living person.[1] It would be valid for a truster to make provision for the erection of a reasonable and suitable memorial to himself, such as a head-

---

[1] Though the spending of trust money always benefits someone, *e.g.* a tradesman or vendor dealing with the trust, such a person is not normally to be regarded as a beneficiary of a trust purpose: *McCaig* v. *University of Glasgow*, 1907 S.C. 231.

stone, or a tomb. This is a concession shown by the law which is based upon "the natural and human sentiments of ordinary people who desire that there should be some memorial to themselves,"[2] and it would follow that the exception should not be extended to other situations in which no identifiable human beneficiary or section of society is given an interest in the trust. It has however been argued by one of the present authors that the exception ought to be extended to include gifts made for the welfare of particular animals.[3] It is a natural and human sentiment for the fond owner of a pet animal to wish to make provision for its wellbeing after the owner's death, and, so long as it satisfies the conditions discussed in this chapter, it is suggested that trustees could competently give effect to such a direction.[4]

Apart from these limited exceptions, the trust purposes will invariably involve the conferring of some benefit (not necessarily financial) on an individual or section of society.

It is clear that every trust must have purposes in order to be valid; but more than this, the law requires that the purposes are legally acceptable. Drafters of trust deeds ought to bear in mind that in order to be acceptable the purposes must satisfy a number of criteria. If these criteria are taken into account when the trust is being drafted, the likelihood of subsequent challenge to the validity of the trust will be greatly reduced. To be legally acceptable, the purposes must satisfy the following criteria.

CERTAINTY

The first and most important criterion that all trust purposes must satisfy is that they be certain, and not vague or unspecified. If it cannot be determined from the trust deed what the truster wants done with the property, the trust will be held void for uncertainty. Various aspects of the trust purposes may be uncertain, for example who is to benefit, or how far they are to benefit, or with what they are to be benefited, or what aims are to be achieved, or what property is to be used in order to achieve these aims. In broad terms however there are two basic types of uncertainty, though it should be emphasised that the result will

---

[2] *Per* Lord Justice-Clerk Aitchison in *Lindsay's Ex.* v. *Forsyth*, 1940 S.C. 568 at p. 572.
[3] See Norrie, "Trusts for Animals" (1987) 32 J.L.S. 386. *Cf.* Mackenzie Stuart at p. 69.
[4] See further, Chap. 1.

be the same in either case, and the trust will be held void. There can be uncertainty either in the sense that the purposes are too vague for the trustees to know what they are being asked to do, or alternatively in the sense that the discretion given to the trustees is so wide that they cannot determine with sufficient accuracy what sort of purposes the truster had in mind.

1. Purposes too vague

A trust deed that is so vague or so ambiguous that the truster's intentions cannot properly be gleaned from it will be held void for uncertainty. Ambiguity on its own is not sufficient to invalidate the deed; it must be quite impossible to know what the truster is directing. It is for the truster to choose the purposes, and if his intention cannot be determined, no one, not even the court, can fill the gap. For example in *Hardie* v. *Morison*[5] a trust was set up for the purchasing of premises in Edinburgh, "to be used as a shop in which one of its objects was the sale of books dealing with the subject of free thought." It was held by Lord Kincairney that this trust was void for uncertainty, owing to the indeterminate nature of the term "free thought." He said:

> "I am not aware that it is a term with any definite or recognised meaning. In carrying out this trust it would not be possible to determine what class of books was meant . . . (T)he mere words of the deed do not indicate whether the testator intended books favourable to free thought or adverse to it."[6]

In order to determine whether a trust purpose is sufficiently clear, Lord Kinnear has said, "the question to be put in each particular case is whether the description of the class to be benefited is sufficiently exact to enable an executor [or trustee] of common sense to carry out the expressed wishes of the testator [or truster]."[7] Lord Justice-Clerk Thomson put it thus: "the test is whether a trustee, approaching the matter with proper care and properly advised, would be able to carry such an instruction out."[8]

In every case what has to be done is to determine the truster's intention. His intention is gleaned from the words used in the

[5] (1899) 7 S.L.T. 42.
[6] *Ibid.* at p. 42.
[7] In *Allan's Ex.* v. *Allan*, 1908 S.C. 807 at p. 814, approved by Lord President Strathclyde in *Bannerman's Trs.* v. *Bannerman*, 1915 S.C. 398.
[8] *Hood* v. *Macdonald's Tr.*, 1949 S.C. 24 at p. 28.

trust deed, and it follows that each deed must be looked at separately in order to determine what each individual truster meant by the words he himself uses. Words will usually be given their normal everyday meaning, though this of course may be affected by particular legal provisions. For example adopted children and illegitimate children will be taken to be included in words such as "children" or "issue" in the circumstances set out in sections 5 of the Law Reform (Miscellaneous Provisions) (Scotland) Acts 1966 and 1968 respectively.

A trust deed will be used "as its own lexicon."[9] By this is meant that the deed is to be read as a whole and that one part of the deed can have its meaning elucidated by another part. In *Russell* v. *Wood's Trs.*[10] an illegitimate child claimed entitlement under a trust set up by her natural father. The father had been married and had legitimate children also. The trust deed made certain provisions in favour of "any children," and in another part made separate but overlapping provision for "any children of our marriage." Lord Cullen held that the use of the two phrases in different parts of the deed showed an intention to benefit two separate classes, one including and one excluding illegitimate children.

The truster's intention governs the interpretation of the deed, so it can sometimes be the case that words will be given meanings that they would not otherwise have, if it can be shown that the truster intended an unusual meaning. This can be illustrated with the case of *Spencer's Trs.* v. *Ruggles.*[11] Here a liferent was created, with the fee going to the liferenter's "lawful issue." It is well established in law today that an adopted child is to be considered the legitimate (*i.e.* the lawful) child of the adopter and will therefore generally be considered the lawful issue of the adopter. In this case the liferenter had an adopted child, but it was held that, in the context of this particular deed, that child was not "lawful issue" within the meaning intended by the truster. The trust deed had declared that the fee was to go to the lawful issue of the liferenter "in the event of [the liferenter] marrying and having lawful issue," and the First Division held that this form of words indicated that the truster intended to restrict the phrase "lawful issue" to lawful issue born of the liferenter's marriage, which an adopted child never could be.

[9] *Per* Lord President Cooper in *Wink's Exx.* v. *Tallent*, 1947 S.C. 470 at p. 478.
[10] 1987 S.L.T. 503.
[11] 1982 S.L.T. 165.

2. Purposes too wide

As an alternative to the purposes being too vague, uncertainty may be constituted by the trust purposes being far too wide. It is perfectly competent for a truster to confer on the trustees a power to choose the individuals who are actually to benefit from a class of potential beneficiaries laid down by the truster, but any discretionary trust of this nature must delimit a sufficiently narrow class so that it is in fact still the truster's purposes that are being carried out, and not the trustees' own. The law does not allow a truster to delegate to his trustees a complete discretion to choose the purposes of the trust.[12] As Lord Justice-Clerk Thomson put it in *Rintoul's Trs.* v. *Rintoul*:

> "The testator must make his will for himself. He cannot leave it to trustees to make a will for him. He must define and identify sufficiently in his will the objects which he wishes to benefit. The underlying reason is that trustees should be able to select within certain defined limits instead of being given an unlimited discretion."[13]

Seldom does this cause difficulty with private trusts, which are normally set up for a limited class of individuals (such as for example "for those of my children deemed worthy by my trustees"); but in public trusts, where purposes tend to be laid down much more broadly, a large number of cases have gone to court on the question of whether a truster's directions in a discretionary trust are sufficiently precise. The basic rule, as always, is that the trustees must be able to determine what the truster had in mind. Mackenzie Stuart suggests as a possible test asking "whether the limits are sufficiently clear to enable the Court to say whether, at any stage, the trustees are in breach of trust."[14] Though each trust deed must be looked at separately, previous decisions do give indications of whether or not certain words or phrases are likely to be regarded by the court as laying down a sufficiently precise class of beneficiary.[15]

---

[12] *Per* Lord Chancellor Halsbury in *Grimond* v. *Grimond's Trs.* (1905) 7 F. (H.L.) 90 at p. 91.

[13] 1949 S.C. 297 at p. 299.

[14] Mackenzie Stuart at p. 109.

[15] Lord Mackay in *Rintoul's Trs.* v. *Rintoul*, 1949 S.C. 297 at p. 302 said this: "It would be absurd . . . [to] take the view of concentrating on the terms of each will, as if there were no prior and helpful decisions . . . On the other hand, it would of course be equally absurd to say that we should blindly follow any decision, unless the general circumstances and the words in both are almost exactly alike."

It has for example long been held that a trust set up for the benefit of "charities" to be chosen by the trustees is sufficiently precise,[16] notwithstanding the very many and diverse types of charitable organisations that exist today. In Scotland the word "charity" bears a much looser meaning than the somewhat artificial definition it bears in English law, and in Scotland it is generally taken to mean the relief of poverty or suffering in any of its forms. Words almost synonymous with "charity" will also be considered valid, such as "benevolent,"[17] or "philanthropic."[18] Other words, such as "educational"[19] will also be considered sufficiently precise to be given effect to.

On the other hand, "religious purposes,"[20] "public purposes,"[21] "social purposes,"[22] or "deserving purposes"[23] are all too vague on their own to delimit the choice given to the trustees.[24] However if these words are further specified, or limited, for example by a denomination within a religion[25] or by locality,[26] this may sometimes provide sufficient guidance to cut down the trustees' discretion and allow them to determine the sort of purpose the truster had in mind.

Often, general words such as the above appear not alone but with other general words, the list being conjoined with either the word "and" or the word "or." This in itself creates difficulties since neither of these words has a single meaning.

Consider for example a trust set up for "educational and religious purposes." This could be interpreted either conjunctively as a gift to a purpose, chosen by the trustees, that is both educational and religious, or disjunctively as a gift to purposes that are educational and additionally to separate purposes that are religious. The distinction is important for two reasons. First, one must be able to identify precisely the class

---

[16] See *Chalmers' Trs.* v. *Turriff School Board*, 1917 S.C. 676; *Wink's Exx.* v. *Tallent*, 1947 S.C. 470; Mackenzie Stuart at p. 112. For such a trust to be valid trustees must be expressly appointed by the truster: see Chap. 2.

[17] *Hay's Trs.* v. *Baillie*, 1908 S.C. 1224.

[18] *Mackinnon's Trs.* v. *Mackinnon*, 1909 S.C. 1041.

[19] *Chalmer's Trs.*, *supra*, n. 16.

[20] *Grimond's Trs.*, *supra*, n. 12.

[21] *Reid's Trs.* v. *Cattanach's Trs.*, 1929 S.C. 727.

[22] *Rintoul's Trs.* v. *Rintoul*, 1949 S.C. 297.

[23] *Campbell's Trs.* v. *Campbell*, 1921 S.C. (H.L.) 12.

[24] For a gradation of the breadth and of the acceptability of these sorts of words, see Lord Mackay in *Rintoul's Trs.*, *supra*, n. 22, at pp. 303–309.

[25] *Bannerman's Trs.* v. *Bannerman*, 1915 S.C. 398.

[26] *McPhee's Trs.* v. *McPhee*, 1912 S.C. 75. But *cf. Turnbull's Trs.* v. *Lord Advocate*, 1918 S.C. (H.L.) 88, in which it was held that a very wide class ("public purposes") could not be saved by a locality limitation.

from which the trustees may choose. And secondly, the validity of the gift may depend upon whether a disjunctive or conjunctive interpretation is adopted. If a disjunctive interpretation of "and" is adopted, all the purposes must individually be valid, otherwise it will not be possible properly to delimit the extent of the trustees' choice, because such a bequest would allow the trustees to choose to benefit an invalidly wide purpose. In the above example it would allow them to choose "religious purposes" to benefit, but that, as shown above, is not guidance enough. On the other hand, if a conjunctive interpretation is adopted, only one of the listed adjectives need be sufficiently precise, because the single purpose is sufficiently delimited by the valid adjective, and the imprecise adjective does not detract from that.

Because "and" is normally used in a conjunctive sense, the presumption will be that this is what is meant[27]; but, since this, like other matters, is determined by the intention of the truster, a disjunctive interpretation can be adopted if the form of the deed, or its language, or even punctuation, suggests that this interpretation was intended. In *McConochie's Trs.* v. *McConochie*,[28] a gift to "educational, charitable and religious purposes" was held void since "and" was interpreted disjunctively because the bequest was "to divide" the property amongst these purposes.[29] Wilson and Duncan have said, "the greater the number of qualifications, the more probable is the construction multiplying the classes within the area of selection and the less probable is the construction multiplying the number of qualifications to be complied with and so diminishing the number of objects within the area of selection."[30]

Like "and," the conjoining word "or" has two meanings. Its primary use is to distinguish two adjectives between which there is an alternative. A bequest to "educational or religious purposes" is a bequest to educational purposes or alternatively to religious purposes (with the trustees being empowered to choose). This disjunctive interpretation, because it is the usual one, will be that which is to be initially presumed.[31] This will result in the above gift being void for uncertainty, since "religious purposes" on its own is too vague, and a disjunctive "or"

---

[27] *Per* Lord Buckmaster in *Caldwell's Trs.* v. *Caldwell*, 1921 S.C. (H.L.) 82 at p. 83.

[28] 1909 S.C. 1046.

[29] *Cf. McPhee's Trs.*, *supra*, n. 26.

[30] Wilson & Duncan at p. 198.

[31] *Rintoul's Trs.*, *supra*, n. 22, *per* Lord Justice-Clerk Thomson at p. 300, and Lord Mackay at p. 303.

requires, like the disjunctive "and," each adjective to be sufficiently precise in order to allow the trustees to know the full extent of the choice open to them. As Lord President Cooper said in *Salvesen's Trs.* v. *Wye*,[32] "the validity of the direction as a whole must be tested on the principle that the strength of a chain is its weakest link."

On the other hand, "or" may be used exegetically, or in an explanatory sense. The foregoing sentence contains an example of the exegetical "or." It is a perfectly correct usage of "or," not to list alternatives, but rather to list synonyms. Lord Justice-Clerk Thomson in *Rintoul's Trs.* said this: "In order to use the word ['or' exegetically] there must be . . . substantial identity between the two words which are in juxtaposition. They must be more or less synonymous in connotation."[33] If this interpretation is adopted only one of a list of adjectives need be sufficiently precise, because the vagueness of the one word is cured by the specificity of the other. In *Wink's Exx.* v. *Tallent*[34] a trust was set up for such "benevolent or charitable societies" as the trustee may choose. It was held that this trust was not void for uncertainty as the vague word "benevolent" was restricted to and interpreted by the sufficiently precise word "charitable." The word "or" will be interpreted exegetically only in exceptional cases. Again, the style, language and punctuation of the deed may be called in aid in order to determine how the truster was using the particular word.

Tax Point

The case of *Jackson's Trs.* v. *Lord Advocate*[35] turned on the exegetical use of the word "or." Here a trust was established for "charitable or benevolent" purposes. In Scots law it did not matter whether an exegetical or a disjunctive interpretation of "or" was adopted, since, both adjectives being sufficiently precise, the deed would be valid in any case. In relation to taxation, with English law governing the trust's charitable status, the difference was fundamental, because in English law "benevolent" purposes would not be "charitable" purposes. The court in *Jackson* held that the Scottish deed had to be interpreted by the principles of Scots Law, and that the "or" was used exegetically: "benevolent" therefore meant "charitable" and the trust's charitable status was preserved.

LEGALITY

A second criterion that the trust purposes must satisfy is that they be legal. Legality in this context is used in two separate senses.

[32] 1954 S.C. 440 at p. 447.
[33] 1949 S.C. at p. 300.
[34] 1947 S.C. 470.
[35] 1926 S.L.T. 358, 10 T.C. 460.

First, the purposes must be legal in the sense that their carrying out will not amount to a breach of the criminal law. A trust set up to finance criminal activity, or an outlawed organisation like the I.R.A., would obviously be invalid. If the purpose itself is not illegal, but the way the trustees carry it out is, this does not invalidate the trust, but it could amount to a breach of trust (as well as a breach by the trustees personally of the criminal law).

The second sense in which legality is used is to invalidate trust purposes that are not criminal but are legally incompetent. A truster can direct his trustees to do only that which legally may be done, and if he instructs them to do something that cannot be done in law, then that purpose fails. This will not necessarily invalidate the whole trust if there are other purposes, and the deed will be read as if the incompetent directions had not been made.

Some purposes that were once competent are no longer so, but occasionally trust deeds contain, usually unintentionally, directions to achieve such purposes. Typically these involve directions to tie up property in trust in such a way as conflicts with the law's discouragement of taking property out of commercial circulation. There is no general prohibition in Scots law on a trust, public or private, continuing in perpetuity, and many Scottish trusts have existed for centuries. However it is not satisfactory to allow large amounts of property to be tied up in trust for long periods of time, for this not only disadvantages the present generation in favour of generations yet to be born, but it also takes property out of commercial circulation, to the detriment of the general economy. Scots law has never suffered from the paranoid fear of perpetuities that so characterises English trust law,[36] but it has compromised the freedom of trusters with economic considerations, first by way of a prohibition on certain purposes designed to inhibit the alienability of capital, and secondly by enforcing periodic distribution of income generated by trust property. The following types of direction will breach these rules, and are thus void for illegality.

1. Entails and successive liferents

Entails, or tailzies, were a common feature of Scots land law for many centuries. They provided a legally efficacious means of

---

[36] The reasons why English law adopted the Rule Against Perpetuities are examined by Burgess, in *Perpetuities in Scots Law*, Edinburgh 1979, The Stair Society, at pp. 41–44.

ensuring that land remained in the hands of the same family for generations. Socially, land in Scotland was traditionally considered to belong to the whole extended family rather than the head of the family who happened to have, for the time being, the legal title. A way of preserving this situation against the inroads of commercialisation was to use the trick of the tailzie, which in effect was a heritable trust. Here land would be passed on to the owner's eldest son, with the condition that it be held complete and passed on to *his* eldest son, with the same condition attached, and so on in perpetuity. This effectively prevented an individual owner from disposing of family land: he was trustee for future generations of his own family.

This was not particularly healthy for society as it depressed the property market and discouraged land improvements. Lord Kames (himself a great eighteenth century land improver)[37] wrote voluminously against the evils of tailzies[38]; and the House of Lords, reflecting the English hatred of perpetuities, used many technical grounds to hold as many as they could to be invalid.[39]

As far as moveables were concerned, the same result as with entails could be achieved by creating a series of successive liferents, with the fee vesting sometime in the distant future.

Entails over land were prohibited by the Entail (Scotland) Act 1914, and successive liferents over moveables restricted by s.9 of the Trusts (Scotland) Act 1921. In relation to deeds executed after November 25, 1968, the law is now contained (for both heritable and moveable property) in section 18 of the Law Reform (Miscellaneous Provisions) (Scotland) Act 1968, for there it is provided that if a person, who was not living or *in utero* at the date of coming into operation of the deed creating the liferent, becomes entitled to that liferent, then on his attaining majority he shall own the property absolutely, and not just a liferent thereto. In other words, indefinite liferents can be conferred on persons alive or *in utero* at the date of the deed, and a series of successive liferents can be set up. If a person not alive or not *in utero* at the date of the deed comes to hold the liferent, that liferent will continue as a valid liferent during the minority of

---

[37] See Kames, *The Gentleman Farmer: Being an Attempt to Improve Agriculture by Subjecting it to the Test of Rational Principles*, Edinburgh 1776; Lehman, *Henry Home, Lord Kames, and the Scottish Enlightenment*, Martinus Nijhoff, The Hague 1971.

[38] See particularly *Elucidations Respecting the Common and Statute Law of Scotland*, Art. XLII, Edinburgh 1777.

[39] See Kolbert & Mackay, *History of Scots and English Land Law*, Geographical Publications London 1977, at pp. 206–219; Burgess, *op. cit.* at n. 36.

the holder,[40] but it will automatically be converted to a right to the fee on the holder attaining majority. Majority for this purpose is achieved at age 18.[41]

2. Accumulations of income

Accumulation is the re-investment (with the capital or otherwise) of the income or part thereof in such a way that the beneficial enjoyment of it is postponed. There are strict limits of time beyond which accumulation is not permitted. Trustees are generally not entitled to accumulate income, unless they have been directed to do so, which direction can either be express, or implied as a necessary consequence of the way the property is to devolve.[42] "The lawfulness of the disposition is judged by the result to which its provisions might lead; if the result might be accumulation beyond the permitted limits, the disposition is to that extent unlawful"; so said Lord Fraser in *Baird* v. *Lord Advocate*,[43] in which the House of Lords decided that the time limits applied to discretionary powers to accumulate as well as to firm directions.[44] Firm directions are commonly found today in, for example, accumulation and maintenance trusts, which are set up for the maintenance of children, with powers to accumulate income over and above that which is needed for that purpose.

If accumulation is directed, expressly or impliedly, it may continue only within certain stated time limits, which were originally laid down in the Accumulations Act 1800 (known as the Thellusson Act), an Act the drafting of which was strongly criticised throughout its existence. Professor Halliday was restrained to the point of generosity when he said, in relation to this much maligned statute, that "many and various have been the terminological sins of our lawgivers."[45]

---

[40] *Per* Lord Sands in *Stewart's Trs.* v. *Whitelaw*, 1926 S.C. 701 at p. 718, discussing s.9 of the Trusts (Scotland) Act 1921.

[41] The Act talks of the person taking the fee absolutely when he becomes of "full age," which is now defined in the Age of Majority (Scotland) Act 1969 to mean 18 years. *Cf.* the definition of majority for the purposes of the legality of accumulations: see *infra*, n. 52.

[42] See the cases collected in Wilson & Duncan at pp. 106/107.

[43] [1979] A.C. 666. at p. 671.

[44] For trusts that take effect after August 3, 1966 (which the trust in *Baird* did not), this rule is now contained in s.6(2) of the Law Reform (Miscellaneous Provisions) (Scotland) Act 1966.

[45] "Trusts (Scotland) Act 1961: Accumulations of Income" (1962) 3 Conv.Rev. 57 at p. 57.

The limits are now contained in section 5 of the much clearer Trusts (Scotland) Act 1961 (which repealed the 1800 Act[46]) and section 6 of the Law Reform (Miscellaneous Provisions) (Scotland) Act 1966. These provisions apply, where appropriate, to *inter vivos* and to *mortis causa* trusts, and they apply to public as well as to private trusts.[47] They are also retrospective. The Hague Convention on the Law Applicable to Trusts, discussed in Chapter 3, and made part of British law by the Recognition of Trusts Act 1987, allows the truster to choose any legal system to govern his trust, or a severable aspect thereof. The accumulation provisions might therefore be avoided by choosing a legal system to govern that does not contain these prohibitions, such as that of the Isle of Man. It is unlikely (though conceivable) that the accumulation provisions will be regarded as mandatory provisions in the sense used by the Convention and thus excluded from its terms by Article 16. The rest of this section will assume that Scots law applies to the power of accumulation.[48]

A direction to accumulate for longer than the appropriate period is legally incompetent and will be given effect to only within that period,[49] with the trustees paying the income arising thereafter to the beneficiary who would have been entitled to it had the illegal accumulation not been directed.[50] This result is usually not what the truster wanted. As a matter of good drafting therefore the drafter ought to bear in mind these statutory time periods, and, if accumulation is desired, ensure that one of the periods is expressly chosen and that the directions do not lead to accumulation beyond the time permitted. Not only does this avoid a possible frustration of the truster's intentions, but it also avoids the difficulties in determining what is to happen to the illegal accumulations. These reasons also suggest that it would be sensible drafting practice to incorporate a clause directing what is

---

[46] For Scotland that is. The 1800 Act was repealed for England by the Law of Property Act 1925, Sched. 7.

[47] It has however been held in England that the rules do not apply to unit trusts, as such schemes do not fall within the mischief for which the rules were designed: see *Re A.E.G. Unit Trusts (Managers) Ltd's Deed* [1957] Ch. 415.

[48] A clear and extensive examination of the law of accumulations can be found in Burgess, *op. cit.*, n. 36, at pp. 162–225.

[49] *Re Clothier* 1971 N.Z.L.R. 745.

[50] Trusts (Scotland) Act 1961, s.5(3). What, more precisely, will happen to the income after the relevant period has expired will depend upon the nature of the gift. Detailed consideration is beyond the scope of this book, but can be found in Mackenzie Stuart at pp. 93–98, Wilson and Duncan at pp. 111–118, and Burgess, *op. cit.* n. 36. See also *Landale's Trs.* v. *Overseas Missionary Fellowship*, 1982 S.L.T. 158.

to happen to accumulated income in the event of the accumulation being found to be illegal, say, because the law changes, or because some eventuality has been overlooked. Further, though there is no authority supporting this, it is suggested that there is nothing in principle to prevent the drafter providing for alternative accumulation periods, for example directing accumulations for the longer of the grantor's lifetime (period (a)) or 21 years from the date of the deed (period (e)). In the absence of such a provision, the periods will be alternative, rather than cumulative.

If accumulation is directed, but no time limit is placed on it, the trustees will apply the most appropriate of the periods, subject to any challenge being made, in which case the court will decide the period. Each accumulation period deals with very different situations. *Carey's Trs.* v. *Rose*[51] (in which there is one of the clearest judicial discussions of the Scots law of accumulations) illustrates well the approach that the court will take in determining the appropriate period, for there the facts of the case were carefully analysed in relation to each period, and by a process of elimination the correct one was determined. The periods are as follows.

(a) *The life of the grantor*

If the trust deed is *inter vivos* and accumulation is directed to begin during the life of the truster, it cannot continue after the truster's death (unless either period (d) or (e) is appropriate). This could potentially be the longest of the accumulation periods, for the truster may survive beyond 21 years, which is otherwise the longest possible period; it is certainly the most unpredictable. This period is seldom chosen today.

(b) *21 years from the death of the grantor*

This period will be appropriate when accumulation is directed to commence on the death of the truster (whether the trust itself is *inter vivos* or *mortis causa*), or when accumulation is implied and the trust is designed to take effect as from death. This is far and away the most common period chosen by trusters in *mortis causa* trusts, and it makes accumulation after 21 years from the date of death illegal. This period was considered the appropriate one in *Carey's Trs.* v. *Rose.* Here a testator directed trustees to hold the residue of his estate until the son of a named nephew reached the age of 21. No directions were given about the income. The son was born two years after the death of the

[51] 1957 S.C. 252.

testator, and the trustees accumulated the income until he was 21; a total of 23 years. The question arose whether the heirs, that is those entitled to the illegal accumulations, were entitled to the income generated during the first two years, or during the last two years. It was held that accumulation was impliedly directed from death, because this period was the only one appropriate to the circumstances of this trust, and consequently the accumulation had to end 21 years after death. The heirs were entitled to the income generated during the last two years.

(c) *The minority of any person living or in utero at the date of the death of the grantor*

This period is intended to deal with the situation where the income is directed to be accumulated from the date of death of the truster and is for the benefit of someone presently in minority or *in utero*. It will end on their attaining majority. By the terms of the Act the person during whose minority accumulation is directed does not need to be the beneficiary (unlike in the case of period (d) below), but if the person is not intended to be a beneficiary, a straight 21 years accumulation under period (b) would be much more straightforward. Minority for this purpose (and for the purposes of periods (d) and (f)) ends when the person reaches the age of 21 years.[52]

(d) *The minority of any person who would, under the terms of the trust deed directing accumulation, be entitled to the income accumulated if of full age*

This period is explained in *Carey's Trs. (supra)* to be intended to cover the situation where accumulation is directed to commence not on the death of the truster but on the termination of a liferent or some other intervening interest, with the accumulated fund going to a beneficiary on that beneficiary's attaining majority. In such a situation it would have been inequitable to terminate accumulation 21 years after the death of the testator (period b) since the liferent may still be extant then, and this would prevent the beneficiary acquiring any accumulated benefit at all. Therefore,

"where the direction to accumulate only begins to operate, owing to the existence of an intervening interest, some years after the date of the

[52] Unlike the provisions restricting successive liferents (see *supra*) the Trusts (Scotland) Act 1961 talks of "minority" rather than "full age," and defines "minority" for the purposes of the Act as lasting till the age of 21 years: s.5(6). This was not reduced to 18 years when the age of majority was reduced in 1969, though it was in relation to the equivalent English statute: see the (English) Family Law Reform Act 1969.

testator's death, the prohibition in relation to the fourth period comes into operation and, while sanctioning accumulations during the beneficiary's minority, prohibits any further accumulation after that beneficiary becomes 21 years of age."[53]

Accumulation under this period will generally be shorter than 21 years, being the length of time between the death of the liferenter and the attaining of majority by the fiar. This is the only period to permit accumulation to commence after the truster's death, and it may also be utilised in an *inter vivos* trust, so that the accumulation commences before the truster's death, and ends after it.[54]

(e) *21 years from the making of the settlement or other disposition; and*
(f) *the duration of the minority of any person living or in utero at the date of the making of the settlement or other disposition*

"Other disposition" could include a resettlement under the variation provisions of section 1 of the Trusts (Scotland) Act 1961, and thus allow accumulation as from the date of the court decree[55] (but only if the variation is so substantial as to amount to a complete resettlement[56]). Periods (e) and (f) were added by the Law Reform (Miscellaneous Provisions) (Scotland) Act 1966, and they only apply to trusts taking effect after August 3, 1966. They were added for a technical reason to avoid problems with the old estate duty regime and are little used today.

MORALITY

A trust purpose that the court deems immoral will be void as being *contra bonos mores*, for the court will not lend its offices to the enforcement of an immoral purpose, notwithstanding that the purpose may not be illegal. It may for example be considered *contra bonos mores* to confer a trust benefit *in consideration of* future extra-marital sexual favours (though it would be very difficult to establish that the benefit was given for that reason).[57]

What is or is not an immoral purpose can only be determined on a case to case basis and previous decisions really are of limited

---

[53] *Carey's Trs.* v. *Rose*, 1957 S.C. 252, *per* Lord President Clyde at p. 258.
[54] Section 5(4) of the Trusts (Scotland) Act 1961 (discussed in fuller detail by Halliday, *op. cit.* note 45).
[55] *Aikman, Petr.*, 1968 S.L.T. 137.
[56] See Chap. 12.
[57] See *Troussier* v. *Matthew*, 1922 S.L.T. 670.

assistance, because concepts of public morality change all the time. In many areas of human activity, sexual and other, there is no longer any code of morality widely accepted by society in general, and it has been concluded from this (in a very different context) that the court ought not to apply what amounts to its own personal prejudices in deciding the legal rights of parties. In *Stephens* v. *Avery* Sir Nicholas Browne-Wilkinson V-C said:

> "The court's function is to apply the law, not personal prejudice. Only in a case where there is still a generally accepted moral code can the court refuse to enforce rights in such a way as to offend that generally accepted code."[58]

Few trust purposes that do not breach the criminal law will today offend a generally accepted moral code. Even a trust that encourages sexual practices of which the state itself disapproves may not today fail as being immoral. It is suggested that such worthy organisations as the Terrence Higgins Trust and the Scottish AIDS Monitor ought not to be regarded as immoral, notwithstanding that a major aim of both trusts is to encourage homosexuals—and others—to practise "safer sex": the purpose of both is to disseminate information about a very dangerous disease, and to educate people on how to avoid it.

It is suggested that in our multi-cultural society there are few things indeed that offend a generally accepted code of morality; and that therefore the courts ought today to be very slow in holding a trust purpose to be void as being *contra bonos mores*.[59]

PUBLIC POLICY

Though not immoral in the sense of offending society, a trust purpose may nevertheless so offend the conscience of the court that it will not give effect to it. The cases have generally involved purposes that are so extravagant or pointless that it would be utterly wasteful to enforce them. In *Sutherland's Tr.* v. *Verschoyle & Ors.*[60] a testatrix had directed her trustees to devote the trust estate to the preservation and display of what she described as her "valuable art collection." The collection was worth about £12,000, but the court held that it was a "heterogeneous con-

---

[58] [1988] 2 All E.R. 477 at p. 481.
[59] The lack of Scottish cases on the issue possibly illustrates that this is the approach taken.
[60] 1968 S.L.T. 43.

glomeration," of no real interest to any section of the public, and that therefore the implementation of the provision would be so grossly extravagant and so completely wasteful as to be contrary to public policy.

Many trust purposes that confer no benefit on any living person or section of the public will fail for this reason, but it is not maintainable to claim that all trusts will fail unless a beneficial interest is created in some person.[61] Trusts for tombstones and, possibly, specified animals will be valid, though there is no living human beneficiary. The development of the law in this area can be seen in the *McCaig* cases[62] and *Aitken's Trs.* v. *Aitken*.[63]

In the first *McCaig* case, a testator attempted to leave much of his property in trust for the building and maintenance of "artistic towers" to be erected on prominent sites throughout his extensive estates, and for statues of his parents and all their nine children to be sculpted in stone and placed in these towers. One such tower was built during his life, on a prominent hill overlooking the town of Oban. His surviving sister (who became the testatrix in the second *McCaig* case) challenged the provision, and the Court of Session held that it was bad and could not be enforced. The Second Division hesitated to hold the provision void solely because it was irrational and wasteful, and held as well that there had been no divestiture of the heir (the sister) because the provisions conferred no beneficial right on anyone.

The second *McCaig* case arose when the sister died seven years later. She left her property (including that which she had succeeded to after her successful challenge in the first case) in trust, directing her trustees to maintain the circular tower at Oban, and to place therein bronze statues of her parents and all their children. The tower was then to be sealed up and entry prohibited to the public. This provision too was challenged, and, although she had no heirs to disinherit, this time the Court of Session had no hesitation in holding it ineffectual as being unreasonably extravagant, the court founding specifically on public policy rather than the failure to confer a beneficial right.[64]

In *Aitken's Trs.* v. *Aitken* a testator whose family had been connected with the town of Musselburgh for some generations, and who himself had twice been elected Champion of the Riding of the Marches for that burgh, directed that a bronze equestrian

---

[61] *Per* Lord Sands in *Aitken's Trs.* v. *Aitken*, 1927 S.C. 374 at p. 380.

[62] *McCaig* v. *University of Glasgow*, 1907 S.C. 231, *McCaig's Trs.* v. *Kirk Session of the United Free Church of Lismore*, 1915 S.C. 426.

[63] 1927 S.C. 374.

[64] See esp. Lord Salvesen 1915 S.C. at p. 434, and Lord Guthrie at p. 438.

statue be erected to his memory, and that certain properties be demolished to make room for it. The First Division found this provision to be contrary to public policy. Lord Sands said this:

> "I take the law applicable to the present case as based upon the *McCaig* cases to be that, if testamentary directions are unreasonable as conferring neither a patrimonial benefit upon anyone nor a benefit upon the public or any section thereof, the directions are invalid."[65]

He also pointed out that it is not for the court to make itself the judge of what would benefit the public: it would be sufficient to save the bequest if only a certain section of opinion regarded the purpose as beneficial.

Lord Blackburn similarly held that to give effect to the deed was contrary to public policy, and he found the provisions in the present case even more objectionable than the directions in the *McCaig* cases, "in respect that they involve the destruction of a valuable rent-producing property in the middle of a burgh without any conceivable benefit to the inhabitants of the burgh."[66] Lord Blackburn also thought the provisions might be self-destructive in the sense that the aim of the truster was to glorify his name, while the effect would be to ridicule it. The statue was to be of "artistic merit," and Lord Blackburn added this piece of delightful, if gratuitous, abuse:

> "Judging from a photograph which was exhibited to us of the testator . . . it would, I think, be impossible for any sculptor with such a subject to produce a statue which faithfully represented the subject and at the same time was of 'artistic merit.' "[67]

Like morality, public policy may potentially be of dangerously wide scope.[68] In *Earl of Caithness* v. *Sinclair*[69] Lord President Dunedin had this to say in dismissing an argument that it was contrary to public policy to make a benefit under a trust conditional on the beneficiary not succeeding to a peerage:

> "I agree with the opinion which has been more than once expressed, that the argument of public policy should be most cautiously applied by judges;

[65] 1927 SC 374 at p. 381.
[66] *Ibid.* at p. 385.
[67] *Ibid.* at p. 384.
[68] Mackenzie Stuart says at p. 76 that whether public policy is applied depends not only on the time of its application, but also on the constitution of the bench.
[69] 1912 S.C. 79.

indeed I would say, should hardly be applied unless there is an exact precedent to bind them."[70]

Sometimes the trust purpose itself is not contrary to public policy, but there is a condition attached thereto that is. For example a benefit under a trust could be made conditional upon the beneficiary turning to crime, or leaving his family. In this sort of case the conditions will be ineffectual and the beneficiary will take the benefit free from the condition.[71] However, the trust itself will remain valid, but only if the nature of the gift and condition is not such that the one is clearly dependent upon the other. This is a matter of the intention of the truster, and if it can be shown that the truster did not intend the purpose to be given effect unless the condition were satisfied, then if the condition is contrary to public policy, so will be the purpose.

---

[70] *Ibid.* at p. 84.
[71] See, *e.g. Re Johnston's Will Trusts* [1967] 1 All E.R. 553, an English case involving a condition attached to a legacy which was interpreted as an encouragement to a wife to leave her husband.

CHAPTER 7

ADMINISTRATION OF THE TRUST

Introduction

ONCE the trust is properly set up with trustees in office and valid purposes established, the trustees must commence the administration of the estate with the aim of achieving these trust purposes. Most trusts, of their nature, impose upon trustees the duty to look after and control the trust estate for an extended period of time, and consequently trustees will possess the powers that allow them to direct the estate towards the end for which the trust was set up. It is somewhat artificial to distinguish between the trustees' powers of administration and their duties to administer, because generally speaking these are interdependent, and are very often simply two sides of the same coin. For example trustees have a duty to ingather the estate, and they have the power to do what is necessary to effect that ingathering.

The way the trust is to be administered will of course depend upon the nature of the purposes to be achieved by the trust. Minimal administration will be involved if the purpose is to keep the estate intact in order to pass it on to a beneficiary at the attainment of a certain age. Much more administration will be required in, for example, a public trust that has on-going charitable aims. Likewise, whether the trustees are conferred a right to exercise their own discretion in certain aspects of the administration will also fundamentally affect how the trust will in fact be run. Because of the wide diversity of possible trust purposes, the range of potential discretion conferred, and the consequent variety of forms of administration, it is difficult to give anything more than the most general guidance on how trustees are to go about administering a particular trust. However there are certain aspects of trust administration that will be applicable to most trusts.[1] It is always to be remembered that the nature of the trust purposes significantly affects the way the trust is to be run.

INGATHERING THE ESTATE

The first duty of the trustees to be fulfilled as soon as possible after they take office is to ingather the estate, that is, to discover the extent, and to take legal possession, of the trust property. Trustees are endowed with the powers necessary to fulfil this duty. They may call for delivery of all the property belonging to the trust held by third parties, and they can ask banks, building societies and the like for statements of account. They are also entitled and bound to do all that is reasonably necessary to recover trust property in the hands of third parties, and this may include calling in debts and raising actions. Failure to do so timeously will amount to a breach of trust. In *Forman* v. *Burns*[2] an executor (who for this purpose is in the same position as a trustee) found amongst the securities of a deceased a promissory note for £250, dated two years previously. He failed to call in the debt immediately, and did nothing until after the debtor had been declared bankrupt. The estate could therefore recover only part of the debt, and the First Division held the executor personally liable for the shortfall.

New trustees are also obliged to call previous trustees to account, if necessary, and to recover any trust property still in their hands.[3]

An important aspect of ingathering the estate is the trustees' taking legal title to the trust property in their own names. The trustees are the legal owners of the estate, and they must therefore do all that is necessary to complete their own title to it:

---

[1] Certain types of trust have statutory rules concerning their administration, the details of which are found in the appropriate legislation: see for example the National Health Service (Scotland) Act 1978, ss.11 & 12 (hospital trusts); the Education (Scotland) Act 1980, ss.104–122 (educational endowments); the Finance Act 1989, Sched. 5 (employee share ownership trusts); and the Law Reform (Micellaneous Provisions) (Scotland) Act 1990, ss.1–8 (charitable trusts).

[2] (1853) 15 D. 362.

[3] Mackenzie Stuart at p. 199.

their appointment to the office merely gives them a personal right to the property, which they should as soon as possible turn into a real right. The precise steps required will of course depend upon the nature of the property and the rules governing transfer of property of that nature. If part of the property is heritable, the trustees must record their title in the Register of Sasines or register it in the Land Register. If the estate contains shares, there must be executed share transfers in favour of the trustees, which must be delivered to the company's registrar,[4] the share certificates being delivered to the trustees. Bank and building society accounts must be transferred to the names of the trustees. Corporeal moveable property must be delivered into the possession of the trustees.

PAYING DEBTS

Other than in *mortis causa* trusts, it is unusual for there to be debts at the commencement of the trust, though there may be if the trust estate consists of a continuing business. Whenever there are debts the trustees must pay them off as soon as possible after the estate has been gathered together. Only after this has been done will the full value of the estate be known, and made available for use in achieving the trust purposes, for the creditors' rights in the trust estate are preferred to those of the beneficiaries. "No trustees are entitled to pay away one shilling of the estate to beneficiaries, until all the truster's debts are paid, and if they do so before ascertaining with certainty that the estate is solvent, they do so at their own risk."[5] If it appears that the estate will not be large enough to pay off all the debts, the trustees should pay all the creditors rateably.[6] If the trust is testamentary, the trustees should wait for six months after the death of the truster before paying any debts,[7] in order to allow creditors time to lodge their claims (though trustees will often pay out before this period if they know the extent of the claims on the estate: any risk in doing so lies on the trustees/executors).

---

[4] In Scotland companies will register shareholders "as trustees," but in England they will not.

[5] Per Lord President Inglis in *Lamond's Trs.* v. *Croom* (1871) 9 M. 662 at p. 668.

[6] Mackenzie Stuart at pp. 207–209.

[7] Except with privileged debts, such as deathbed and funeral expenses, which can be paid at once: Wilson & Duncan at p. 454.

Tax Point
One of the debts that the trustees may be subject to is liability for IHT incurred when the trust is set up. Generally the trustees will be liable for any IHT payable on the trust fund, although exceptionally the truster himself may undertake the tax burden when the tax is immediately payable on the setting up of an *inter vivos* trust (IHTA 1984, ss.199 & 200).

Once the estate has been ingathered, and the debts (including any tax liabilities) have been paid, the trustees can then begin to administer the estate in accordance with the truster's directions, and for the achievement of the purposes he laid down. In doing so, they must always keep the trust estate under their own control, and must keep it separate from their own property.

MAKING DECISIONS

Throughout the course of administering the trust, the trustees will inevitably be called upon to make decisions concerning various matters, including investment, distribution, sale or purchase of property. In doing so they must bear in mind not only the interest of the beneficiaries, but also the rights and duties of the trustees amongst themselves.

1. Consultation

Each and every trustee has a right to take part in the decision making process. Making decisions is a joint effort, and the trustees therefore have a duty to meet together and to consult with each other. It would be a clear breach of trust either for trustees to exclude one of their own number from their deliberations,[8] or for one or more of the trustees to refuse to take part in the administration of the trust.[9] All trustees must be given reasonable notice of any meeting of trustees, and must be given an opportunity to express their own opinion on any matter requiring a decision to be made. However the duty to consult with each other will be interpreted reasonably, and the trust administration will not be allowed to grind to a halt just because one or more trustees cannot be consulted. This was made clear in the case of *Malcolm* v. *Goldie*.[10] Here one of a number of trustees

---

[8] Per Lord Kinnear, in *Malcolm* v. *Goldie* (1895) 22 R. 968 at p. 971.
[9] *MacGilchrist's Trs.* v. *MacGilchrist* 1930 S.C. 635.
[10] *Supra*, n. 8.

had emigrated to Australia without resigning from the trust, and the other trustees, without attempting to consult him, assumed new trustees into the trust.[11] When this assumption was challenged some years later, the Court upheld its validity. Accepting that there is a duty to consult, Lord Kinnear in the First Divison said this:

> "The consultation of a trustee by his co-trustees does not in strictness mean that they are to obtain his separate opinion only, but it means that they are all, like other deliberative bodies, to meet together to deliberate; and therefore I am not prepared to assent to the proposition that where a trustee cannot attend, his co-trustees are bound to obtain his opinion before they can arrive at any conclusion, they being a quorum of trustees without him. But then I do not at all doubt that they are bound to give him an opportunity of attending the meeting . . . If he is accessible it would be quite wrong not to give him notice of a meeting; but then if the trustees are aware that he is resident in Australia, and that he does not intend to come back, to give notice of the meeting would be mere futile formality. I do not see any reason whatever for holding that the business and administration of the trust is to be interrupted for the sake of any such unmeaning form."[12]

2. The quorum

It is not essential in every case that all the trustees take part in all acts of administration. One or more of the trustees may be absent, or ill, or otherwise unable to take part in the decision making process; but nevertheless the administration may be continued, so long as a quorum of trustees participates. The quorum may be laid down by the trust deed and, if specified, is usually a majority of trustees for the time being, but it may be more, or less. If there is nothing expressed in the trust deed to the contrary, section 3(c) of the Trusts (Scotland) Act 1921 provides that a majority of the trustees accepting and surviving shall be a quorum. A majority is, of course, the smallest number that makes more than half the total. For example the quorum of three trustees is two, as must be the quorum of two trustees.

It is unusual for a truster to have specified anything other than a majority to be the quorum, but sometimes he will have appointed a *sine quo non* trustee, that is a trustee without whom no act of administration can be undertaken nor any decision made.[13] This is not common in modern practice, but it might be

---

[11] On assumption of Trustees, see Chap. 5.
[12] (1893) 22 R. 968 at p. 972.
[13] See Wilson & Duncan at p. 301.

thought appropriate, for example, if one of the trustees is the
father or guardian of the beneficiaries. If a specified number is
laid down as a quorum, and the total number of trustees falls
below this number, the quorum provision becomes inoperative,
and the trust may continue with the lesser number.[14]

3. Majority decison making

Unlike English law, which requires all trustees to agree to any act
of administration, Scots law allows trust decisions to be made by
majority vote. While all trustees must be consulted, they need
not all agree to any decision or act of administration, and a
majority has power to bind the trust estate. Unanimity would
only be required if the appointment of the trustees were joint *i.e.*
each appointment made dependent on all the others, but this is
highly unusual in modern practice: majority rule is the norm. If
there is an even number of trustees, and they are equally split,
the act of administration being considered cannot be undertaken,
and neither group will be able to bind the trust. If there is a
deadlock threatening the continued running of the trust, the
court may be petitioned by any interested party to appoint new
trustees.[15] It would obviously save time and expense if the
trustees could instead agree to the assumption of a new trustee to
resolve such a deadlock.

As pointed out above, the majority can bind the trust estate,
and in so doing they may impose liabilities on the whole body of
trustees, including any who disagree with the action taken. A
minority has no right to prevent a majority from carrying out any
proper act of administration, and if the minority trustees wish to
avoid any personal liability that may flow from such an act, they
must resign from office or otherwise expressly disassociate themselves from the particular decision with which they disagree.[16]
Only if the majority's actions amount in some way to a breach of
trust, or are undertaken in *mala fides*, will the minority have title
to prevent them from so acting. In *Reid* v. *Maxwell*[17] a minority
of trustees was held entitled to raise an action to prevent the
majority assuming new trustees in a secretive and underhand
manner. In no other situation will a minority be able to represent
the trust.

[14] See Chap. 5 for the circumstances in which trustees will be obliged to assume
new trustees.
[15] See, *e.g. Taylor & Ors, Petrs.*, 1932 S.C. 1.
[16] Wilson & Duncan at p. 305.
[17] (1852) 14 D. 449.

It has been suggested[18]—though tentatively—that while decisions affecting the trust can be reached by a majority of trustees, a majority may not necessarily be able to bind the trust, at least in relation to heritable conveyancing. It cannot be denied that the common law required all trustees to sign documents that were to bind the trust, nor that there is no statutory provision expressly reversing this rule. However, for a number of reasons, that tentative suggestion would be an illogical position for the law to adopt (though that does not in itself make the suggestion wrong). For one thing, section 3(c) of the Trusts (Scotland) Act 1921 provides that a majority will be a quorum, and the recognised power of a majority to make a decision would be an empty power if the majority did not also have the power to carry that decision into effect. It would mean that a minority could effectively prevent a majority from acting and this would render the established Scottish rule of majority decison making quite meaningless.[19] Secondly, it would be inconsistent with the cases discussed in the previous paragraph, for it would imply that the majority trustees could not bind their co-trustees. Thirdly, these cases talk of trustees having a duty merely to consult with co-trustees: the authorities would surely have said that trustees had to receive the signatures of all co-trustees, had this been the rule. To express a duty of consultation surely by implication excludes a duty to obtain consent. Finally a rule to the effect that all trustees must sign documents before the trust can be bound would be inconsistent with section 7 of the Trusts (Scotland) Act 1921, which protects the validity of some transactions[20] which suffer from an internal procedural irregularity, including the failure of a majority to consult with their co-trustees. It is this section (though admittedly its meaning and effect are opaque), together with s.3(c), that probably overturns the common law rule. Burns, at least impliedly, suggests that a majority of trustees in Scotland can execute deeds.[21]

TAKING ADVICE

In the course of administering a trust the trustees are often called upon to make decisions concerning matters about which they are

---

[18] Gretton, "Trust and Executry Conveyancing" (1987) 32 J.L.S. 111, at p. 118.
[19] It is assumed in *Green's Encylopaedia*, 1933 edition, Vol. 15, at paras. 437 and 438, that a quorum can execute deeds that will be binding on all the trustees.
[20] See Chap. 11.
[21] Burns, *Conveyancing Practice*, 4th ed., W. Green, Edinburgh 1957 at pp. 313/314, following the 3rd ed. (1926) at pp. 307/308.

not competent to make proper judgments. In this situation they will have a duty to take advice from some person who can make such a judgment, be it a lawyer, an accountant, or a stockbroker. The duty to take advice does not amount to a duty to follow that advice, otherwise there would be an unlawful delegation of the power to make decisions.[22] Rather, the trustees, in their deliberations, must make such use of the opinions of appropriate experts as would the reasonably prudent man. In some situations the trustees are expressly directed by statute to take advice. Section 6(2) of the Trustee Investments Act 1961 directs trustees to take advice on whether investments they intend to make are satisfactory; and this advice must come from a person reasonably believed by the trustees to be qualified by his ability in and practical experience of financial matters.[23]

As well as the obligation to take advice on certain matters, the trustees may, if they wish, choose to employ suitable persons to carry out the day to day running of the trust. Indeed they will be duty bound to do so in circumstances in which the reasonably prudent man would employ an agent.[24] Trustees ignorant of the art of book-keeping really ought to employ an accountant to keep the trust accounts. This however amounts to a delegation only of the day to day running of the trust: trustees cannot delegate their decision making powers nor pass on their responsibilities under the trust.[25] The trustees remain personally liable for the running of the trust and they must therefore properly supervise the agent's administration. The trustees must always make the final decisions and bear responsibility therefor, and they may be held to account for the maladministration of anyone they appoint.

KEEPING ACCOUNTS

The trustees' obligation is to pay over to the beneficiaries the trust estate less only that expenditure which they can prove was

[22] *Per* Lord Murray in *Martin* v. *City of Edinburgh District Council*, 1988 S.L.T. 329 at p. 334.

[23] This matter is dealt with more fully in Chap. 8.

[24] Enc. 24, 190. Indeed s.4(1)(*f*) of the Trusts (Scotland) Act 1921 empowers trustees "to appoint factors and law agents and to pay them suitable remuneration," unless such would be at variance with the terms or purposes of the trust. Power to employ financial advisers is implied by the terms of s.6 of the Trustee Investments Act 1961. It is to be noted that if trustees are themselves to be remunerated, this must be authorised by the trust deed itself: see Chap. 9. Any such remuneration paid to a professional trustee will be taxed as income under Sched. D., case II: *Jones* v. *Wright* 13 T.C. 221.

[25] *Per* Lord President Normand in *Esdaile* v. *Inland Revenue* (1936) 20 T.C. 700 at p. 709. See also the opinion of the First Division in *Scott* v. *Occidental Petroleum (Caledonia) Ltd.*, 1990 S.L.T. 882.

properly incurred. The keeping of accounts allows for that proof, and accordingly the trustees should keep full and proper accounts detailing their intromissions with the trust estate.[26] Trustees can be called upon to produce accounts at any time by the beneficiaries, and if they do not respond to such a request, an action for accounting can be raised,[27] the expenses of which, if successful, will be personally charged to the trustees. In England it is provided by section 22(4) of the Trustee Act 1925 that, in the general case, accounts should be audited every three years. This is probably a sensible rule of thumb in Scotland also, although there is no such statutory requirement. The expenses of an audit would be a proper charge against the trust estate.

Occasionally the nature of the trust is such that it is clear that the truster did not intend any accounts to be kept. This can be seen for example in *Leitch* v. *Leitch*.[28] In that case a farmer died, leaving a young wife and large family. The farmer's father, with whom he had shared the farm, assigned to the widow the lease of the farm "for behoof of herself and her family." She continued residing there, bringing up her family, and, with their help, running the farm. Some years later one of the children raised an action for accounting, but the First Division dismissed the action as irrelevant, holding that the nature of the trust, being to provide the widow and her family with a home and secure future for so long as the widow wished to live at the farm, indicated that the truster did not intend a formal trust to be established nor accounts to be kept. This conclusion is likely to be followed only in exceptional cases.

INVESTMENT

This important aspect of trust administration is dealt with in Chapter 8.

DISTRIBUTION

Throughout the existence of the trust, trustees may from time to time be called upon or may decide to distribute part of the trust

---

[26] Indeed with charitable trusts there is a statutory duty to keep accounts: ss.4 and 5 of the Law Reform (Micellaneous Provisions) (Scotland) Act 1990.
[27] See Chap. 10.
[28] 1927 S.C. 823.

estate or the income therefrom to the beneficiaries. Though this can occur without bringing the trust to an end, the most significant moment of distribution is at the termination of the trust and this whole topic is more conveniently dealt with in the final chapter of this book.

MISCELLANEOUS POWERS

The powers that the trustees may rely upon in administering a trust come from two main sources: the trust deed, and the Trusts (Scotland) Act 1921. If a power to do a certain act is granted by the trust deed then the only challenge relating to that power will concern the way it is exercised. These powers may be expressly granted or they may be implied, for example, if they are necessary for the achievement of the specified aims of the trust. Powers that are neither expressed nor necessarily implied cannot be exercised by the trustees. For example in *Esdaile* v. *Inland Revenue*[29] a power to advance capital to the liferentrix was held not to imply a power to make loans to her. In addition the 1921 Act lays down various powers which will be implied into every trust deed (subject to the qualification shortly to be discussed).

Section 4 of the 1921 Act (as amended) gives a long list of powers, including power to sell trust property, power to grant leases of heritage, power to borrow on the security of the trust estate, power to pay debts due by the trust, and power to discharge trustees who have resigned. There is also, by section 4(1)(*ee*)[30] a power to purchase residential accommodation reasonably required by any of the beneficiaries. This is the only statutory power to purchase heritage, and is clearly very limited.[31] It follows that if trustees wish to purchase heritage of any other sort or for any other reason, they must rely on authority given in the trust deed, or, exceptionally, apply to the court (see *infra*).

Tax Point
It should however be noted that the CGT main residence exemption is available where trustees hold heritage which is occupied as the only or main residence of the beneficiary (CGTA 1979, s.104).

There are various other powers specified in section 4, and for the full list reference should be made to the Act itself.

---

[29] (1936) 20 T.C. 700.
[30] Added to the list by s.4 of the Trusts (Scotland) Act 1961.
[31] See *Bristow, Petr.*, 1965 S.L.T. 225.

The section 4 powers will be implied into all trust deeds, so long as the exercise of such power would not be "at variance with the terms or purposes of the trust." The word "terms" is not synonymous with the word "purposes" and consequently whether the exercise of the power is at variance with either must be considered separately.[32] The "terms" of the trust are the actual words used, either in the deed creating the trust or in the judical decree appointing the person to the office of trustee.[33] To be at variance with the terms of the trust the power must be "at variance with the express language by which the trust or appointment is created,"[34] *i.e.* the power must be positively withheld, or at least be so clearly against the expressed wishes of the truster as to be absolutely inconsistent with the language used. The "purposes" of the trust, being the aims to be achieved, are a good deal wider than the "terms," but "can only be implied from the language by which the trust is created."[35] It also embraces the necessary administration of the trust.[36] An act that inhibits in some way either the achievement of the specified aims or the underlying ultimate purpose of the trust is likely to be considered to be at variance with the purposes. Lord President Cooper read the words "at variance with the purposes of the trust" as equivalent to the phrase "involving a variation of the purposes of the trust."[37] It has also been stated that "not at variance with the purposes" is not the same as "necessary for the purposes"[38]: it follows that the section 4 powers are available to trustees even if they are not strictly necessary for the achievement of the aims of the trust.

EXTENSION OF POWERS

While the trustees can rely upon the powers granted by section 4 (when appropriate) and the powers conferred by the trust deed (so long as they are exercised properly) without further authority, the court possesses the jurisdiction to extend the powers of trustees in certain situations. This jurisdiction comes from two sources.

---

[32] *Leslie's J.F.*, 1925 S.C. 464; *Marquess of Lothian's C.B.*, 1927 S.C. 579.
[33] *Leslie's J.F. supra* n. 32.
[34] *Per*, Lord Blackburn in *Marquess of Lothian's C.B.*, *supra*, n. 32, at p. 587.
[35] *Ibid.* at p. 588.
[36] *Per* Lord Russell in *Tennent's J.F.* v. *Tennent*, 1954 S.C. 215 at p. 229.
[37] *Ibid.* at p. 225.
[38] *Per* Lord Sands in *Marquess of Lothian's C.B.*, *supra*, n. 32 at p. 586.

1. The Trusts (Scotland) Act 1921

If the trustees wish to exercise a power listed in s.4, but that power is at variance with either the terms or the purposes of the trust, and therefore cannot be exercised, the trustees may petition the court for authority under section 5 of the 1921 Act to exercise any of the section 4 powers. The court may grant this authority so long as the exercise of the power is "in all the circumstances expedient for the execution of the trust." There seems to have been very little judicial discussion of the meaning of the phrase "expedient for the execution of the trust," but one can easily imagine a situation in which a power sought would not satisfy this test. For example, in *Conage's J.F.*[39] a petition under section 5 was dismissed when a judicial factor asked permission to sell the heritable property in a trust, one of the aims of which was to preserve this property as a family estate. This was deemed not expedient for the execution of the trust.

Often petitions under section 5 are refused as unnecessary. This can happen if the court considers that the power sought under section 5 is already conferred by section 4 (because it is not at variance with the terms or purposes of the trust), or indeed is already contained in the trust deed. For example in *Cunningham's Tutrix*[40] a petition for authority to sell two tenements held purely for investment purposes and which were falling into disrepair was dismissed as unnecessary since this amounted to a proper act of administration in preserving the trust estate. The effect of such a refusal was described by Lord Blackburn in the following terms:

> "The dismissal of the petition as unnecessary would amount to a judicial finding that the exercise of the power . . . was not at variance with the purposes of the deed or appointment; would provide the petitioner with some guide in his future actings; and might dispense with the necessity of repeated applications to the Court."[41]

Trustees are not to be criticised if the petition is dismissed as unnecessary; consequently they may charge the expenses of raising the action to the trust.[42] On the other hand, the court has been impatient with petitions brought in cases in which there is

[39] 1948 S.L.T. (Notes) 12.
[40] 1949 S.C. 275.
[41] *Marquess of Lothian's C.B.*, *supra*, n. 32 at p. 588.
[42] *Cunningham's Tutrix*, *supra*, n. 40.

no real doubt that the trustees already have the power sought, but which are raised solely to give the trustees a feeling of extra security.[43] Given the onerous nature of the trustees' potential liabilities if they exercise powers they do not have, the raising of a petition for court sanction is perfectly understandable, but in a clearly frivolous case the trustees may well be held liable to pay the expenses of the action themselves. The section 5 petition is properly brought either when the section 4 power is clearly not available to trustees, or when there is real doubt whether it is available or not.

Section 16 of the 1921 Act also allows for the powers of the trustees to be extended, by empowering the court to authorise trustees to advance any part of the capital of the trust to minor beneficiaries for the purpose of their maintenance or education if the income of the trust is not sufficient or not available to do so. This authorisation can be given in the absence of such authority in the trust deed, but cannot be given if the trust deed expressly prohibits such advances.

2. The nobile officium and section 1 of the Trusts (Scotland) Act 1961

Exceptionally, when section 5 of the 1921 Act cannot be used (say, because the power sought is not one listed in section 4, or because, though listed, its exercise cannot be proved to be expedient for the execution of the trust) the Inner House may grant authority through the *nobile officium* to do an act which the trustees do not otherwise have the power to do. This course is not open to trustees if section 5 can be used instead.[44]

Previously the court took the view that it was incompetent to grant trustees powers which they had not been granted either by statute or by the trust deed.[45] Occasionally however the court has, in exceptional cases, been willing to grant powers if these are necessary to prevent the total defeat of the purposes of the trust. In *Anderson's Trs.*[46] authority was given to trustees to purchase a farm, even although they had no power to purchase heritage either under the trust deed or under statute.[47] The trust estate

---

[43] See *Marquess of Lothian's C.B.*, *supra*, n. 32, and *Tennent's J.F.* v. *Tennent*, *supra*, n. 36.

[44] *Tennent's J.F.* v. *Tennent*, *supra*, n. 36.

[45] See *Hall's Trs.* v. *McArthur*, 1918 S.C. 646.

[46] 1921 S.C. 315.

[47] Section 4 of the 1921 Act now gives the very limited power, described above, to purchase heritage, but that would not have covered this case.

had consisted of a lease of a farm, and the trust purpose was to maintain the farm until such time as the truster's nephew, who was currently at agricultural college, attained the age of majority and took over the running of the farm. However the landlord decided to sell the farm, and gave first option to the trustees. They did not have the power to purchase the farm and inability to do so threatened to destroy the main purpose of the trust. The trust was saved by the Second Division granting the authority that was lacking. Lord Justice-Clerk Scott Dickson pointed out that unless the powers were granted, the main purpose of the trust-deed would be completely frustrated, and he continued:

> "In these circumstances I think we may grant the powers that the petitioners ask for, on the ground that it is only by doing so that the main purpose of the trust can be carried out, and that there could really be no doubt that, if the truster had foreseen the position of things which has now come about, he would have made provision for it."[48]

However the court was careful to emphasise the exceptional nature of this case, and warned that it could not be used as a precedent.

The power of the Scottish court to involve itself in the administration of a trust is a good deal more limited than the power of the Chancery Court in England,[49] and it is rather difficult precisely to identify the extent of the Court of Session's jurisdiction under the *nobile officium* to grant powers of administration to trustees.[50] In *Gibson's Trs.*[51] a Court of Seven Judges extended trustees' powers of investment under the *nobile officium* because a case of "strong expediency" had been made out. Lord Anderson felt that "mere expediency" might be sufficient,[52] because that was all that was required for the court to exercise its powers under section 5 of the 1921 Act. However, the court also decided that it could not grant any powers expressly withheld by the truster. However the court can grant powers not listed in section 4. In *Anderson's Trs.*[53] the power to purchase heritage was granted, even though this was not a statutory power.

Given the uncertainties of the scope of the *nobile officium*, the better course today would probably be to petition the court for a

---

[48] 1921 S.C. 315 at p. 322.

[49] See the discussion in *Hall's Trs.* v. *McArthur, supra,* n. 45.

[50] For a discussion of this issue, see Mackenzie Stuart "*The Nobile Officium and Trust Administration,*" 1935 S.L.T. (News) 1.

[51] 1933 S.C. 190.

[52] *Ibid.* at p. 210.

[53] *Supra,* n. 48.

variation under the terms of section 1 of the Trusts (Scotland) Act 1961.[54] This has been the course adopted in relation to trustees' powers of investment. It has been held that the limitations on such powers contained in the Trustee Investments Act 1961 can be extended by an application under section 1[55]; and this would suggest that an application under section 1 of the 1961 Act could also grant powers wider than those contained in section 4 of the 1921 Act.

[54] Discussed in Chap. 12.
[55] *Henderson, Petr.*, 1981 S.L.T. (Notes) 40 (discussed further in Chap. 8).

CHAPTER 8

THE POWER AND DUTY OF INVESTMENT

Introduction

If the trustees are called upon to hold the trust estate for longer than a minimal period of time, they will be duty-bound to use the estate in such a way as protects its value in both notional and real terms. Unless the purposes can be fulfilled by maintaining the trust property as it stands until such time as it is passed on to the beneficiaries, one of the trustees' most important duties is to invest the trust estate in such proper investments as are authorised either by statute or by the trust deed itself. A trustee who fails to invest properly will be liable to account to the beneficiaries for the income that the estate, properly invested, would have generated.[1]

Proper investments, in relation to trusts, are investments that are not speculative or hazardous: the trustees are not allowed to take any risk with the property to which they do not have the beneficial right. They must therefore perform a rather nice balancing act, attempting to provide a proper return on the estate without compromising the safety of the funds. This is made all the more important by the fact that it often happens that the beneficiaries entitled to the capital are different from the beneficiaries entitled to the income. Some investments (particularly in certain sectors of the stock market) produce primarily capital

---

[1] *Melville* v. *Noble's Trs.* (1896) 24 R. 243. See also *Manners* v. *Strong's J.F.* (1902) 4 F. 829 in which it was held that no liability for failure to invest attached to a judicial factor who had concluded, correctly, that prices at the time he could have invested were unduly high.

appreciation with little or no income; others (such as deposits in banks and building societies) produce income with little or no capital appreciation. In determining the type of investment to make, the trustees must bear in mind the nature of the respective interests of the various beneficiaries and ensure that the interests of one are not prejudiced in favour of those of another.

APPROPRIATION OF INVESTMENTS

All the beneficiaries are entitled to have their interests secured by the whole fund. It follows as a general rule that trustees may not appropriate particular investments to particular beneficiaries. Only sometimes may they do so: the power and duty to appropriate investments "is limited to cases where either the method of distribution of the estate makes it essential that there should be appropriation, or the intention of the truster to that effect can be reasonably inferred."[2] The truster may, and in formal trusts normally will, expressly provide that certain investments are to be appropriated for the benefit of specified beneficiaries, in which case any loss or appreciation on the investment is borne by the particular beneficiary and not the whole estate. Likewise, if all the beneficiaries agree that this be done, the trustees would be entitled to appropriate. Once intimated to the beneficiaries, the appropriation is irrevocable.[3]

Alternatively it can sometimes be inferred from the nature of the provisions that the truster intended appropriation. If for example there are directions for immediate distribution of part of the estate and postponed payment of the remainder, it can be inferred that the truster intended appropriation, for otherwise those entitled to the immediate distribution would not know their full shares until the ultimate distribution has taken place.

Tax Point
It has been stated by Lord President Cooper that appropriation of investments in this way will effectively create "a number of subordinate trusts."[4] However, it is unlikely that these "subordinate trusts" will be treated as wholly separate funds for the purposes of Capital Gains Tax: see *Roome* v. *Edwards*.[5] If they were to be so treated, the chargeable gains and allowable losses would be calculated separately, with the appropriate annual exemption being deducted separately.

[2] Mackenzie Stuart at p. 286.
[3] *Warrack's Trs.* v. *Warrack*, 1919 S.C 522.
[4] *Per* Lord President Cooper in *Duncan's Trs.*, 1951 S.C. 557 at p. 561.
[5] [1982] A.C. 279, *per* Lord Wilberforce at pp. 292–293.

DEVELOPMENT OF THE POWER OF INVESTMENT

Trustees have never by the law of Scotland been allowed completely unfettered discretion over the investments they may make with trust funds, and it has always been the case that trustees may only place the funds in "authorised investments," and even then only if the investments are safe enough and provide income enough to satisfy the interests of all classes of beneficiary. Authority may come from the law, or, as is more common in current drafting practice, from the trust deed itself.

At common law trustees had the duty, and therefore the power, to invest the funds in their charge. However, superseding that power was the almost absolute duty not to subject the funds to any risks at all. At common law, with the primary all important duty being to preserve the trust estate intact, it was an absolute rule that the only investments the trustees could make were in low return, low risk securities such as fixed interest Government Bonds, War Stock and the like. A wider list of securities was provided by the Trusts (Scotland) Act 1921, in section 27 of which the Court of Session was given the power to add to the list of recognised trustee investments; but still the types of investments permitted provided a very low return, though high security for the capital investment. While inflation remained constantly very low for lengthy periods of time, this appeared to be the sensible approach: many great speculative disasters have destroyed trusts that contained powers going beyond statutorily permitted classes of investment. The failure of the Darien Scheme at the turn of the eighteenth century, the collapse of the City of Glasgow Bank in 1878, and the Stock Market Crash of 1929 provide some of the more spectacular examples.

Since the Second World War however there have been long periods of high inflation, and this resulted in a number of trust funds losing their value in real terms. It began to be felt that the legal position was too narrow to allow trustees properly to protect the funds under their charge. Parliament therefore passed the Trustee Investments Act 1961, section 1(1) of which, for the first time, allowed all trustees to invest trust funds in equities and other securities that would provide a return sufficient to ward off the ravages of inflation. Such securities, known as "wider-range investments" do, of their nature, carry a higher risk, and for that reason the Act lays down a fairly sophisticated procedure through which trustees must go if they wish to invest funds in the higher risk areas. The wording and layout of this important statute is at times opaque and hard to follow: it could never be described as being user-friendly.

INVESTMENT UNDER THE TRUSTEE INVESTMENTS ACT 1961

By section 2(1) of the 1961 Act, if trustees wish to make any investment in wider-range investments they must split the trust fund into two parts that are equal in value at the time of the division.[6] Once split, the fund may not be split again, and property may not be transferred from one part to the other, unless a compensating transfer of the same value is made in the opposite direction. Before making the split, the trustees must value the property, and, by section 5(1), if in doing so they obtain a valuation in writing from a person reasonably believed to be qualified to make it, such valuation shall be conclusive in determining whether the split has been properly made.

Once the split has been made, the two parts, known as the narrower-range part and the wider-range part, shall be administered as if they were quite separate funds. If new property comes into the trust itself this too must be split equally between the two parts, or placed in one part with a compensating transfer of half its value to the other part[7]; but any income arising or capital appreciation generated solely by the property in one part shall be treated as belonging to that part, and no compensating transfer need, or indeed can, be made in order to keep the two parts of the same value. It follows that one part may, through time, become very different in value from the other part.

For example, if a truster adds to the trust fund after it has been set up and the split made, the property he adds must also be split, or added to one part with a compensating transfer of half its value made to the other part. Dividends or interest earned on investments which come into the trustees' hands as capital must similarly be split.[8] If property in one part increases in value, for example through an increase in share price, no compensating transfer is necessary. Similarly, if a company in which shares are held in one part makes a bonus issue, this is added to the holding

---

[6] By s.13 the Treasury may in the future increase the proportion of the funds initially to be put into the wider-range part, but to a figure no greater than three to one in relation to the narrower-range part; and if this happens, funds already split may be split again to reflect the new proportions.

[7] s.2(3).

[8] *Ibid.*

in that part. On the other hand, if a company offers a rights issue, whereby the trustees may purchase extra shares at an advantageous price, this is not in itself a return, *i.e.* is not an accrual for the purposes of section 2(3). If the trustees wish to take up such a rights issue, they may do so,[9] but must ensure that the narrower-range part also increases accordingly. They may use money in the wider-range part to make the new investment, but must allocate half of the investment to the narrower-range part (selling half the newly acquired investment and re-investing in narrower-range investments if necessary).

The investments that may be made under the Act are classified into three different types, listed in three separate parts of Schedule 1. Part I and Part II list what are known as narrower-range investments. The Act's innovation comes with Part III, for there are listed what are called wider-range investments, these being the types of investments not permitted before the passing of the 1961 Act.

THE SEPARATE FUNDS

1. The narrower-range part

The part of the trust estate known as the narrower-range part may be invested, in such proportions as the trustees think fit, in those investments listed in Part I and Part II of Schedule 1 of the 1961 Act.

Part I contains the sort of investments allowed at common law and includes such things as National Savings Certificates, and deposits in the National Savings Bank. (For a full list, see the Act itself). The capital value of these investments will tend to remain, notionally, static. Trustees may invest the trust funds in Part I investments at their own absolute discretion and they are not obliged to obtain any advice before doing so.

Part II contains roughly the sort of investments that were permitted under the Trusts (Scotland) Act 1921, and now includes such things as government securities, fixed interest securities issued by the E.C., U.K. company debentures, deposits in a building society and heritable securities. (For a full list see the Act itself). The capital value of Part II investments may well fluctuate, and for that reason, the trustees' discretion to invest in

---

[9] s.4(1)(p) of the Trusts (Scotland) Act 1921.

Part II investments is rather more limited than with Part I investments in that, before investing in Part II investments, the trustees must obtain advice (see *infra*).

2. The wider-range part

The part of the trust estate known as the wider-range part may be invested, in such proportions as the trustees think fit, in those investments listed in Parts I, II and III of Schedule 1 of the 1961 Act. Though they may thus invest all the wider-range part in narrower-range investments, there is only point in splitting the fund if they intend to invest at least part of the funds in Part III, wider-range, investments. Part III includes shares in qualifying companies, shares in building societies, and units in Unit Trust Schemes. Advice of the same nature as required for Part II investments must be obtained before the trustees make any Part III investment (see *infra*).

There are strict qualifications on the companies that can be invested in as Part III investments. The company must be incorporated in the United Kingdom[10]; it must be quoted on the stock exchange[11]; its shares must be fully paid up or required to be fully paid up within nine months of the issue[12]; it must have a total paid up share capital of not less than £1m[13]; and it must have paid a dividend on all its shares entitled to rank for a dividend in each of the preceding five years.[14] These provisions are designed to ensure that if the trustees do decide to invest part or all of the wider-range part in wider-range securities, they will only choose fairly large British companies that have consistently performed well enough to declare dividends in recent years.

3. Special-range property

It is of course still open to a truster to provide wider powers of investment in the trust deed than is allowed for under the 1961 Act. He may specify that the trustees make certain investments, or authorise or direct them to hold the investments he has made

---

[10] Sched. 1, Part III, para. 1.
[11] Sched. 1, Part IV, para. 2(*a*).
[12] Sched. 1, Part IV, para. 2(*b*).
[13] Sched. 1, Part IV, para. 3(*a*).
[14] Sched. 1, Part IV, para. 3(*b*). Note that no level of dividend is laid down, unlike with a number of Part II investments.

himself. Alternatively, a truster may waive any or all of the conditions on Part II and Part III investments. Any such specified investments are put into a separate fund, and are known as special-range property.[15] Once that fund is created, the remainder of the estate is invested in narrower-range investments, or, if the trustees wish to make wider-range investments, the remainder of the estate is split into two and invested in accordance with the principles described above. If the whole of the trust estate falls into the special range, the 1961 Act has no applicability, and the trustees take all their authority to invest from the trust deed. It is common, indeed usual, for trust deeds today to specify that trustees are to have wider powers of investment than those given in the 1961 Act, and it is therefore only a small minority of trusts to which the Act will apply.

INSTRUCTIONS FROM THE TRUSTER

It can be seen from the above that certain very common types of property holding are not statutorily recognised as being trustee investments. Land holdings for example are a common and valuable type of property that individuals can own. However trustees have no express power to hold land nor to invest the trust property in land (except for the limited purpose permitted under section 4(1)(ee) of the Trusts (Scotland) Act 1921). It follows that if a trust estate is to consist in land, or, say, in shares in a private company, the drafter of the trust deed must take care to ensure that express power to make such investment is included in the deed.

It is indeed open to the truster to provide that the trustees are to have the fullest powers of investment as if they were beneficial owners of the trust estate. If the whole trust fund is covered by such a provision, there will be no need to split the fund in terms of section 1(2) of the Trustee Investments Act 1961. Similarly the truster may restrict the powers of investment that the trustees would otherwise have, for example by prohibiting investments in such concerns as armaments manufacturers, distillers, or turf accountants. The movement towards "ethical investments" has been growing in recent years.

The court has tended to interpret investment clauses that grant wider powers strictly and any ambiguity in the wording will be resolved in favour of security for the funds. For example, in

---

[15] s.3 and Sched. 2.

Moss's Trs. v. *King*,[16] a trust deed granted "the fullest powers
. . . of investment" to trustees, but the First Division held that
this clause could not mean the fullest powers of investment that
an unrestricted owner would have, but rather only the powers of
investment granted by the common law to one under fiduciary
duties such as a trustee. Lord President Cooper put it thus·

> "It was not seriously maintained that this clause fell to be read literally as
> meaning all that it might appear to say, and any such construction would be
> impossible for it would make nonsense of the trust. The trustees are only
> trustees, and they hold and administer the estate in that capacity and with
> the overriding fiduciary obligations of all trustees."[17]

This clause was therefore held to mean virtually nothing, for it
gave no more power to the trustees than did the law itself. It is
unclear whether a clause such as the one in *Moss' Trs.* would
today be taken to mean that the trustees must follow the
provisions of the 1961 Act, or whether they could depart from its
terms. If a truster intends to confer upon his trustees wider
powers, he must do so in the most unequivocal and unambiguous
fashion.

If the trust estate as originally passed to the trustees consists in
whole or in part of investments, these will not be covered by the
1961 Act, as it is not the trustees who have made the investments. In that situation trustees need not sell and re-invest the
estate in accordance with the provisions of the Act. There is
however no presumption that the original constitution of the
estate is to be retained, and the trustees are no more entitled to
continue a truster's speculations than to indulge in them themselves.[18] Even when trustees have been given clear and express
powers by the trust deed, it does not necessarily follow that they
will be fulfilling their duty in relation to investment by following
such instructions.

There is a difference between an authorised investment and a
proper investment, and trustees may only make proper investments. A proper investment is one that is both authorised *and*
does not subject the trust estate to unreasonable risk. The
trustees must pay regard to the changing economic climate and
the potential dangers that even authorised investments can carry.

---

[16] 1952 S.C. 523.
[17] *Ibid.* at p. 527. *Cf.* the English case of *Re Harari's Settlement Trusts* [1949] 1
All E.R. 430.
[18] *Brownlie & Ors.* v. *Brownlie's Trs.* (1879) 6 R. 1233.

An authorisation in the trust deed to retain the trust securities
does not absolve the trustees from the duty to protect the estate,
and a failure to pay attention to how the securities are faring in a
changing market could result in liability for breach of trust. In
Clarke v. *Clarke's Trs.*[19] trustees were authorised to retain the
investments that the truster himself had made. They did so,
giving no fresh or periodic consideration to the propriety of
keeping these shares. The shares gradually lost their value and
the trustees were held liable for the loss to the trust estate. Lord
Cullen said:

> "It is the plain and undoubted duty of trustees who continue to hold shares
> of such a nature, or other kinds of assets, to keep a prudent and business-
> like eye upon them, and to revise the situation from time to time, instead of
> going to sleep upon the matter and continuing to hold either in blind
> confidence or without giving any such consideration to the matter as an
> ordinary prudent man would give."[20]

Similarly, in *Thomson's Trs.* v. *Davidson*,[21] it was held that even
the most peremptory instruction by the truster to retain investments could not be taken to prohibit trustees from exercising
"the most characteristic function which falls to be discharged by
every trustee—the preservation of the trust estate."[22] This suggests that trustees are duty bound to realise hazardous investments even when prohibited from doing so by the trust deed
itself[23]; and if they are so bound then there can be no need to go
to court to obtain authorisation (under section 5 of the Trusts
(Scotland) Act 1921 or section 1 of the Trusts (Scotland) Act
1961) to depart from the terms of the deed.

Indeed the duty to take care of investments and to realise
authorised and *previously* proper investments might conceivably
result in the trustees being liable for failure to get rid of
investments authorised by the 1961 Act itself. If for example a
particular class of investment in Part III of Schedule 1 becomes
insecure, owing to a fluctuating economic situation, the trustees
would not be able to rely upon the fact that it qualifies under
Schedule 1 to avoid personal liability if, in the circumstances, it
was unreasonable for them not to have noticed the dangers. The
list of investments in Schedule 1 has the same effect as a list of

---

[19] 1925 S.C. 693.
[20] *Ibid.* at p. 711.
[21] 1947 S.C. 654.
[22] *Ibid.* at p. 658, *per* Lord President Cooper.
[23] *Stevenson's Trs., Petrs.*, 1924 S.L.T. 792, *per* Lord Ashmore at p. 793.

investments in the trust deed itself: they are authorised, but only become proper when, having exercised their obligation of diligence, the trustees reasonably decide that the trust funds are safe enough in such an investment.

If a truster grants wider powers of investment to the trustees than are allowed for by the general law, such wider powers will not transmit to a judicial factor appointed to the trust estate. Though a judicial factor is in terms of section 2 of the Trusts (Scotland) Act 1921 a trustee, he is nonetheless different from a normal trustee because he takes all his authority from the court and not from the truster. So it was held by the Second Division in *Carmichael's J.F.*,[24] in which Lord Wheatley pointed out that the truster's conferring of wide powers of investment indicates a clear element of *delectus personae*, which would not be present once a judicial factor is appointed. On the other hand, a *curator bonis*, who administers the estate of an *incapax* is in a quite different position, though also, in terms of section 2 of the 1921 Act, a trustee. A curator does not take real title to the estate under his charge, as a trustee does. "In exercising his power of management the question which the curator would have to ask himself is, what would the ward have done if he had been of full capacity?"[25] It follows that if the ward would have maintained investments not permitted under the Trustee Investments Act 1961, the *curator bonis* may likewise maintain such investments. So it was held in *Fraser* v. *Paterson* (*No. 2*),[26] in which Lord Jauncey allowed a *curator bonis* to retain investments in a family company when it was clear that this was what the ward wished. He said this:

"I conclude that the primary duty of a *curator bonis* is to preserve and manage the curatory estate for the benefit of the ward and that what may be for the benefit of the ward will not necessarily result in the maximising of the estate nor the conversion thereof into trustee investments."[27]

In light of an earlier House of Lords case[28] however, Lord Jauncey did restrict his remarks to a *curator bonis* wishing to retain the ward's investments rather than making new investments with the ward's estate.

[24] 1971 S.L.T. 336.
[25] *Per* Lord Kilbrandon in *Burns' C.B.* v. *Burns' Trs.*, 1961 S.L.T. 166 at p. 167.
[26] 1988 S.L.T. 124.
[27] *Ibid.* at p. 125.
[28] *Hutton* v. *Annan* (1898) 25 R. (H.L.) 23.

THE NATURE OF ADVICE

Before making any investments authorised in Part II or Part III of Schedule 1 of the 1961 Act, or otherwise authorised by a special power in the trust deed (however expressed), the trustees are directed by section 6(2) to obtain advice on the question of whether the investment is satisfactory having regard to the need for diversification and the suitability of the proposed investment to the trust. Proper advice is defined in section 6(4) to mean:

> "the advice of a person who is reasonably believed by the trustee to be qualified by his ability in and practical experience of financial matters; and such advice may be given by a person notwithstanding that he gives it in the course of his employment as an officer or servant."

The advice must be given or subsequently confirmed in writing.[29]

By section 6(3) the trustees must also periodically obtain and consider advice on the desirability of retaining investments made, whether the investments were made under the terms of the 1961 Act or otherwise. This subsection gives to the trustees the power to determine at what intervals such periodic advice ought to be obtained; but since this obligation reflects the common law duty in relation to advice it follows that advice should be obtained as often as the prudent and reasonable trustee would obtain it. At common law the prudent and reasonable trustee kept a continual check on all the trust investments, paying regard to the changing economic climate and realising investments that had become less secure: he did not "go to sleep" on the issue and blindly retain everything that was once proper.[30] Section 6(3) of the Trustee Investments Act 1961 gives statutory effect to this principle. A yearly re-appraisal is probably a sensible strategy to adopt.

A failure in this duty to obtain advice can amount to a breach of trust, as is shown in *Martin* v. *City of Edinburgh District Council*.[31] Here a District Council was the trustee of various trusts. The ruling group within the Council decided to withdraw all Council funds and trust funds under the Council's control from South Africa. They took advice, but only on how the disinvestment policy could be implemented, not on whether it should be implemented. It was held that this amounted to a breach of trust, because the Council had not obtained advice

[29] s.6(5).
[30] *Per* Lord Cullen in *Clarke* v. *Clarke's Trs.*, 1925 S.C. 693, at p. 711.
[31] 1988 S.L.T. 329.

from professional advisers on whether or not it was in the best interests of the trusts and of the beneficiaries to disinvest from South Africa. It did not matter that the trust funds had in fact increased in value through the change in investment: it had been done without taking advice on its effects on the beneficiaries and therefore had been done for the wrong reasons.

Section 6(6) provides that the requirement to obtain advice before investing or retaining investments does not apply where one of two or more trustees is the person giving advice. This has the effect, not of obviating the necessity for advice, but of allowing one co-trustee (if he is qualified) to give the required advice to the other trustees. It is implicit in the wording that a single trustee may not give advice to himself. Likewise the advice may be given by a trust employee lawfully exercising the powers of a trustee so long as such officer or servant is reasonably believed by the trustees to be qualified by his ability in and practical experience of financial matters to give such advice.

Advice need not be taken under s.6 in relation to the suitability of investing in a loan on heritable security.[32]

Section 3 of the Financial Services Act 1986 provides that no person shall carry on an investment business in the United Kingdom unless he is an "authorised person," and by Schedule 1, para. 15 of that Act the giving of investment advice of the nature required by trustees will constitute "investment business." Trustees must therefore obtain the advice only from persons authorised under the 1986 Act. These are defined by the 1986 Act to include members of self-regulating organisations[33] and persons authorised by recognised professional bodies[34] (such as, for example, the Law Society of Scotland). Schedule 1, para. 22(4) however provides that a trustee giving advice to co-trustees will not be subject to the 1986 Act, except where he is remunerated for doing so (*i.e.* remunerated for giving advice rather than remunerated for acting as a trustee).

Once the advice has been obtained the trustees' duty is to consider it carefully and then to make a decision whether to follow it or not. Trustees would be acting in breach of trust if they simply followed whatever financial advice they received without giving consideration to it, for that would amount to an unlawful delegation to the financial adviser of their own duty to make decisions. Nor are the trustees to displace their own

[32] s.6(7).
[33] 1986 Act, s.7.
[34] 1986 Act, s.15.

discretion with "an arithmetical calculation of maximum profit," for this too would amount to such unlawful delegation.[35] The welfare of the beneficiaries is the paramount consideration, and this may sometimes involve the trustees in determining matters on grounds other than purely financial ones.[36]

DUTY OF CARE IN INVESTMENT STRATEGY

The standard of care expected of trustees in making and carrying out investment strategy is the same standard of the ordinary prudent trustee as is applied to all other aspects of trust management.[37] However, the 1961 Act also imposes certain duties of care in making investments, to be followed whether or not the investments are those authorised by that Act. Section 6(1) provides:

> "In the exercise of his powers of investment, a trustee shall have regard—
> (a) to the need for diversification of investments of the trust, in so far as is appropriate to the circumstances of the trust;
> (b) to the suitability to the trust of investments of the description of investment proposed and of the investment proposed as an investment of that description."

Both conditions restate the common law duty of care. The need for diversification is a sensible economic strategy always followed by prudent investors. This duty is all the more important the larger the fund is, but its application could be awkward if the fund is so small as to make diversification counter-productive (taking account of the administration charges of investing a number of very small sums in different places).[38]

Trusts are commonly set up with the sole purpose of holding a single insurance policy.[39] Section 6(1)(a) will not prevent this,

[35] *Per* Lord Murray in *Martin* v. *Edinburgh District Council*, 1988 S.L.T. 329 at p. 334.

[36] See the English cases of *Re Weston's Settlements* [1968] 3 All E.R. 338, *Re Remnant's Settlement Trusts* [1970] 2 All E.R. 554; *Cowan* v. *Scargill* [1984] 3 W.L.R. 501 at pp. 514/515.

[37] See Chap. 10.

[38] In the English case of *Cowan* v. *Scargill* (*supra*) Sir Robert Megarry V-.C. said this at p. 515: "the reference to 'circumstances of the trust' plainly includes matters such as the size of the trust funds: the degree of diversification that is practicable and desirable for a large fund may plainly be impracticable or undesirable (or both) in the case of a small fund."

[39] The 1961 Act itself does not permit investment in life assurance policies, though they have become a very common form of investment for individuals today. If a trust is to hold such an investment, express authority must be given.

because diversification in that situation would hardly be "appropriate to the circumstances of the trust."

Unit trusts are investments which in themselves spread the risk amongst a large number of holdings; but a trust investment in one unit trust is unlikely thereby to satisfy the diversification requirement. This requirement would seem to demand that the trust property be invested in a number of separate holdings, *i.e.* be under the control of a number of different investment managers, or be in different sectors. The aim is to prevent the whole fund collapsing when a single holding collapses. Though going a long way towards this aim, unit trusts do not in themselves give absolute protection from collapse.

The suitability consideration is also a common law requirement,[40] and it will depend on the trust purposes whether an investment is suitable for a trust. This requirement probably infers that the investment must be such as to protect the interests both of the class of beneficiaries entitled to the income and the class entitled to the capital. An investment would not be "suitable" if there were both classes, but it provided only capital appreciation, or only income. Menzies points out[41] that the funds should not be tied up if there is a possibility of distribution being required before they can be withdrawn.

Though there is no case illustrating the point, suitability probably also goes further than purely financial considerations, and section 6(1)(*b*) may be taken to impose a duty on the trustees to have regard to the social purposes of the trust. An investment in a company running, say, sex shops, would be unsuitable for a trust for the education of young children. A trust fund for cancer research really ought not to invest in cigarette or tobacco companies.

A suitable investment will normally be one that provides an income, this being the generally accepted meaning of the word "investment." In *Moss's Trs.* v. *King*,[42] a question arose about whether the purchase of a house to let free to a beneficiary was an "investment." It was held that it was not, Lord President Cooper saying,

"I respectfully agree with P. O. Lawrence J. in *In Re Wragg*[43] that to 'invest' *prima facie* means 'to apply money in the purchase of some property from

---

[40] See Menzies at pp. 386–388.
[41] *Ibid.* at p. 387.
[42] 1952 S.C. 523.
[43] [1919] 2 Ch. 58.

which interest or profit is expected and which property is purchased in order to be held for the sake of the income which it will yield' . . . If the trustees were to apply trust funds in buying and furnishing a house for the occupation of Mrs. King rent-free or on uneconomic terms, it would be a mere simulate device to describe the transaction as a trust 'investment'."[44]

However, it is suggested that this cannot be an absolute rule, and a trust whose purpose envisages only a capital appreciation for postponed payment may well have as a suitable "investment" the purchase of a corporeal moveable that is expected to increase in value (*e.g.* some collector's piece like an oil painting or an antique). Such an "investment" must, of course, satisfy the prudence condition that pervades this whole subject.

Tax Point
In making investment decisions, trustees should always bear in mind the possibility of CGT being incurred if trust investments are sold realising a chargeable gain. For example, if trustees sell a shareholding in a particular company, a chargeable gain would arise if the value of the shareholding has increased faster than the rate of inflation (and an allowable loss will be incurred if the value has not kept up with inflation).

It should be noted however that the realisation of many authorised trustee investments under the 1961 Act will not give rise to a CGT charge. Some investments, like bank and building society deposits, are outside the ambit of a CGT charge (CGTA 1979, s.135). Others, like savings certificates and gilt-edged securities are statutorily excluded from the charge (CGTA 1979, ss.71 & 67). A similar result is achieved with building society share accounts (Finance Act 1988, s.113). As a rule of thumb, narrower range investments are not the sort of investment that attracts CGT.

Where other property held as a trust investment is to be sold, trustees may be able to take advantage of one of the following: (a) the so-called "chattels exemption" (for corporeal moveables worth under £6,000: CGTA 1979, s.128); (b) the private residence exemption (where a home owned by the trust is occupied by a beneficiary under the terms of the trust: CGTA 1979, s.104); or (c) retirement relief (where a trust beneficiary aged over 60 or retiring on ill-health grounds has been involved in a business owned by the trust: Finance Act 1985, s.70).

EXTENSION OF POWERS OF INVESTMENT

The trust deed may be varied if this has the consent of all beneficiaries and potential beneficiaries. Section 1 of the Trusts (Scotland) Act 1961 gives the court power to grant such consent on behalf of specified classes of beneficiary,[45] and this provision

---

[44] 1952 S.C. 523 at p. 527.
[45] See Chap. 12.

may therefore be used to enlarge the powers of investment that trustees have been given by the trust deed.[46]

There has been an argument over whether the powers the court can grant under this section can go beyond that which is permitted in the Trustee Investments Act 1961. The question was first discussed in England in relation to the equivalent power granted to English trustees under the Variation of Trusts Act 1958. In *Re Kolb's Will Trusts*[47] it was held that the English courts should not grant powers beyond those envisaged in the 1961 Act unless there were "special circumstances" to justify it. In *Mason* v. *Farbrother*[48] it was held that special circumstances did exist, being the rate of inflation since 1961, and the fact that the fund in question, being a pension fund, was very large and was in the nature of a public rather than a private trust. In *Trustees of the British Museum* v. *Att. Gen.*,[49] an application brought under the Variation of Trusts Act 1958 was allowed and the "special circumstances" rule in *Re Kolb* was disapproved.

The Court of Session has been equally equivocal in its approach. In *Inglis & Ors, Pet's.*,[50] the First Division held that the court had no authority to grant any wider powers than those envisaged by the Trustee Investments Act 1961. Lord President Clyde, quoting Mackenzie Stuart[51] with approval, said this:

> "Parliament has seen fit in the Trustee Investments Act to define categories of investment in which trustees have authority to place trust funds. It would be quite contrary to principle for this Court to proceed at its own hand to add to these categories and to give trustees power to invest in still wider classes of stocks and shares than Parliament has authorised."[52]

But in *Henderson, Petr.*,[53] the Court, faced with the authority of *Inglis*, convened a bench of five judges and approved a petition

---

[46] Which power is expressly preserved by s.15 of the Trustee Investments Act 1961.

[47] [1961] 3 All E.R. 811.

[48] [1983] 2 All E.R. 1078. This action was raised under s.57 of the (English) Trustee Act 1925, which allows English trustees to apply to the court for wider powers than the law or the trust deed gives them.

[49] [1984] 1 All E.R. 337.

[50] 1965 S.L.T. 326.

[51] Mackenzie Stuart at p. 256.

[52] 1965 S.L.T. 326 at p. 327. See also *Carmichael's J.F.*, 1971 S.L.T. 336, in which the Second Division refused to grant a judicial factor wider powers than "the usual powers" of investment. Wider powers had been exercised successfully by the original trustees, but it was held that this was no reason why the court should "fly in the face of the protection which Parliament and the courts have sought to give trust estates when a judicial factor is appointed" (*per* Lord Wheatley at p. 340).

[53] 1981 S.L.T. (Notes) 40.

brought under section 1 of the Trusts (Scotland) Act 1961 which asked for approval on behalf of minor and unascertained beneficiaries of an arrangement varying the trustees' powers under the deed by providing the additional power to purchase, sell, let or borrow on security of heritable property in Scotland or real property elsewhere. It may now be taken that *Inglis, Petr.* is overruled, and that the Scottish court will, if the circumstances justify it, approve an extension of the powers of investment even beyond those laid down in the Trustee Investments Act 1961. The onus will be on the trustees to show why the extra powers are necessary, and to show that the proposed increase in powers will be used prudently and reasonably.

AVOIDANCE OF THE STATUTORY SCHEME

The policy behind the Trustee Investments Act 1961 is to protect, in form at least, one half of the original trust fund, while at the same time allowing riskier but potentially more lucrative investments to be made with the other half. In this way, the Act tries to ensure that a balance is kept between the need for reasonable safety and the need for a proper return. However, it should be pointed out that the great majority of trust deeds specifically avoid the provisions of the 1961 Act by laying down that the trustees are to have absolute discretion over the investments they make.

Also, within the Act itself there are provisions that make it possible to avoid the statutory scheme so carefully constructed. First, there is no need ever to make any compensating transfer after the initial split has been made; if the two funds have followed different investment strategies, it is almost inevitable that they will become of different values, which disparity may become very great as time goes on. Secondly and more immediately, section 2(4) of the Act declares that where property falls to be taken out of the trust fund, the trustees have a discretion over the choice of property to be taken out. Any current drawings, or payments or distributions to beneficiaries, may be made from, say, the narrower-range part, until that is all used up, leaving only the wider-range part.

It is fashionable to criticise the strictness of the 1961 Act, on the ground that it was passed at a time of vastly different economic circumstances from those which exist today. This criticism is not really justified, because the possibility is always available for a truster in setting up a trust to grant much wider powers than the Act allows. For trusts created both before and after the 1961 Act, the avoidance tactics mentioned above may be adopted. Also, a petition under section 1 of the Trusts (Scotland) Act 1961 may be used by trustees to obtain wider powers than those granted by either the trust deed or the Act.

Nor is the position too liberal, for governing the whole subject, superseding both the trust deed and the Act itself, is the trustees' onerous duty to act in the way that is best for the trust. They cannot avoid the policy of the Act, or make or keep any investment, unless this is expedient for the trust itself, and they have considered, after taking any necessary advice, the best interests of the beneficiaries. This is not to suggest that trustees effectively become cautioners, but their duty of diligence in investment strategy is a fundamental one and it is that which provides the real protection for the beneficiaries.

CHAPTER 9

TRUSTEES' PROBITY

Introduction

THROUGHOUT the course of administration of the trust, it is the duty of the trustees to bring to their office a high degree of probity. Their office involves their having the legal ownership of property, the beneficial right to which is in someone else; and it follows that they must perform their duties with an honesty and an integrity that will ensure proper protection of the rights of the beneficiaries. Not only must they act as a reasonable trustee would act, but they must maintain at all times a separation of their personal interests from the interests of the trust. This obligation is designed to avoid any possibility of a conflict between the trustees' own interests and own personality, and the interests and personality of the trust. Further, in carrying out the administration of the trust, trustees must not allow themselves to be influenced by factors extraneous to the trust: their sole consideration is the welfare of the beneficiaries and the estate under their charge. The trustees' duty to act as reasonable trustees will be considered in Chapter 10. This chapter will examine two aspects of the trustees' probity: the duty of trustees not to permit a conflict of interests between themselves and the trust, and the duty of trustees to be motivated by proper considerations.

AUCTOR IN REM SUAM

Any trustee who permits a conflict to arise between his personal interests and those of the trust is said to be *auctor in rem suam*, or actor in his own cause, and as such is in breach of trust.

126

There are a number of reasons why the law prohibits trustees from being *auctor in rem suam*. First, trustees act in a fiduciary capacity which would be compromised by allowing personal considerations to be brought in. Secondly and more obviously, if a trustee were allowed to act in a personal capacity in a transaction with the trust, his personal interest could clearly clash with his trust duties. Thirdly, trustees have opportunities to acquire information regarding the trust property that is not open to third parties, giving the trustees an unfair advantage, which they may turn to their own profit, even unconsciously. In another context this would be described as insider dealing, which, of course, is not tolerated by the law. Fourthly, the trust is always entitled to independent advice and representation, and this would not always clearly be the case if the trustees were allowed to give advice on matters that might affect themselves.

The duty to advance the interests of those whom they represent irrespective of personal considerations is a duty that applies to all fiduciary relationships, such as that of guardian and child, or agent and principal, but possibly its most significant application is in relation to trusts, for unlike other fiduciaries, trustees hold the legal title to property that someone else has the beneficial right to, and for that reason the potential for fraud and dishonesty, as well as mere clash of interests, is all the greater.

The point of the principle of *auctor in rem suam* is to prevent the possibility of any conflict arising, rather than to provide for the consequences of such a conflict. "The criterion . . . ," said Lord Dunedin,[1] speaking for the Privy Council, "is not what was done, but what might be done." The principle is of such strong application that any transaction that breaches it will not be cured by the passing of any prescriptive period.[2] Nor will it be a defence that the other trustees concurred, nor that the trustee acted in *bona fide* or for the benefit of the beneficiary.[3]

CONSEQUENCES OF BEING AUCTOR IN REM SUAM

Scots law has long regarded the concept of *auctor in rem suam* as a first principle of equity, and it has many consequences. First and

[1] In *Wright* v. *Morgan* [1926] A.C. 788 at p. 798.
[2] *Magistrates of Aberdeen* v. *Aberdeen University* (1877) 4 R. (H.L.) 48, *per* Lord O'Hagan at p. 54, affirming the Court of Session on this point at (1876) 3 R. 1087. See also Prescription and Limitation (Scotland) Act 1973, Sched. 1(1)(*f*).
[3] *Per* Lord Hunter in *Inglis* v. *Inglis*, 1983 S.L.T. 437 at p. 440. See also *Aberdeen Railway Co.* v. *Blaikie Bros.* (1854) 1 Macq. 461.

foremost, the trustee who allows himself to become *auctor in rem suam* will be in breach of trust, the remedies for which are discussed in Chapter 10.

Secondly, a constructive trust[4] is created over any profit which a trustee makes, for it is irrebuttably presumed that he holds on behalf of the trust any benefit he acquires from his position. The trustee "cannot plead otherwise: to do so would be to plead his own breach of trust."[5]

Thirdly, any transaction in which a trustee is *auctor in rem suam* will be open to reduction. The transaction itself is not void, but is voidable.[6] Any beneficiary may challenge the transaction, so long as he has both title and interest to do so.[7] Likewise it may be challenged by any co-trustee,[8] or by a judicial factor appointed to a trust estate.[9] The truster may challenge, at least when he may have a reversionary right in the trust estate.[10] Creditors of the truster have also been held entitled to challenge,[11] though again a reversionary right in the trust is required. On the other hand, third parties to the trust have no title to challenge.[12] If the transaction is challenged by someone entitled to do so, the onus will be on the trustee to prove that he was not *auctor in rem suam*, or that he can rely on one of the limited defences discussed below.

APPLICATION OF THE PRINCIPLE

The following rules illustrate how the Scottish courts have applied the principle.

1. Trustees may not transact with the trust estate

The most obvious application of the principle is a prohibition on trustees transacting in their personal capacity with the trust estate. For example, they cannot purchase property from the trust (even in

---

[4] For which see Chap. 4.

[5] Mackenzie Stuart at p. 175. See also *Laird* v. *Laird* (1858) 20 D. 972, *Magistrates of Aberdeen*, *supra*, n. 2.

[6] Mackenzie Stuart at p. 188.

[7] *Ibid.* at p. 189; *Johnston* v. *Macfarlane*, 1987 S.L.T. 593.

[8] As in *Cherry's Trs.* v. *Patrick* (1911) 2 S.L.T. 313.

[9] *Henderson* v. *Watson* 1939 S.C. 711.

[10] Mackenzie Stuart at p. 189.

[11] *Bon-Accord Marine Assurance Co.* v. *Soutar's Trs.* (1850) 12 D. 1010.

[12] *Per* Lord Johnston in *Hall's Trs.* v. *McArthur*, 1918 S.C. 646 at p. 651.

a public auction), nor can they sell their own property to the trust. Trustees cannot borrow money from the trust estate,[13] nor can they lend to it.[14] This is so even when the transacting trustee distances himself from the decision making of his co-trustees. The reason is not hard to understand. In a sale the seller's interest is in obtaining the highest price while the buyer's interest is in obtaining the lowest price; in a loan the lender's interest is in obtaining the highest rate of return on the greatest security while the borrower's interest is in giving the lowest rate of return on the least security. The clash of interests is obvious here.

The classic example illustrating this rule is the case of *Magistrates of Aberdeen* v. *University of Aberdeen*.[15] Here Aberdeen Town Council were trustees of a fund set up to finance two professorships at the University of Aberdeen. Part of the trust property consisted of a strip of coastal land. Through an intermediary the trustees sold this land to the Council (themselves in another guise), and the Council then exercised the right, which attached to the land, of applying for certain salmon fishing rights from the Crown. They obtained these rights, and used the income therefrom for municipal purposes. Some 70 years after the sale of the land, the University challenged the sale, and the House of Lords had no difficulty in reducing "this strange and indefensible transaction."

Indirect dealings are struck at as much as direct dealings. While there is nothing to prevent a trustee purchasing property from a third party who had obtained the property from the trust,[16] such a purchase could be challenged if it appears that the scheme was set up in a pre-arranged manner in order to get around the rule. In *Clark* v. *Clark's Exx.*[17] executors (who for this purpose are in the same position as trustees) entered into an agreement to sell part of the heritable estate of the deceased to certain third parties. After the conclusion of missives the third parties assigned their right to receive the property to one of the executors in her personal capacity. The assignation was reduced by Lord Mayfield on the ground that the transaction was one in which there was a conflict between the executrix's duty and her personal interest.

The principle of *auctor in rem suam* does not automatically prevent a trustee from transacting with a beneficiary, even in relation to the latter's interest in the trust estate. However in this situation, because the trustee may possess information the benefici-

---

[13] *Croskery* v. *Gilmour's Trs.* (1890) 17 R. 697.
[14] *Wilson* v. *Smith's Trs.* 1939 S.L.T. 120.
[15] (1877) 4 R. (H.L.) 48.
[16] *Wright* v. *Morgan* [1926] A.C. 788.
[17] 1989 S.L.T. 665.

ary lacks, or may unduly influence the beneficiary, the transaction will stand only if the trustee can prove that he has acted fairly and honestly, and that the beneficiary fully understands the nature and implications of the transaction.[18]

2. Trustees may not use their position to personal advantage

A second application of the principle is to prevent trustees from obtaining any advantage or acquiring any profit from their position in the trust. Any such profit will be held on a constructive trust. Again it does not matter whether the trustee's interests will actually harm the estate: the mere possibility is enough.

If a trustee has power to exercise a discretion, he must never exercise it in his own favour. This is illustrated by the case of *Inglis* v. *Inglis*.[19] Here an executor was also one of the deceased's potential heirs in intestacy. Part of the estate consisted of an agricultural lease, and section 16 of the Succession (Scotland) Act 1964 allows executors to transfer the interest in agricultural leases to any of the deceased's potential heirs in intestacy. The executor transferred the lease to himself, and when this was challenged he argued that the statutory provisions in section 16 qualified the rule that he must not be *auctor in rem suam*. Though this was accepted in the sheriff court, the Second Division disagreed, and it was pointed out that section 20 of the Act puts executors in the same position as trustees, and that therefore there was nothing on the face of the Act to qualify the rule. Either the conflict ought to have been avoided by the defender not seeking confirmation as executor[20] or the lease ought to have been transferred to someone other than the defender.[21]

3. Trustees are not entitled to remuneration

A third application of the principle is the assumption that, as a general rule, trustees will act gratuitously and will not receive

---

[18] *Dougan* v. *Macpherson* (1902) 4F. (H.L.) 7, Mackenzie Stuart at pp. 195–196.

[19] 1983 S.L.T. 437.

[20] Per Lord Hunter at p. 441.

[21] Though this will not always be a good course, *e.g.* if there is no other "near relative" of the deceased tenant and it is thought that the landlord will exercise his right to recover possession under s.21 of the Agricultural Holdings (Scotland) Act 1949 effectively removing the asset.

remuneration for performing their duties under the trust. It is considered that "a man is not to be the judge of what is proper remuneration for himself,"[22] and also that trustees ought to act because they want to act and not just because they are getting paid for doing so. Consequently trustees are entitled to reimbursement only of their own out of pocket expenses incurred in the course of administering the trust.

Indirect remuneration will be prohibited as much as direct payment if it is clearly referable to the trustee's position in the trust.[23] For example, a partner in a firm of solicitors who is a trustee will not be entitled to keep the profits his firm makes from undertaking legal work for the trust: if his firm charges, he will hold that proportion of the fees to which the partnership agreement entitles him on a constructive trust for the beneficiaries.[24] On the other hand it has been held that a salaried employee remained entitled to his salary from a firm when the firm's assets became trust estate and the employee became a trustee—his salary was paid because he was an employee of the firm, not because he was a trustee of the firm's assets.[25]

There are two sorts of indirect remuneration that require special mention: (a) commission, and (b) directors' fees.

(a) It is common for solicitors and accountants to hold agencies with insurance companies or building societies, whereby they receive commission on insurances taken out or funds placed on behalf of clients. If the solicitor is a trustee and takes out insurance for the trust or places trust funds in a building society, and receives commission for doing so, that commission should be held on a constructive trust for the beneficiaries, and must not be kept by the solicitor or his firm. Though there seems to be no Scottish decision directly holding this, it must logically follow from the principle, because commission is clearly remuneration obtained with the use of trust funds. A trustee must be in the position to give unfettered advice about such matters, and the possibility of his earning commission might easily influence the advice he gives. In the English case of *Williams* v. *Barton*,[26] the defendant was a clerk in a firm of stockbrokers and part of his salary was commission for business he could bring to the firm. He was trustee of an estate and employed his own firm to value the securities in the estate. It was

---

[22] *Per* Lord Justice-Clerk Hope in *Fegan* v. *Thomson* (1855) 17 D. 1146 at p. 1148.
[23] See Mackenzie Stuart at pp. 172–173.
[24] *Henderson* v. *Watson*, 1939 S.C. 711.
[25] *Lawrie* v. *Lawrie's Trs.* (1892) 19 R. 675.
[26] [1927] 2 Ch. 9.

held that the commission referable to that valuation was earned through his position as trustee, and therefore was held on a constructive trust. An analogy might be drawn with the Scottish case of *Cherry's Trs.* v. *Patrick*[27] in which a trustee who was a wholesale supplier of alcoholic liquor made profits by trading with public houses that were part of the trust estate: it was held that these profits were held on a constructive trust and could not be retained by the trustee. It is difficult to see any difference between such profits and commission of the sort described above.

(b) Trustees, as legal owners of the trust estate, may be entitled to exercise rights attaching to ownership. If the trust holds shares with voting rights, trustees will be able to vote at company meetings, and even influence the running of the company. Indeed it has been held in England that trustees may sometimes be bound to influence the running of a company, if this is necessary to protect the value of the trust's shareholding.[28] They may do so by using the trust's shareholding to vote themselves onto the company board, and thus incidentally become entitled to directors' fees. The question arises whether they may keep such fees. In England directors' fees earned by trustee/directors are considered to be held on a constructive trust for the beneficiaries, but only when there is a clear causal connection between their position as trustees and their appointment as directors.[29] However the English approach may not be persuasive in Scotland since in England the court has an ultimate power to sanction payments that would otherwise be *auctor in rem suam*[30]: such a power does not lie with the Scottish court (see *infra*). The only Scottish case concerned with trustee/directors' fees is that of *Elliot* v. *Mackie & Sons*.[31] Here directors of a company were qualified for their position through their holding shares in the company as trustees. In the Outer House Lord Moncrieff held that the fees earned were fees "acquired by services rendered by the directors to the company and are not profit earned by the trustees by use of the property of the trust." This was upheld by the First Division, Lord Carmont expressing the view that,

"The payment of directors' fees . . . cannot legitimately be said to be 'in respect of a qualification afforded by shares,' but in respect of services rendered

[27] (1911) 2 S.L.T. 313.

[28] *Bartlett* v. *Barclays Bank Trust Co.* (*No.* 1) [1980] 1 All E.R. 139.

[29] *Re Macadam* [1946] Ch. 73; *Re Gee, Decd.* [1948] Ch. 284. See also Riddall at pp. 305–306.

[30] For a discussion of this power, see *Re Keeler's Settlement Trusts* [1981] 1 All E.R. 888.

[31] 1935 S.C. 81.

to the company by a director on the board whose title involved the holding of certain shares."[32]

Consequently these fees were *not* held on a constructive trust. However, though there is no authority one way or the other, the matter might be treated differently if the trustees used their shares not simply as a qualification but actually to vote themselves onto the board. If they did so specifically in order to protect the interests of the trust, as they may in some circumstances be bound to do, it would be more logical to regard the fees paid to them as earned in the service of the trust rather than in the service of the company.

While the general rule is that there is no entitlement to remuneration, this aspect of the principle is probably nowadays honoured more in the breach than in the observance. Many trustees are professional people, such as solicitors and accountants, and their duties as trustees involve tasks that they would perform in their day-to-day professional practice. It is perfectly open to such people (or any other person) to refuse to act as trustee unless remuneration is given. Consequently (as will be discussed in the next section) it is common for trust deeds to contain a remuneration clause authorising payment, or permitting the retention of commission, or a clause giving the trustee a legacy in lieu.

WAYS AROUND THE PRINCIPLE

There are three methods by which a trustee can do things that would normally render him *auctor in rem suam*, and a fourth that is sometimes mooted.

1. Authorisation in the trust deed

A truster may envisage and can make provision for the trustee becoming *auctor in rem suam*, and can grant express authorisation in the trust deed for the trustee to do something that would breach the principle. This is commonly met with when solicitor/ trustees are given express power to charge remuneration for acting in their professional capacity, or when, for example, trustees hold interests in family businesses in which individual trustees are already involved.

Any such provision will however always be read in the strictest light, and will confer no greater power to the trustee than is clearly

[32] *Ibid.* at p. 94. See also Lord Morison at p. 92.

intended by the truster. In *Johnston* v. *Macfarlane*[33] a truster left property in trust, and the trust deed contained a clause allowing the trustees to sell the property to "any beneficiary." There were three beneficiaries, one of whom was also a trustee. The trustees sold the property to the beneficiary who was a trustee, and when this was challenged the court reduced the sale on the ground that the trustee was *auctor in rem suam*. The clause founded upon did not expressly grant the trustees authority to sell to one of their number, and the court refused to imply such authorisation from the mere fact that the truster knew that one of the beneficiaries was also a trustee. Lord Justice-Clerk Ross stated:

> "A trustee will only be permitted to enter into transactions in which he has or may have a personal interest which conflicts with his fiduciary duty if the truster has expressly provided for such a situation."[34]

and he accepted the Lord Ordinary's proposition that such a transaction "would require the clearest and unambiguous authorisation."[35] He also pointed out that even if the law were to accept implied authorisation, such would not be appropriate here, because other parts of the deed granted rights to beneficiaries, but had expressly included beneficiaries who were also trustees: an implication of authorisation could not be drawn in one part of a deed when express authorisation is given in other parts.

All the judges in *Johnston* emphasised that authorisation in the trust deed had to be *express*. From this it might be inferred that *implied* authorisation will never be accepted as sufficient, and that indeed was the line of argument put forward by counsel for the pursuer in *Johnston*. However such a conclusion was not held in so many words by the judges. Such a conclusion would be contrary to previous authority[36]. In *Lewis's Trs.* v. *Pirie*[37] the First Division inferred from a power to appoint one of the trustees as the trust's law agent a power to pay that trustee the remuneration of a law agent. In *Coat's Trs.*[38] the First Division held that a power to sell to "any beneficiary" (the situation in *Johnston* v. *Macfarlane*) included a power to sell to trustees who were beneficiaries. It may well be that all *Johnston* v. *Macfarlane* decided was that no authorisation

---

[33] 1987 S.L.T. 593.

[34] *Ibid.* at p. 595.

[35] 1985 S.L.T. 339 at p. 341.

[36] And is also contrary to the position in England: see *Re Sykes* [1909] 2 Ch. 241.

[37] 1912 S.C. 574.

[38] 1914 S.C. 723, as explained in *Hall's Trs.* v. *McArthur*, 1918 S.C. 646.

could be implied from the facts of that particular case and that the court will be slow to draw any such implication. In principle, it is suggested that if the intention of the truster is unambiguous and is clearly to the effect that the trustees may deal with the trust estate, then this should be sufficient notwithstanding that it is not expressed in so many words. However, drafters of trust deeds should bear in mind the dangers made evident in *Johnston* and if the intention of the truster is to allow trustees to act in ways that might breach the principle of *auctor in rem suam*, authorisation should in practice be spelt out clearly and unambiguously.

2. Authorisation by the beneficiaries

The principle of *auctor in rem suam* is designed to protect the beneficiaries, and they are entitled to waive that protection if they so wish. The trustee may defend a challenge based on *auctor in rem suam* by proving that he had obtained the free and fully informed consent of all the beneficiaries and potential beneficiaries to the transaction at issue. This defence will not be available if any beneficiary or potential beneficiary cannot, for whatever reason, provide consent; and if there is undue pressure on any to give consent, the court is likely to hold that consent invalid. The onus is on the trustee to show that all the beneficiaries consented, and that they were fully aware of the implications of what they were doing.[39]

3. Resignation

There is in general nothing to prevent an ex-trustee transacting with the trust estate. Thus if a trustee wishes to serve his own interests before those of the trust, the correct thing for him to do is to resign from his trusteeship. If he does resign he should do so well ahead of the conflict of interest arising, for the court will look closely at any transaction in which a trustee resigns specifically in order to further his own interests. Resignation will not protect a transaction that was set up while the trustee was still in office.[40] If a challenge is made to a transaction with an ex-trustee, it is the ex-trustee who has the onus of proving that the transaction was fair and ought therefore to be upheld.[41]

[39] *Taylor* v. *Hillhouse's Trs.* (1901) 9 S.L.T. 31.
[40] *Aberdeen Railway Co.* v. *Blaikie Bros. supra*, n. 3, *Wright* v. *Morgan supra*, n. 1, *Clark* v. *Clark's Exx.*, *supra*, n. 17.
[41] *Aberdeen Railway Co. supra*, n. 3. This is one of the few circumstances in which the court will pay regard to the fairness of the transaction.

4. Authorisation by the court?

The Court of Session has no power under the *nobile officium* to authorise a trustee to do acts that would otherwise render him *auctor in rem suam*. This is an important difference between the power of the court in Scotland and the court in England, for the latter can grant such authorisation.[42] The difference was said in *Hall's Trs.* v. *McArthur*[43] to be a consequence of the fact that the Court of Chancery is a court that takes a much more active role in actually administering trusts than the Court of Session; and the Scottish rule was explained on the basis that the right to challenge belonged to the beneficiaries and that right could not be taken away by the courts.[44]

In *Coat's Trs.*[45] a petition was brought for authority to allow a trustee to bid for part of the trust estate at a public auction, and the First Division granted authority. However, despite appearances, this case is not authority for the proposition that the court can authorise a transaction that would otherwise render the trustee *auctor in rem suam*. The decision was explained in *Hall's Trs.* v. *McArthur*, in which it was stated that all the beneficiaries in *Coat's Trs.* had consented to the trustee bidding in the auction,[46] and that all the court did was to "give their *imprimatur* to this concurrence."[47] The reason given in *Hall's Trs.* as to why the issue was taken to court in *Coat's Trs.* was because the method of sale desired by the trustees was different from that laid down in the trust deed, rather than that the trustee had no right to purchase the trust estate.[48] It was made plain in *Hall's Trs.* that the court will not give authority, and that *Coat's Trs.* cannot be used as a precedent.

THE PRINCIPLE OF PROPER MOTIVATION

In administering the trust, and particularly in making investment decisions, the paramount motivation of the trustees must be

[42] See Moffat & Chesterman at pp. 354–358.

[43] 1918 S.C. 646.

[44] *Per* Lord Skerrington at p. 654.

[45] 1914 S.C. 723.

[46] Actually, all that appears from the report, in both *Session Cases* and in the slightly fuller *Scottish Law Reporter*, (1914) 51 S.L.R. 642, is that no one lodged answers to the petition, although all persons interested in the estate were served with the petition.

[47] *Per* Lord Johnston 1918 S.C. 646 at p. 652.

[48] Again, this is by no means clear from the case reports of *Coat's Trs.* themselves.

directed towards the welfare of the trust estate, or the interests of
the beneficiaries. Their duty is to carry out the purposes of the
trust, and in doing so they may create a number of different
consequences. However, they are entitled to be motivated only by
those consequences that are relevant to the trust itself. As a result,
trustees cannot allow themselves to be decisively influenced by
matters or consequences that are extraneous to the terms or
purposes of the trust. Nor can they bind their decision making to
the policies of other bodies, or to principles and prejudices they
accept in their personal affairs. A trustee, like anyone else, is of
course entitled to have political affiliations and moral opinions; but
in administering the trust, he must distance himself so far as is
practicable from his own affiliations and opinions. For example a
trustee is not allowed to determine investment strategy on the basis
of his approval or disapproval of particular sectors of the stock
market; he must determine his investment strategy by considering
the terms and purposes of the trust and the welfare of the trust
estate.[49]

The importance of this principle became apparent in the English
case of *Cowan* v. *Scargill*.[50] Here a pension fund had been set up for
the benefit of retired miners and their dependents. There were 10
trustees, five appointed by the National Coal Board, and five
appointed by the National Union of Mineworkers. The president of
the latter body was *ex officio* one of the Union's nominees. Shortly
after the election of a new president, the Union adopted a policy of
disinvesting its own funds from overseas investment, and also of not
increasing its current holdings in industries that were in direct
competition to the coal industry in Britain. The five Union
appointees wished this policy to be applied to the pension fund, but
the five Board appointees objected, and raised an action for
declaration that to adopt such a policy would be a breach of trust.
The court held that the Union nominees were attempting to use the
trust to further the aims of the Union, and that to do so would be a
clear breach of trust. Sir Robert Megarry, V-C, said this:

> "Trustees may have strongly held social or political views. They may be firmly
> opposed to any investment in South Africa or other countries, or they may
> object to any form of investment in companies concerned with alcohol,
> tobacco, armaments or many other things. In the conduct of their own affairs,

[49] For investment, see Chap. 8. On the issue of allowing personal views to
determine investment strategy, see the amusing piece of fiction "The Lawyer's Tale:
A Question of Ethics" (1989) Pensions Management 61.
   [50] [1984] 3 W.L.R. 501.

of course, they are free to abstain from making any such investments. Yet under a trust, if investments of this type would be more beneficial to the beneficiaries than other investments, the trustees must not refrain from making the investments by reason of the views that they hold."[51]

A similar Scottish case is that of *Martin* v. *Edinburgh District Council*.[52] Edinburgh District Council was controlled by the Labour Party, the policy of which was not to invest in South Africa. The Council adopted this as its own policy and, further, decided that where it held South African funds as trustee, it would disinvest these funds also. When this was challenged,[53] it was held in the Outer House that the Council was in breach of trust in that it had failed to consider whether the policy was for the benefit of the beneficiaries. As in *Cowan* v. *Scargill*, the trustees had bound themselves by a policy made in another capacity and for reasons extraneous to the trust. However Lord Murray was careful to point out the limits to which *Cowan* v. *Scargill* could be taken. He said:

"[It was argued that] trustees have a duty not to fetter their investment discretion for reasons extraneous to the trust purposes, including reasons of a political or moral nature, and presumably matters of conscience. If this proposition [taken from *Cowan* v. *Scargill*] means that a trustee has a duty to apply his mind genuinely and independently to a trust issue which is before him, and not simply to adhere to a decision which he has made previously in a different context, or to a policy or other principle to which he is committed, then I can accept it. But if it means that each individual trustee in genuinely applying his mind and judgment to a trust decision, must divest himself of all personal preferences, of all political beliefs, and of all moral, religious or other conscientiously held principles, then I do not think that this proposition is either reasonable or practicable. What he must do, I think, is to recognise that he has those preferences, commitments or principles but nonetheless do his best to exercise fair and impartial judgment on the merits of the issue before him. If he realises that he cannot do that, then he should abstain from participating in deciding the issue . . . or, in the extreme case, resign as a trustee."[54]

It should be pointed out that this extremely clear statement of the law is not restricted to investment decisions.

As with *auctor in rem suam*, the trustees may do that which this principle would otherwise forbid, if they have authority to do so, either from the beneficiaries or the trust deed. The same considerations as have already been discussed would be relevant.

---

[51] *Ibid.* at p. 514.
[52] 1988 S.L.T. 329.
[53] In both *Cowan* and *Martin* the remedy sought was merely declarator. In other circumstances, *e.g.* if loss had been caused, the other remedies for breach of trust might have been appropriate: see Chap. 10.
[54] 1988 S.L.T. 329 at p. 334.

CHAPTER 10

TRUSTEES' LIABILITIES TO BENEFICIARIES

Introduction

A TRUSTEE'S liability towards the beneficiaries is to pay them their due, and to carry out the purposes of the trust as a careful and prudent trustee would do. If he fails to do so, he will be in breach of trust and liable for any loss caused by such a breach. Trustees are also liable to account to the beneficiaries for their intromissions with the trust estate, and will be liable to make up any shortfall which has been caused by a breach of trust.

BREACH OF TRUST

Breach of trust is a concept which is very wide in its scope, and it includes much more than simply dishonest dealing with the trust property, though that, of course, is the clearest example of a breach. Breach of trust may for example consist in a failure to invest the trust estate in accordance with the trust deed or the law, or a failure to account for any intromission, or a failure timeously to discharge a security, or a failure timeously to call in a debt,[1] or a failure to take proper advice when that is required,[2] or the making of a loan from the trust estate to one of the trustees,[3] or the payment of the trust estate to the wrong beneficiaries,[4] or a failure to prevent a company in which the

---

[1] As in *Forman* v. *Burns* (1853) 15 D. 362.
[2] As in *Martin* v. *Edinburgh District Council*, 1988 S.L.T. 329.
[3] As in *Croskery* v. *Gilmour's Trs.* (1890) 17 R. 697.
[4] For which see Chap. 14.

139

trust has a controlling interest, and in which the trust estate is substantially invested, from indulging in speculation as a result of which the value of the company's shares (and thus the trust estate) substantially diminishes.[5] Indeed, it includes any form of bad management or neglect or dilatory carrying out of the trust purposes, or anything that causes the trust estate to diminish in value, which a trustee acting reasonably could have avoided. Additionally, a breach of trust may be constituted by some act that goes against the terms or purposes of the trust, even although that act results in an increase in the value of the trust estate: for the aim of a trust is the achievement of purposes rather than the maximisation of profit.

Though not in itself a crime, breach of trust can sometimes result in criminal liability, if for example it involves embezzlement.[6] Even when carrying out his duty under the trust, the trustee remains subject to the criminal law, and there could never be a situation in which the fulfilment of a trust duty necessitates a breach of the criminal law. Such a conflict may not be immediately apparent. For example, a trustee has a duty to adopt a careful and prudent investment policy. If he comes into possession of information concerning the future performance of a particular investment, the utilisation of which for his own benefit would amount to insider dealing contrary to the Companies Securities (Insider Dealing) Act 1985, to use this information in satisfaction of his duty to the trust would itself amount to insider dealing and thus be illegal.

Liability for breach of trust may be enforced by the beneficiaries or any beneficiary against any trustee who has committed the breach. If the breach was committed by a former trustee, the existing trustees should enforce that liability, failing whom any beneficiary may do so. It has been held that if a former trustee has been discharged the discharge will have to be reduced before action can be taken against him.[7]

Liability for breach of trust is, according to Walker, an obligation *sui generis* and not wholly analogous either to a contractual or delictual obligation.[8] Nevertheless the determina-

---

[5] As in *Bartlett* v. *Barclays Bank Trust Co.* (*No. 1*) [1980] 1 All E.R. 139.

[6] See Smith, "Constructive Trusts in the Law of Theft" [1977] Crim.L.R. 395, and Glanville Williams, "Innocuously Dipping into Trust Funds" (1985) 5 Leg. Stud. 183.

[7] *Hastie's J.F.* v. *Morham's Ex.* 1951 S.C. 668. On reduction of discharge, see Chap. 14.

[8] *Civil Remedies*, at p. 1067. Though see Wilson and Duncan at p. 384: "The liability is *ex delicto* or *ex quasi delicto*."

tion of the duty of care required, and whether it has been breached, follows general delictual principles. The true test for establishing whether a trustee is in breach of trust is to ask "has it been shewn that the trustee failed to exercise that degree of diligence which a man of ordinary prudence would exercise in the management of his own affairs?"[9] This is an objective standard and it is no defence for a trustee charged with breach of trust to show that he brought to the management of the trust estate the same care and attention as that which he gives to his own affairs: rather the trustee's actions must be measured against the standard of the ordinary prudent man of business.

In the English first instance decision of *Bartlett* v. *Barclays Bank Trust Co. (No. 1)*,[10] the judge stated *obiter* that a corporate trustee carrying on a specialised business of trust management, which holds itself out as being skilled as a trustee, will be subject to a higher standard of care and diligence than a non-corporate trustee. There is no authority for this proposition in Scots law,[11] and certainly the high authority from last century laying down the standard of the ordinary prudent man[12] makes no such qualification. It is suggested that the approach in *Bartlett* ought to be resisted. The standard of care required is designed to protect the beneficiaries, and from their point of view, it is wholly fortuitous whether or not the trustee is corporate or non-corporate, professional or non-professional. The corporate trustee does not hold itself out to the beneficiary, but to the truster. Also, there is authority in the delict cases for suggesting that an amateur performing a function requiring skill and competence will be subject to the same standard as that expected from the professional,[13] for the standard is determined by the nature of the task rather than by the competence of the performer.[14] This is as it should be in trust law also.[15]

---

[9] *Per* Lord Herschell in *Raes* v. *Meek* (1889) 16 R. (H.L.) 31 at p. 34. See also Lord Watson in *Learoyd* v. *Whiteley* (1887) 12 App.Cas. 727 at p. 733; and Lord Atkinson in *Buchanan* v. *Eaton*, 1911 S.C. (H.L.) 40 at p. 45.

[10] [1980] 1 All E.R. 139.

[11] Except that Wilson and Duncan at p. 385 makes this proposition without comment, citing only the previous English first instance decision of *Re Waterman's Will Trusts* [1952] 2 All E.R. 1054.

[12] See n. 9.

[13] See *Macintosh* v. *Nelson* 1984 S.L.T. (Sh. Ct.) 82.

[14] In *Wilsher* v. *Essex Area Health Authority* [1986] 3 All E.R. 801 (C.A.) Mustill L.J. said this at p. 813: "This notion of a duty tailored to the actor, rather than to the act which he elects to perform, has no place in the law of tort." (This decision was overruled on another point at [1988] 2 W.L.R. 557).

[15] Bearing in mind that the professional person or body will be subject to the rules of his or its profession, in whatever task it undertakes (which could be more onerous than a trust responsibility).

REMEDIES FOR BREACH OF TRUST

One of the major differences between Scots and English law is that in the latter, a beneficiary has real rights in the trust property. This gives him extensive proprietorial remedies for breach of trust.[16] The Scottish beneficiary on the other hand has only personal rights against trustees, and he can follow trust property only to the extent that he can establish that the person who comes to hold the property is a constructive trustee over that property. Even then his right is a claim *in personam* against such a person, not a claim *in rem* over the property.[17]

The personal rights vested in the beneficiaries can be enforced in the following ways.

1. Interdict

Any beneficiary or co-trustee will be able to interdict a trustee who threatens to carry out an act that amounts to a breach of trust; and if the breach has occurred, and is a continuing one, the pursuer can seek an interdict to prevent its continuation.[18] However, if the breach was constituted by some single act and there is nothing to indicate that it will be repeated, interdict will not be available.

2. Damages

A trustee will be liable (in the sense of having to pay) for a breach of trust only if that breach causes loss to the trust estate. If it does so, the amount of liability is determined by the extent of the loss suffered by the estate. "The precise nature of the breach of trust and the degree of fault are quite immaterial to the measure of damages, the sole question being *restitutio in integrum*."[19] For exaample if the breach consisted in the failure to invest the trust estate, the damages will be the income that the estate would have generated, or the capital growth that would have been obtained, had the estate been invested properly. In *Forman* v. *Burns*[20] an executor had failed to call in a debt for

---

[16] See Riddall at pp. 326–337, Moffat & Chesterman at pp. 452–459.
[17] Menzies at p. 808.
[18] Menzies at p. 727.
[19] Walker at p. 1072.
[20] (1853) 15 D. 362.

£250 until after the debtor was sequestrated. The estate eventually recovered £50, and the executor was held liable to make up the shortfall of £200. Interest will be payable, and, if the trustee has acted dishonestly, this may be quantified at a compound rate.[21]

Tax Point
Interest is regarded as income and subject therefore to income tax.[22] There may be a tax liability on the capital sum of damages awarded. It has been held in England that this liability only arises with damages for breach of trust at the point of distributing the trust estate, and not (as with other actions for damages) when the award is made. It follows from this that in assessing the damages due from the trustee, the defendant will not be entitled to have a deduction made for the tax due.[23] This point has not yet been discussed in a Scottish case and it remains to be seen whether this approach will be followed in Scotland.

Though the standard of care in breach of trust will be determined delictually, the extent of the restitutionary obligation flowing therefrom is more absolute. The limitations to delictual liability will not apply: *e.g.* questions of foreseeability, remoteness of damage, *novus actus interveniens*, etc, will be irrelevant in assessing damages.[24] "The principles embodied in this approach do not appear to involve any inquiry whether the loss was caused by or flowed from the breach. Rather the inquiry in each instance would appear to be whether the loss would have happened if there had been no breach."[25] It will however be open to the trustee to establish (and he will have the onus of proof[26]) that his breach of trust did not in fact cause the loss, by showing that the loss would have occurred even had he carried out his duties properly.[27]

---

[21] See *Lees' Trs.* v. *Dun* 1912 S.C. 50, 1913 S.C. (H.L.) 12.

[22] *Lees' Trs.*, *supra*, reported as *Schulze* v. *Bensted* (1915) 7 T.C. 30. For a fuller discussion of the point, see Lord Normand in the House of Lords case of *Westminster Bank Ltd.* v. *Riches* (1947) 28 T.C. 159.

[23] *Bartlett* v. *Barclays Bank Trust Co.* (*No. 2*) [1980] 2 All E.R. 92. In *Re Bell's Indenture* [1980] 1 W.L.R. 1217 it was held that a trustee who was in breach of trust and liable in damages therefor had to pay the full amount of the loss to the trust, and could not deduct a sum in respect of the estate duty that would have been paid on the trust fund had he not been in breach (by misappropriating the trust assets).

[24] This position can be justified since these concepts were developed in the context of delictual liability to avoid the dangers of unlimited liability—a trustee's liability on the other hand will have a natural limit, being the size of the estate (or what its size should be). For a fuller discussion, see the Australian case of *Re Dawson* [1966] 2 N.S.W.R. 211.

[25] *Ibid.* at p. 214.

[26] Menzies at p. 685.

[27] *Carruthers* v. *Carruthers* (1896) 23 R. (H.L.) 55.

As has been seen a breach of trust can lead to a benefit rather than a loss, particularly if the breach consists in an unauthorised investment. Damages as such will not be available, as that remedy is only apt when there is a loss.[28] However the trustee of course will be obliged to account for the extra profit he makes, for he will hold that extra profit on constructive trust for the beneficiaries. If one unauthorised investment leads to a profit while another leads to a loss, the trustee cannot set off the one against the other, and the beneficiaries may claim the profit, and demand that the trustee reimburses the loss from his own pocket. *Bartlett* v. *Barclays Bank Trust Co. (No. 1)*[29] is authority for suggesting that English law adopts a slightly different position. In that case a trust corporation was found to be in breach of trust for failing to prevent a company in which it had a controlling interest from speculating in hazardous property development schemes. One such scheme, around the Old Bailey in London, proved a disaster and much money was lost, but by "sheer luck" another such scheme, in Guildford, "paid off handsomely." Though accepting that all the English textbooks state that gains cannot be set off against losses from different breaches (as the Scottish textbooks also state), the judge did just that in assessing damages in this case. There is authority for suggesting that a set off will be permitted if the breaches of trust are in essence part of the same transaction,[30] and this may explain the decision in *Bartlett*, for there the breach was not two separate speculative investments but rather the failure to prevent the company adopting a policy of speculation—a single breach. However, Walker[31] suggests that gains must be accounted for and losses must be reimbursed whether they come from distinct and separate breaches of trust, or from the same breach. It is therefore unclear whether *Bartlett* will be followed on this point in Scotland, but it is suggested that the law should certainly go no further, and ought not to hold, for example, that a course of related dealings amounts to a single transaction.

A trustee cannot set off his generally beneficial administration of the estate against a loss from a particular breach of trust,[32] though this may be relevant to the question of whether relief under section 32 of the Trusts (Scotland) Act 1921 ought to be granted[33] (see *infra*).

---

[28] Walker at p. 1072.
[29] [1980] 1 All E.R. 139.
[30] Underhill, *The Law of Trusts and Trustees* at p. 479; Mackenzie Stuart at p. 375.
[31] At p. 1072.
[32] *Clarke* v. *Clarke's Trs.* 1925 S.C. 693.
[33] *Fogo's J.F.* v. *Fogo's Trs.* 1929 S.C. 546.

3. Accounting

The trustees' primary obligation is to carry out the trust purposes in accordance with the terms of the trust deed. "A beneficiary is entitled to receive from the trustee the share of the trust estate to which he is entitled on the footing that the trust has been properly administered, and a trustee must therefore account to the beneficiary for that share."[34] An unwarranted refusal by the trustee to pay the beneficiaries their entitlement can be remedied by an action of count, reckoning and payment.[35]

Likewise, a beneficiary can recover any shortfall in his entitlement through this action. If that shortfall is constituted by a breach of trust the beneficiary may either bring this action, or an action for damages. The action for count, reckoning and payment can also be used when the action for damages is inappropriate, such as when a breach of trust leads to a profit. Such a profit can be recovered by the beneficiary through this action, as can any benefit the trustee acquires by becoming *auctor in rem suam*, or which he otherwise comes to hold constructively for the trust.

If there are losses for which the trustee is liable, in essence the action for count, reckoning and payment will have the same effect as an action for damages, and the recoverable losses will be calculated in the same way. However, there is one significant advantage that an action for count, reckoning and payment has over an action for damages, as was made clear in the case of *Hobday* v. *Kirkpatrick's Trs.*[36] Here, trustees had failed to pay out a share of residue on a certain date in 1973. An action for count, reckoning and payment was raised in 1979, more than six years later. The defenders claimed that in essence this was an action for damages, and therefore had prescribed in terms of the Prescription and Limitation (Scotland) Act 1973, section 6 of which provides a prescriptive period of five years for the raising of an action based on an obligation to make reparation. Lord Cowie held that an action for damages for breach of trust was indeed an obligation to make reparation within the terms of s.6, and thus subject to the five year prescriptive period; but that in an action for count, reckoning and payment the pursuer is *not* asking for damages (*i.e.* is not asking for compensation), but

---

[34] Walker at p. 1069.
[35] As in, *e.g. Mackenzie's Ex.* v. *Thomson's Trs.*, 1965 S.C. 154. In this case the trustees had attempted to withhold payment of the estate until they received a discharge because they were, *in another capacity*, representative of and liable for the breaches of the predecessor trustee.
[36] 1985 S.L.T. 197.

rather for the restoration to the trust estate of the value it has lost. The obligation on a trustee to account for intromissions does not prescribe,[37] though his liability for any shortfall is subject to the long negative prescription of 20 years. The action in *Hobday* was therefore still competent.

4. Removal of trustees

If the breach of trust is particularly flagrant, or the trustee refuses to discontinue a breach of trust, the court may in such exceptional circumstances remove the trustee from office, and appoint a new trustee. The court may be petitioned by any person having an interest in the trust (*i.e.* any beneficiary, any trustee, or, if appropriate, the truster). A clear case for removal would be if the trustee embezzles the trust funds: in *Wishart & Ors, Petrs.*[38] a trustee was removed from office when he absconded with the trust funds and was never seen again. The main consideration will be the welfare of the beneficiaries. In *MacGilchrist's Trs.* v. *MacGilchrist*[39] a petition for removal of a trustee was granted to the trustees when the defender had continuously neglected the business of the trust and indeed had failed to take any part in the administration of the trust. Lord President Clyde pointed out that mere negligence, even if it caused loss to the trust estate, was not necessarily sufficient ground for removal of a trustee; but in this case a gross misconception of trust duty which was difficult to reconcile with good faith was a sufficient ground for removal. The standard is therefore rather stricter than for a simple claim for damages.[40]

LIABILITY FOR CO-TRUSTEES AND FOR OMISSIONS

Section 3(*d*) of the Trusts (Scotland) Act 1921 provides that, unless the contrary be expressed, all trusts shall be held to include a provision that "each trustee shall be liable only for his

---

[37] See Schedule 3(*e*) of the Prescription and Limitation (Scotland) Act 1973, which also renders imprescriptable a trustee's liability for *fraudulent* breach of trust.

[38] (1910) 2 S.L.T. 229.

[39] 1930 S.C. 635.

[40] *Cf. Dick & Ors. Petrs.* (1899) 2 F. 316, in which the court did not remove a trustee who had refused to co-operate with his co-trustees, to the detriment of the trust, but who gave the court an undertaking that he would in future co-operate.

own acts and intromissions and shall not be liable for the acts and intromissions of co-trustees and shall not be liable for omissions." This is declaratory of the common law and probably creates no protection from liability greater than trustees would have had if the provision had not been enacted.[41] It has been held that this subsection infers that trustees will not be liable for the acts and intromissions of their predecessors.[42]

A trustee can be made liable for the breaches of trust of his co-trustees, notwithstanding s.3(d), in a number of ways, so long as he himself commits a breach of his own duty. Trustees are assumed to act as a body, and this imposes a duty on each of them to oversee the actions of the others. Trustees are not entitled, whether through good nature, or embarrassment, or ignorance, or indolence, to allow co-trustees free reign to do as they think fit. A failure to prevent a co-trustee committing a breach, in circumstances in which a trustee of ordinary prudence would not have so failed, will amount to a breach. To authorise a co-trustee to commit a breach, either expressly or impliedly, will in itself be a breach by a trustee, as might a failure to attend trust meetings at which a breach is instigated.[43]

All the trustees who are in breach of trust (which may not be all the trustees in the trust) are jointly and severally liable for the loss caused to the trust estate, so a beneficiary may go against any one, or a few, or all of them. The proportion of fault *inter se* is irrelevant, and any trustee who pays off the beneficiary is entitled to an equal contribution from all other trustees who are liable. There is no equivalent in Scotland (yet)[44] to the English statute[45] that allows the court to allocate liability amongst trustees in breach to such extent as it regards just and equitable.

It is difficult to know what is meant to be covered by the provision that a trustee will not be liable for omissions, for in a strict sense, most forms of breach of trust are omissions. A failure to invest, or a failure to take proper advice, or a failure to call in a debt, are all omissions, but all are clearly breaches of trust for which a trustee will be liable, notwithstanding section 3(d). With these failures however, there is a clear pre-existing duty to act, and the exclusion of liability for omissions will probably (again following general delictual principles) cover only omissions to do things where there is no positive duty to act.

[41] Stair, 1:12:17; McLaren, at para. 2267.

[42] *Mackenzie's Ex.* v. *Thomson's Trs.*, 1965 S.C. 154.

[43] For a fuller discussion on this whole issue, see Bogert, "The Liability of an Inactive Co-Trustee"(1920) 34 Harv.L.R. 483.

[44] See Scottish Law Commission Report No. 115: *Civil Liability—Contribution*.

[45] Civil Liability (Contribution) Act 1978, s.2(1).

LIMITATIONS ON LIABILITY

1. Immunity clauses

Most trust deeds contain clauses purporting to limit a trustee's liability to the beneficiaries for breach of trust. While immunity clauses can provide a certain amount of protection to a trustee who causes loss to the trust estate but is nevertheless acting in good faith, or who has committed a mere error of judgment,[46] the court will interpret such clauses narrowly, and it is probable that they will not provide any protection for a trustee who acts in "positive breach of trust,"[47] or in bad faith, or carelessly.[48]

There is authority to suggest that an immunity clause will be ignored to the extent that it attempts to exempt trustees from liability for *gross* negligence[49] though, if the words are sufficient, it may provide protection for a trustee guilty of *mere* negligence. In the medical negligence case of *Hunter* v. *Hanley*,[50] where for the purposes of delict the First Division defined gross negligence out of existence,[51] both Lord President Clyde and Lord Russell accepted that the concept of gross negligence was probably still extant in Scotland for the purpose of determining the extent of protection that immunity clauses provide for trustees.

2. Statutory limitations: section 31[52]

Section 31 of the Trusts (Scotland) Act 1921 provides for the possibility of relief for a trustee who commits some breach of trust at the instigation of a beneficiary. It provides that if a trustee acts in breach of trust at the instigation or request or with the written consent of a beneficiary, the court[53] may, at its own discretion, make any such order as it thinks fit to apply all or any

---

[46] *Knox* v. *Mackinnon* (1888) 15 R. (H.L.) 83, *per* Lord Watson at p. 86.

[47] *Wyman* v. *Paterson* (1900) 2 F. (H.L.) 37, *per* Lord Macnaghten at p. 41.

[48] *Clarke* v. *Clarke's Trs.*, 1925 S.C. 693.

[49] *Knox* v. *Mackinnon* (n. 46); *Raes* v. *Meek* (n. 9); *Carruthers* v. *Carruthers* (n. 27); *Wyman* v. *Paterson* (n. 47).

[50] 1955 S.C. 200.

[51] See Norrie, "Common Practice and the Standard of Care in Medical Negligence" 1985 J.R. 145.

[52] Sections 29, 30 and 33 also provide certain limitations in very special circumstances, but these are outwith the scope of this work.

[53] By which is meant any court of competent jurisdiction in which a question relative to the actings, liability or removal of a trustee comes to be tried: s.32(2).

part of the interest of that beneficiary in indemnifying the trustee for the amount he has to pay as a consequence of that breach of trust. This is a statutory formulation of a similar common law principle, which was based on personal bar. It does not confer on the trustee a right of personal action against the beneficiary,[54] but rather allows the court to authorise the trustees not to pay that beneficiary his full entitlement. If the trustee is liable for more than the instigating beneficiary's interest, he must suffer the excess loss himself.

There is a similar provision in England,[55] based on the English common law rule, which itself is not totally superseded by statute. At common law in England it was not necessary for the beneficiary to recognise that what he was requesting amounted to a breach of trust, so long as he understood the nature of the act he was instigating; and some English writers suggest that this principle also holds good in relation to the statutory provision.[56] However, there is clear authority in Scotland to the effect that, in order for the section 31 relief to be granted, it must be shown that the beneficiary understood not only the nature of the act he was requesting, but also that for the trustee to perform that act would amount to a breach of trust.[57] In *Henderson* v. *Henderson's Trs.*,[58] a beneficiary had expressed a hope to the trustees that the trust estate would be invested in Canada. The trustees invested in a Canadian lumbering company, which proved economically disastrous. The trustees were held in breach of trust for adopting an imprudent and hazardous investment, and they claimed that they were entitled to be indemnified from the beneficiary's interest under the statutory predecessor to section 31 (which was in identical form). The First Division held that as the beneficiary had not requested the trustees to commit a breach of trust, the statutory relief could not be granted. The beneficiary had clearly been relying on the trustees to ensure that it was in their power to make such an investment, and that it was otherwise proper and sufficient. The request to invest in Canada did not amount to a request to invest in Canada in an unauthorised manner. Lord President Balfour said:

"It was for [the trustees] and not for [the beneficiary] to see to the legality and sufficiency of the investment, and [the beneficiary] did not, in my

---

[54] Menzies at p. 785, Mackenzie Stuart at p. 384, Walker at p. 1080.
[55] Trustee Act 1925, s.62.
[56] Riddall at p. 349. Moffat & Chesterman at p. 447.
[57] *Henderson* v. *Henderson's Trs.* (1900) 2 F. 1295; *Cathcart's Trs.* v. *Cathcart* (1907) 15 S.L.T. 646; Mackenzie Stuart at p. 384.
[58] (1900) 2 F. 1295.

judgment, do anything to discharge them of this responsibility and take it upon himself. . . .

Nor is it, in my view, established either that he was aware that it was a breach of trust, or that he was cogniscant of the facts which would have made it a breach of trust."[59]

It is suggested that the better approach is to insist, as the Scottish courts insist, on knowledge on the part of the beneficiary that what he asks the trustee to do amounts to a breach of trust. For it is only in that situation that it would be equitable to penalise the beneficiary by idemnifying the trustee from his interest in the trust estate.

It was also emphasised in *Henderson* that this provision does not give trustees an absolute right to idemnity, but only empowers the court to grant it, if it sees fit. Here it was held that even had the section been applicable, the court would not have exercised its discretion in favour of the trustees because of the obviously speculative nature of the Canadian investment.

3. Statutory limitations: section 32

Section 32 of the 1921 Act provides that where it appears to the court[60] that a trustee is or may be personally liable for any breach of trust, but has nevertheless acted honestly and reasonably and ought fairly to be excused for such breach, the court in its discretion may relieve the trustee wholly or partly from personal liability for it. Both honesty and reasonableness must be established (and it is for the trustee to prove this), and the court must further be satisfied that it would be fair to excuse the trustee. Though there are no cases defining "dishonesty," it probably serves to exclude any trustee who acts for reasons other than his *bona fide* conclusion of what is in the interests of the trust. Since negligence is, by definition, unreasonable behaviour, any trustee who is negligent in the performance of his duties under the trust would also be unable to claim relief under this section. In *Clarke* v. *Clarke's Trs.*,[61] a trustee had in all honesty left a sum of money on deposit receipt for two years, instead of investing part of it in an annuity for which the trust had provided. It was held that this was not a reasonable course of action since it meant that the

---

[59] *Ibid.* at p. 1310.
[60] By which is meant any court of competent jurisdiction in which a question relative to the actings, liability or removal of a trustee comes to be tried: s.32(2).
[61] 1925 S.C. 693.

annuity would be chargeable to the whole fund rather than only to the part that ought to have been invested: relief under section 32 was refused.

It is not clear from the wording of the section whether, once honesty and reasonableness are proved, the court will always regard it as fair to grant relief, or whether fairness is a third condition that must be established. In *Clarke* only honesty and reasonableness were discussed, and the court seems to have assumed that "fairness" was not a further issue. On the other hand, Mackenzie Stuart[62] regards "fairness" as a third condition and says "relief granted to the trustees will generally be to the prejudice of the beneficiaries or the creditors, and fairness to all parties concerned must be observed in modifying the legal position of the trustee." It seems likely that the additional qualification of fairness is meant to indicate that, as with section 31, there is an ultimate discretion on the part of the court, which does not need to grant relief, even though the conditions of honesty and reasonableness are satisfied, if, taking everything into consideration, including the hurt to the beneficiaries, it decides that it would be inappropriate to grant relief. It has been held in England[63] that once honesty and reasonableness are established, the court should normally grant relief, and that it is only when special circumstances exist that it will be considered not fair to grant relief. This seems a sensible approach.

A common example of when relief ought to be granted is where the trust deed is ambiguous and the trustees adopt one reasonable interpretation, which later turns out to be wrong.[64] In *Fogo's J.F.* v. *Fogo's Trs.*,[65] relief would have been granted had the liferentrix in that case been held to be a trustee, because her general administration of the liferented estate had resulted in a great increase in its overall value since she received it.

Mackenzie Stuart[66] suggests on the basis of English authority that section 32 relief will not be granted to non-gratuitous trustees. There is no authority for such a proposition in Scotland and the Privy Council case Mackenzie Stuart founds upon[67] was modified in *Re Pauling's Settlement Trs. (No. 1)*[68], where the ratio

---

[62] At pp. 381/382. *Cf.* Wilson and Duncan at p. 392.
[63] *Perrins* v. *Bellamy* [1898] 2 Ch. 521, *per* Kekewich J.
[64] As in *Perrins, supra.*
[65] 1929 S.C. 546.
[66] Mackenzie Stuart at pp. 382/383.
[67] *National Trustees Company of Australasia* v. *General Finance Company of Australasia* [1905] A.C. 373.
[68] [1963] 3 W.L.R. 742.

of the earlier case was stated to be that where a banker undertakes to act as a paid trustee of a customer and so deliberately places himself in a position where his duty to the trust conflicts with his interest as a banker, the court should be very slow to relieve such a trustee under the statutory provisions. Doubtless the Scottish court would accept this as a statement of principle.

CHAPTER 11

TRUSTEES' LIABILITIES TO THIRD PARTIES

Introduction
Proper Relations
Improper Relations

Introduction

In the course of performing their duties under the trust, trustees will inevitably come into contact with third parties, that is strangers to the trust, through intromitting with the trust funds, or otherwise using the trust estate to achieve the purposes of the trust. Trustees' relations with third parties may in themselves be perfectly proper, in the sense that the power to enter into such relations does exist in terms either of the trust deed or of the Trusts (Scotland) Act 1921.[1] On the other hand, the relations may be improper in the sense that it is *ultra vires* (*i.e.* not within their power) for the trustees to enter into them. In both cases the trustees may find themselves personally liable to fulfil the obligations arising from the relationship with third parties; but different considerations apply in each situation, and they must be examined separately.

PROPER RELATIONS

When trustees enter into relations with third parties which they are entitled to enter into, and liability ensues from such a relationship, in order to deny their own personal liability arising from such a relationship it is not sufficient for it to have been properly entered into on behalf of the trust. The general rule is that trustees entering into any relationship are assumed to be undertaking personal liability therefor, and that third parties may go against the trustees as individuals (and not *qua* their position as trustees). Trustees acting for the trust act jointly and severally, and so their personal liability is joint and several.[2] This is a liability to fulfil contractual obligations as well as to pay for any breach; liability for breach is concurrent with liability for execution.[3]

[1] See Chap. 7.
[2] Unless some of the trustees take steps to disassociate themselves from the action, and the third parties accept this: see Mackenzie Stuart at p. 362.
[3] *Per* Mackenzie Stuart at p. 367.

153

The rule of personal liability is justified on the ground that the trustees are in the best position to know the full extent of liabilities that the trust estate can bear, this being something about which the third parties will have little knowledge. Indeed, the trustees are duty-bound to be aware of such matters. Consequently third parties are assumed to be relying on the good faith and credit worthiness of the trustees as individuals. If the trust funds are not sufficient to meet the trust liabilities, the trustees are responsible for explaining why not.[4] Also, the trustees are the legal owners of the trust estate and any liabilities arising from the exercise of the rights of ownership ought to be enforceable against the legal owners.[5]

The presumption is that the trustees undertake personal liability. That presumption can be overturned, though this must be done expressly, and will never be implied. To undertake an obligation "as trustee" will usually not be enough to overturn the presumption of personal liability, for this may simply be a descriptive term rather than one showing that the trust estate only is to be bound.[6] In *Muir* v. *City of Glasgow Bank*, Lord Chancellor Cairns said this:

> "Whether in any particular case the contract of an executor or trustee is one which binds himself personally, or is to be satisfied only out of the estate of which he is the representative, is . . . a question of construction, to be decided with reference to all the circumstances of the case, the nature of the contract, the subject matter on which it is to operate, and the capacity and duty of the parties to make the contract in one form or in the other."[7]

It must be established (and the onus lies with the trustees) that the third party knew that the intention was to bind only the trust estate, and that the third party accepted the relationship on that basis. This is a heavy onus, but will be satisfied by the contract containing such words as "I bind not myself but only the trust estate," or by the warrandice clause containing such words as "we as trustees foresaid grant warrandice from our own facts and deeds only; and bind the trust estate under our charge and beneficiaries interested therein in absolute warrandice."[8] The

---

[4] *Per* Lord Neaves in *Brown* v. *Sutherland* (1875) 2 R. 615 at p. 620.

[5] Mackenzie Stuart at p. 358.

[6] *Per* Lord Gifford in *Brown* v. *Sutherland, supra* n. 4, at p. 621.

[7] *Muir* v. *City of Glasgow Bank* (1879) 6 R. (H.L.) 21 at pp. 22/23.

[8] In *Horsbrugh's Trs.* v. *Welch* (1886) 14 R. 67 it was indicated that a conveyance of heritage with the words "I grant warrandice as trustee" was probably insufficient to exclude the trustee's personal liability in absolute warrandice. It is to be noted that trustees are not obliged to grant absolute warrandice and can be required only to grant warrandice from their own facts and deeds: the point here is that if the warrandice is to be limited, this must be done expressly. See further Halliday, Vol. 1, paras 4.28–4.52.

onus will not be discharged simply by showing that the third party knew that the trustees were acting as trustees: he must be shown to have accepted the obligation on the basis of liability being limited to the extent of the trust estate. It follows that trustees must be careful in entering into obligations to ensure that it is understood by all parties that they are not to be bound personally. Lord Penzance in *Muir* said this:

> "To exonerate [the trustee] it would be necessary to shew that, upon a proper interpretation of any contract he had made, viewed as a whole, in its language, its incidents and its subject-matter, the intention of the parties to that contract was apparent, that his personal liability should be excluded, and that, although he was a contracting party to the obligation, the creditors should look to the trust-estate alone."[9]

The presumption of personal liability is applied particularly strongly in relation to the liabilities attaching to share holdings in companies. Shareholders may be called upon to pay the uncalled-up portion of the company's share capital, and trustees who hold such shares may find themselves personally liable, even though they are registered (as they can be in Scotland) in the company books "as trustees." The reason for this is a consequence of company law rather than trust law.[10] To limit shareholders' liabilities to the extent of the trust estate they represent would be to create an unauthorized class of shareholders with liabilities more limited than the other shareholders, and it would be *ultra vires* for a company to accept shareholders on such a basis.[11]

There is an exception to the general rule in relation to transactions with the solicitors to the trust or with co-trustees. Both classes of individual are assumed to know the extent of the trust estate and they cannot therefore be held to be relying on the creditworthiness of the trustees personally. Consequently in transactions with individuals from either class, the presumption is reversed and it is assumed that only the trust estate is to be liable.[12]

If trustees have had to pay from their own pockets any liability properly undertaken on behalf of the trust, they are entitled to claim indemnity from the trust estate. Indeed they are entitled to pay their personal liability out of the trust funds, realising the estate if necessary, before going to their own funds, and in

---

[9] (1879) 6 R. (H.L.) 21 at p. 31.
[10] Mackenzie Stuart at p. 366.
[11] *Muir* v. *City of Glasgow Bank, supra* n. 7.
[12] *Ferme, Ferme & Williamson* v. *Stephenson's Trs.* (1905) 7 F. 902.

practice it is only when the trust funds are insufficient to meet the liabilities undertaken by the trustees that the trustees will have to pay from their own pockets. Trustees are not bound to become bankrupt if the estate from which they are entitled to relief is able to relieve them.[13] The liability of the trust estate is determined by the liability of the trustees, not by the trustees' ability to pay.[14]

IMPROPER RELATIONS

Sometimes trustees, whether deliberately or accidentally, do things on behalf of the trust which they are not actually entitled to do, because neither the trust deed nor the law grants them the necessary authority. In such a case the trustees are clearly in breach of the trust, and liable to the beneficiaries as such. However this does not necessarily mean that the transaction itself is void, for the law gives some limited protection to third parties in such transactions.

As was explained in Chapter 7 the trustees' powers of administration come from two main sources, the trust deed, and the Trusts (Scotland) Act 1921. Before 1961, third parties entering into a transaction with trustees had to satisfy themselves, by examining the trust deed and considering the 1921 Act, that the transaction was actually permitted; and if it was not permitted by either the trust deed or the 1921 Act, it was void, and the third party would lose any real right he would have acquired. Often there was doubt whether the trustees had power, say, to sell part of the trust estate, because it was unclear whether the power of sale was "at variance with the terms or purposes of the trust" and therefore unclear whether such a power could be implied under section 4 of the 1921 Act. The problems were compounded if there were no deed of trust but simply the appointment, judicial or otherwise, of a tutor or curator, or judicial factor. In such cases of doubt it was necessary to go to court under section 5 of the Trusts (Scotland) Act 1921 for a determination of the existence of the power. This was costly both in terms of time and money, and many third parties preferred not to deal with trustees at all, to the consequent detriment of some trusts.

Since the coming into force of section 2 of the Trusts (Scotland) Act 1961 there has been a limited protection for certain

[13] Per Lord Deas in Cuningham v. Montgomerie (1879) 6 R. 1333 at p. 1339.
[14] Ibid., per Lord President Inglis at p. 1338.

transactions entered into by trustees when they are not in fact authorised to do so. A transaction that gives effect to any of the acts listed in paragraphs (*a*) to (*ee*) of section 4(1) of the Trusts (Scotland) Act 1921 will have its validity protected, and more importantly any title acquired by a third party cannot be challenged by either the third party or any other person on the ground that the act in question was at variance with the terms or purposes of the trust (that is, on the ground that the trustees did not have the power under section 4).

It is important to note that this protection of transactions is limited in a number of ways.

First, it gives protection only to third parties by ensuring the legal enforceability of the obligations in their favour. The undertaking of the obligation may remain a breach of trust, and the trustees will still be personally liable to the beneficiaries and any co-trustees for such a breach.[15] It follows that a petition under s.5 may still be necessary in order to determine whether the trustees have the power to enter into the transaction, but this will be for their own protection rather than for the protection of the third parties.

Secondly, the transaction has to be one whereby the action performed is one of those listed in the first six paragraphs of section 4(1) of the 1921 Act. These powers are to sell the trust estate, to grant feus, to grant leases, to borrow money on security of the trust estate, to excamb any part of the trust estate, or to purchase suitable residential accommodation for any of the beneficiaries. A transaction involving any other act will not be protected by section 2 of the 1961 Act.

Thirdly, the 1961 Act protects transactions only from challenge on the ground that the act was at variance with the terms or purposes of the trust. It follows that if the challenge is raised on any other ground, the transaction is not protected by section 2. For example a purchaser from a *curator bonis* of a minor may still have his title reduced on the ground of minority and lesion.[16]

Finally, transactions entered into by trustees who are acting under the supervision of the accountant of court are not protected unless the accountant has previously given his consent to the transaction. It has been held that this does not permit the accountant to give powers that the trustees do not already have, and his consent is only valid for transactions which are not at variance with the terms or purposes of the trust.[17] However in

---

[15] s.2(2).
[16] This example was given by Halliday (1962) 3 Conv. Rev. 29 at p. 31.
[17] *Barclay (Mason's Curator)* 1962 S.L.T. 137; Halliday, *op. cit.* n. 16 at p. 31.

such circumstances the section 2 protection would not be necessary in any case, and it is difficult to see what effect section 2 is left with in these circumstances.[18]

A further protection to certain transactions is given by section 7 of the Trusts (Scotland) Act 1921, which provides that where a deed purports to be granted by a body of trustees, but it is in fact granted only by a quorum, the deed is not void and its validity cannot be challenged on the ground of some procedural irregularity. Such procedural irregularities would be constituted by a failure to consult with all the trustees or the absence of one or more trustees at a meeting where the transaction was considered, or a failure to obtain consent or concurrence from one or more of the trustees, or any other omission or irregularity of procedure on the part of the trustees or any of them in relation to the granting of the deed. Again there are limitations. Only persons acting onerously and in good faith can rely on this section; it only gives protection from challenge based on the ground or grounds mentioned; it only protects deeds purporting to be granted by a body of trustees[19]; and, again, the liability of the granters of the deed to co-trustees and beneficiaries is unaffected.

Likewise, but only in relation to executors, section 17 of the Succession (Scotland) Act 1964 protects from challenge title to, or any interest in, security over heritable property which has been obtained for value by a third party acting in good faith, if it has been obtained from an executor or a person deriving title directly from an executor. The protection is limited to challenges made on the ground that the executor's confirmation was reducible or has in fact been reduced, or that the executor should not have transferred title to the person from whom the third party, acting in good faith and for value, obtained title.

---

[18] See further, Halliday, *Conveyancing Law and Practice*, Vol. 1, at paras. 2.27 and 2.83.

[19] It is unclear what is meant here by "body of trustees." It could mean the whole number of trustees, or it could mean that portion of the trustees that have authority to bind the trust (normally a majority). It is suggested that the former interpretation is more likely, for the point of the protection is to deal with cases in which only some trustees acted while the third party assumed that all the trustees were acting.

CHAPTER 12

VARIATION OF PRIVATE TRUSTS

THE COMMON LAW POSITION

THE essence of a trust is that it provides a means whereby the original owner of property can control what happens to that property even after he has divested himself of title to it. A truster gives away his property, to the trustees, and it is the truster who lays down what the trustees are to do with the property, what purposes they are to achieve with it, and who is to benefit from it.

It followed at common law that once the trust came into existence the trustees could neither alter the actual purposes of the trust nor administer the trust in any way other than that directed by the truster. Similarly, the truster himself could not alter the trust purposes or modes of administration: once the trust became effective the truster had alienated the trust property away from himself, and he had no right thereafter to change his mind about the gift to which he had given effect. To vary a trust is to alter the rights of those who have or may potentially have interests in the trust property, and it is considered unjust that a person's interest or potential interest could be affected to their detriment without that person's consent.

These rules could be avoided in only very limited ways. For example, the truster could (and still can) reduce the necessity for requiring a variation by conferring on the trustees wide powers of appointment (*i.e.* a wide discretion to name individuals from a group specified by the truster to receive a part of the trust estate). Any beneficiary who is capax could (and still can) assign his interest in a trust to a third party or to another trust: this might achieve all that a proposed variation could achieve. Alternatively, an actual variation could (and still can) be carried out at common law if all the beneficiaries and potential beneficiaries were identified, were fully capax, and were in total agreement upon the issue: they together could direct the trustees to utilise the property in some way not envisaged by the original trust deed.

The Court of Session, through the *nobile officium*, had a very limited power to alter the terms of a private trust when that was necessary to prevent a complete breakdown of the trust.[1] This was limited to the granting of powers to trustees that they did not otherwise have, and it was certainly not equivalent to the English courts' common law "emergency and salvage" jurisdiction to vary the very purposes of private trusts, nor to the statutory jurisdiction under section 57 of the (English) Trustee Act 1925 to authorise any act of administration that is expedient for the trust as a whole.

The rule that all beneficiaries and potential beneficiaries had to consent to the variation of the trust meant that in a large number of cases the trust could never be varied at all. Whenever any beneficiary was incapable of consenting, for example because he or she was mentally incapax, or was a child, or had not yet been born, any proposed variation of the trust was effectively prevented. Similarly, whenever the trust involved an alimentary liferent it could not be varied, due to the rule in Scots law that alimentary liferents cannot be revoked, even by capax adults. Obtaining a variation was all the more difficult owing to the fact that even those who had remote contingent interests had to provide consent, if, potentially, their interests could be affected. This created practical difficulties, because of the potential size of that group, because members of that group might be not yet born or might be incapable of consenting, and because those who were capable of consenting had an equal right of veto to those who were actually benefiting from the trust.

There was a slight statutory modification to this position in the Trusts (Scotland) Act 1921, section 5 of which allows the court, on petition of the trustees, to grant them authority to do any of the acts mentioned in section 4 of the 1921 Act. Section 4 lays down the general powers of administration that all trustees are assumed to have unless such power is expressly withheld by the trust deed itself: if any of these powers are indeed withheld, the court can nevertheless grant the power in terms of section 5, so long as it is satisfied that, in all the circumstances, it would be

[1] See Elliott in Wilson & Duncan at pp. 149/150; Mackenzie Stuart, "*The Nobile Officium* and Trust Administration," 1935 S.L.T. (News) 1.

expedient for the execution of the trust for the trustees to have the power requested.[2] Likewise, section 16 of the 1921 Act allows the court to authorise the advance of part of the capital of the trust, if this is necessary for the maintenance or education of beneficiaries not of full age, notwithstanding that there is no power to do so in the trust deed itself.

The 1921 modifications were merely matters of administration, and in no circumstances did the court have the right to vary the actual purposes, or alter the nature or value of the interests of the beneficiaries in the trust. Only when all the beneficiaries and potential beneficiaries could agree and did agree could the trustees go against the truster's wishes in these respects.

THE PUSH FOR REFORM

The common law rule was inflexible and led to much hardship, particularly in periods of rising inflation and rapidly altering taxation rules. A trust set up one year in a tax advantageous manner may the very next year become tax disastrous: yet the disaster had to be borne unless all beneficiaries and potential beneficiaries could and did agree to alter the provisions of the trust deed to obviate the tax consequences. The facts of *Colville, Petr.*[3] illustrate this, for there the burden of estate duty payable on the termination of the liferent had increased from a top rate of 20 per cent. at the time the trust was set up to a top rate of 80 per cent. by the date of the court hearing.

In English law, the position was much the same, although the English courts' power to sanction variation was, as stated above, somewhat greater than in Scotland. One circumstance in which the English court could sanction a variation was when litigation concerning rights under an English settlement was compromised by the parties before judgment. The English court could (indeed had to) approve the compromise, which would normally involve some readjustment of the various interests under the trust, and that approved compromise would be binding on all beneficiaries, even those not party to the court action. For this reason it became advantageous for trustees to find some matter in the trust upon which to litigate. Such litigation became more and more

---

[2] Because s.5 petitions are restricted to the s.4 powers, this procedure is very much more limited than the English provisions under s.57 of the Trustee Act 1925.

[3] 1962 S.L.T. 45.

fictitious, the more variations became desired, usually for tax avoidance reasons. Eventually the fiction of litigation was dropped, and, by the middle years of this century, trustees were simply asking the court to sanction a "compromise" that was in reality a variation. At first the Court of Chancery granted such requests, thus acquiring for itself a new jurisdiction to vary private trusts, which it exercised for almost 20 years.

Eventually, however, one such case was taken to the House of Lords, and that chamber held, in *Chapman* v. *Chapman*,[4] that the Court of Chancery had no such jurisdiction: the power of the court was restricted to sanctioning real compromises in cases of actual dispute. So abruptly ended the Court of Chancery's acquired powers of variation.

The new jurisdiction however had proved too useful to be given up lightly: trusts were (and are) often set up for tax reasons, and variation had been found to be an essential element in the equitable administration of trusts. The outcry at the decision in *Chapman* v. *Chapman* led directly to the passing of the English Variation of Trusts Act 1958, which conferred upon the Court of Chancery in England the very power denied it by the House of Lords.

As far as Scotland was concerned, one can do no better than to allow the late Professor Halliday to take up the story.

> "Once the benefit was conferred upon English beneficiaries in 1958 there was no effective answer to the recommendation, cogently argued in the report of the Scottish Law Reform Committee, that the equally taxridden beneficiaries north of the Tweed should have a similar indulgence, however alien to our former ideas of jurisprudence. Thus it has happened that the decision in *Chapman*, which related to a technical question of the jurisdiction of the Court of Chancery and scarcely occasioned a ripple of comment in Scotland at the time, has resulted in a major and unprecedented extension of the powers of the Court of Session."[5]

The Inner House of the Court of Session was granted power to approve and authorise variations in private trusts by section 1 of the Trusts (Scotland) Act 1961, which power is in addition to any that it possessed before the passing of that Act.[6]

Though the motivation behind the Scottish provisions is the same as that behind the English legislation, there are significant

---

[4] [1954] A.C. 429.

[5] Halliday, "The Trusts (Scotland) Act 1961: Variation of Trusts," (1962) 3 Conv. Rev. 1 at p. 2.

[6] s.1(5) (referring primarily to the power under s.5 of the Trusts (Scotland) Act 1921).

differences in the wording of the two statutes, and for this reason English cases must be read with care.

THE TRUSTS (SCOTLAND) ACT 1961

Section 1 of the Trusts (Scotland) Act 1961 allows the trustees or any of the beneficiaries[7] to petition the court for it to sanction a variation of the terms or purposes of the trust. This section is in two separate parts, with different substantive rules applying to each. Section 1(1) allows the court to *approve* any arrangement varying or revoking all or any of the trust purposes or enlarging the powers of the trustees of managing or administering the trust estate. Section 1(4) allows the court to *authorise* any arrangement varying or revoking any trust purpose that entitles any of the beneficiaries to an alimentary liferent of or alimentary income from the trust estate or any part thereof. The difference between approval and authorisation is as follows.

Section 1(1) does not alter the substantive common law rule that all beneficiaries and potential beneficiaries must consent to the variation: all it does is to allow the court to give consent or approval on behalf of persons within certain categories, and in this way provide the nexus required for variation. The jurisdiction "remains essentially a curatorial function under which the court is acting in place of minor, incapable or unborn beneficiaries in granting consents on their behalf which might have been granted by themselves if they had been in existence or *sui juris*."[8] The court does not *order* variation under section 1(1), and the court's decree is not sufficient authority for the trustees to act upon the varied terms[9]: they must also obtain the consent of all the other beneficiaries, and if any other beneficiary cannot or does not consent, the variation is not legally efficacious.[10] (Having said which, however, the normal practice is for the petition under section 1(1) to have appended thereto all the other necessary consents. The gathering of these consents may cause great practical difficulties, and the Act does nothing to help in that respect.)

Section 1(4), on the other hand, constitutes a substantive alteration of the common law, for it allows for the variation and

---

[7] Which includes potential beneficiaries: s.1(6).
[8] Elliott, in Wilson & Duncan at p. 155.
[9] *Per* Buckley J. in *Re Suffert's Settlement* [1960] 3 All E.R. 561 at p. 563.
[10] *Knocker* v. *Youle* [1986] 2 All E.R. 914.

revocation of alimentary liferents, which cannot, at common law, be revoked. Under this subsection the court *authorises* that which would otherwise be legally incompetent, and the court's decree will be sufficient authority for the trustees to apply the trust funds to the new, varied, purposes insofar as they supersede the alimentary provisions previously laid down. (Having said which, however, if, as will almost invariably be the case, the renunciation of a liferent affects the interests of other persons, those others must also consent to the variation of their right, or have that consent provided under section 1(1).)

The reported variation cases in Scotland predominantly concern alimentary liferents, though the provisions in section 1(1) will apply to a much broader range of trusts. In a previous age liferents were more often alimentary than not, but modern trusts tend to be considerably more flexible. Not only should this give more significance to section 1(1) in the future, but that very flexibility may itself obviate the necessity to go to court at all.

1. Section 1(1): the classes

Section 1(1) lays down three different classes of person on whose behalf the court may grant consent to a variation of the trust purposes.

First, there is any beneficiary who is incapable of consenting by reason of nonage or other incapacity. "Nonage" covers those in pupillarity, "other incapacity" covers those who are mentally incapable of providing consent, and section 1(2) provides that those over the age of pupillarity but below the age of 18 (*i.e.* minors)[11] are incapable of consenting by reason of nonage, even when they act with the concurrence of a curator, administrator at law, or other guardian. When granting consent on behalf of a minor the court must take such account as it thinks appropriate of the minor's attitude to the arrangement. If the court grants consent on behalf of anyone in this first class, the arrangement cannot subsequently be reduced by the person on whose behalf consent was given, on grounds of minority and lesion.[12]

Secondly, the court may grant consent on behalf of any person who may in the future become a beneficiary, *i.e.* is at present merely a potential beneficiary. This is the only circumstance in

---

[11] See *Forbes* v. *House of Clydesdale Ltd.*, 1988 S.L.T. 594, *per* Lord Davidson at p. 596.
[12] s.1(3).

which the court can grant consent on behalf of persons who themselves may be capable of consenting; but this class is significantly reduced by a proviso to the effect that consent cannot be given by the court if the contingent beneficiary is capable of consenting *and* he or she would be an actual beneficiary had the immediate contingency occurred at the date of the petition. This has the effect of ensuring that the court can provide consent only on behalf of potential beneficiaries who are more than one contingency away from becoming actual beneficiaries. If they are only one contingency away, they must give their own consent. Imagine, for example, a trust set up for the benefit of "A, whom failing B, whom failing C." A, being an actual beneficiary, must give his own consent (unless he is not a capax adult). B, being only one contingency, A's death, away from benefit, must give his own consent (unless he is not a capax adult) because he is within the terms of the proviso. C, being more than one contingency, the deaths of both A and B, away from benefiting may have his consent given for him by the court, whether he is a capax adult or not: because, had the immediate contingency (B's death) occurred by the date of the petition, C would not yet be a beneficiary, for he still awaits A's death, and he is therefore not within the proviso.[13]

Thirdly, the court may grant consent on behalf of "any person unborn." This includes children *in utero* and those not yet conceived nor even thought about. There may be a difference between the child *in utero* and the potential child yet to be conceived, in that the likelihood of conception is a matter that will be relevant in determining whether the condition about to be discussed is satisfied.

2. Section 1(1): the condition

The court will grant consent on behalf of anyone in the above three classes only if it is of the opinion that the carrying out of the arrangement would not be prejudicial to those on whose behalf consent is being sought. The petitioner must set forth in the petition the effect on that person which the proposed arrangement will have, and must satisfy the court that this does not amount to prejudice.

---

[13] There is an identical proviso in the English legislation, and this has been judicially discussed a number of times in the English courts: see, *e.g.*, *Re Suffert's Settlement* [1960] 3 All E.R. 561; *Knocker* v. *Youle* [1986] 2 All E.R. 914.

A distinction must be noted here between the law of Scotland and the law of England. In Scotland the court must be satisfied that there is no prejudice, whereas in England the court must be satisfied that the arrangement will cause some positive benefit to the beneficiary on whose behalf approval is sought.[14] It would appear from this that approval will be easier to obtain in Scotland than in England. A variation with no effect on a beneficiary could certainly be sanctioned in Scotland,[15] while in England in that circumstance it would have to be argued that benefit accrues to the beneficiary by having the trust run the way that others wish it.[16]

"Prejudice" normally means some financial prejudice, and it will be difficult to satisfy the court that there is no prejudice if the arrangement is to the beneficiary's financial detriment. In *Pollok-Morris & Ors., Petrs.*[17] a petition was made to vary a trust so that the number of beneficiaries be increased to include the truster's adopted children, who were not originally covered. The petition to provide consent on behalf of the beneficiaries who were still minor was rejected, on the ground that to decrease the share of the estate that would come to the minor beneficiaries constituted a "possible prejudice," and this made it impossible for the court to hold that the arrangement would not be prejudicial. (Capax adults may, of course, consent to arrangements to their own prejudice, so the variation proposed in *Pollok-Morris* could go ahead once all the children grew up and, of their own volition, consented to the variation.)

The court will be unable to state that no prejudice will occur even when there is merely a risk of prejudice. This might be obviated by the trustees taking out insurance to cover for the potentiality that would constitute prejudice. This could be used, for example, to protect remote contingent fiars when the arrange-

---

[14] Variation of Trusts Act 1958, s.1. "Benefit" reflects the same requirement in certain earlier pieces of English legislation conferring limited powers of variation on the English courts: see, *e.g.*, s.64(1) of the Settled Land Act 1925, and s.53 of the Trustee Act 1925.

[15] See Lord President Clyde in *Colville, Petr.* 1962 S.L.T. 45 at pp. 51/52: "We can still approve where the variation puts the person in question in no worse position than before."

[16] Having said which, however, it should be pointed out that the English court is often quite liberal in defining what is a "benefit": see, *e.g.*, *Re C.L.* [1968] 1 All E.R. 1104, and *Re Remnant's Settlement Trusts* [1970] 2 All E.R. 554. In the former case it was held that it would benefit an incapax for the court to consent to that which the incapax would have consented to, had she been of full capacity.

[17] 1969 S.L.T. (Notes) 60.

ment is designed for immediate payment to existing fiars,[18] or to protect remote contingent beneficiaries who cannot be traced.[19]

Tax Point
A risk of prejudice might sometimes occur where the variation consists in the termination of a liferent. For should the liferenter die within seven years of the variation, Inheritance Tax will be payable on the portion of the trust fund received by any beneficiary (except the ex-liferenter). This risk could be avoided by the trustees arranging short term assurance on the life of the ex-liferenter to protect the beneficiary. (See *Colville, Petr.*,[20] where term assurance was taken out to protect a pupil beneficiary against a similar risk under the estate duty regime.) The court may not insist on this in every case, for "risk of prejudice" is to be determined from the exact circumstances of each case, and insurance may be considered appropriate, or not, depending upon such factors as the age and state of health of the ex-liferenter, and the size of premium required.

Loss of a potential benefit may not necessarily amount to "prejudice." Prejudice must be established on the balance of probabilities.[21] It may be prejudicial to deny a person one contingency away from benefit of a full right to a whole trust fund but it is not necessarily prejudicial to deny a person such a right who is 100 contingencies away, for he is losing something he almost certainly will never get, and therefore, on balance, will not be prejudiced. The likelihood of a child being conceived and being born alive is infinitely variable, but will often have to be borne in mind as creating a future potential beneficiary.

The court may exceptionally give approval on behalf of a beneficiary to arrangements which are to that beneficiary's financial detriment, because financial considerations are not necessarily the only relevant factors. In the English case of *Re Remnant's Settlement Trusts*[22] a trust deed contained a forfeiture clause, excluding from benefit any potential beneficiary who was or became a Roman Catholic or who married a Roman Catholic. A variation was sought to remove this forfeiture clause, on behalf of a number of minor beneficiaries of the same family, some Roman Catholic and some Protestant. There was no difficulty with the Roman Catholic beneficiaries, for the removal of the

---

[18] As was the case in *Robertson & Ors., Petrs.* 1962 S.L.T. 156.

[19] As in *Morris, Petr.* 1985 S.L.T. 252. The English courts have expressed a willingness to take risks on behalf of infants if it is one that adult beneficiaries would take: see *Re Cohen's Will Trust* [1959] 1 W.L.R. 865 (a position approved by Halliday, *op. cit.* n. 5 at p. 3).

[20] 1962 S.L.T. 45.

[21] Elliott in Wilson & Duncan at p. 158.

[22] [1970] 2 All E.R. 554.

forfeiture clause was clearly to their benefit; but the court also approved the variation on behalf of the Protestant beneficiaries, notwithstanding that their interests would of necessity be diminished by letting in the Roman Catholics. The court held that the Protestant beneficiaries received benefit in the removing of a source of possible family dispute and in the encouragement of their matrimonial liberty. If such is a benefit in England, an arrangement of this nature ought not to be regarded as prejudicial in Scotland.

It should also be noted that even if there is clearly no prejudice, this does not automatically entitle the petitioner to succeed, for the words "the court may if it thinks fit" as they appear in section 1(1) (and again in section 1(4)) clearly confer a discretion on the court.

3. Section 1(4): alimentary liferents

Alimentary liferents (which do not exist in England and for which there is therefore no provision made in the English statute) cannot be assigned or renounced once they have been accepted. Section 1(4) of the Trusts (Scotland) Act 1961 qualifies this rule by allowing the court to authorise an arrangement varying or revoking a trust purpose which involves the revocation of an alimentary liferent.

There are two conditions that must be satisfied before the court will grant authorisation to the variation under section 1(4).

First, the court must consider that the carrying out of the arrangement would be "reasonable." This is somewhat broader than the "no prejudice" test under section 1(1), for even a prejudicial variation may be reasonable in the context of an alimentary liferent, if, say, the liferenter has other sufficient sources of income. The statute provides that in determining reasonableness the court shall have regard to all the liferenter's sources of income, and "such other factors, if any, as the court considers material." In *Bergius' Trs., Petrs.*[23] the liferent which the petitioners sought to have revoked was contingent and for that reason the sources of income available to the liferentrix when the liferent opened to her were a matter of speculation. Accordingly the court held that it was not in a position to determine whether the proposed arrangement was reasonable or not, and the petition for variation was refused. In *Lobnitz, Petr.*[24]

[23] 1963 S.C. 194.
[24] 1966 S.L.T. (Notes) 81.

the petition was continued to allow for the production of an actuarial report valuing the petitioner's interest in the liferent. Without that, the court could not determine the question of reasonableness, as the value of the liferenter's interest was "obviously a material circumstance." In *Colville, Petr.*[25] the effect of the variation on the fiars of the liferented funds, and the tax liability the unvaried trust would attract, were both considered to be other material factors.

The second condition is that consent to the variation must be obtained. Section 1(4) requires consent from the liferenter only. However, when the fiars are in nonage or otherwise incapable of consenting themselves, the court has insisted that its approval under section 1(1) is also required,[26] and the arrangement will therefore have to satisfy that subsection's no prejudice test as well as the reasonableness test.[27] If the court requires to give consent for fiars who cannot themselves consent, it would logically follow that those who can consent must do so also, notwithstanding that section 1(4) requires only the consent of the liferenter.

Tax Point

When the arrangement varying an alimentary liferent is designed to save tax for the fiars, the normal practice has been to confer on the ex-liferenter a sum equivalent to the actuarial value of the liferent that is being revoked and the fiars will receive immediately the sum which it is estimated that they would receive if the alimentary liferent had run its course. However if the tax saving for the fiars is less than the actuarial value of the liferenter's interest, such an arrangement would cause financial prejudice to the fiars. In such a case the court might be willing to deem reasonable the giving to the liferenter of a sum less than the actuarial value of his interest, on being satisfied that his income is otherwise satisfactory: either that, or it could not authorise the variation.

Contingent alimentary liferents, *i.e.* those that have not yet become interests in possession, can be revoked at any time before enjoyment, and therefore authority under section 1(4) is not required, and any petition for such authority will be refused as unnecessary.[28] Likewise alimentary liferents can be assigned or renounced insofar as they are excessive for the liferenter's needs, and to that extent again the court's authorisation is not necessary.

[25] *Supra* n. 20.

[26] *Colville, Petr., supra* n. 20; *Robertson & Ors., Petrs.*, 1962 S.L.T. 156.

[27] See *Findlay & Anor., Petrs.*, 1962 S.L.T. 209; *Robinson, Petr.*, 1962 S.L.T. 304.

[28] *Findlay & Anor., Petrs., supra* n. 27.

There may however be practical problems in determining what is an excess, and in cases of doubt it is probably safer to ask the court to determine the matter under section 1(4).

VARIATION OR RESETTLEMENT?

It was sometimes said that the 1961 Act allows the court to *vary* an existing trust, but not to *create* a new trust.[29] The line between a substantial variation and a new settlement may be slim indeed. It has been held that the assets of a Scottish trust may be transferred, by means of a section 1(1) petition, to the jurisdiction of the English court[30]; and it has been held in England that the court can sanction the winding up of an English trust and the resettlement of the trust property as a Canadian trust.[31] If all the beneficiaries agree to the winding up of a trust then the trustees cannot prevent this.[32] Should not the court be able to provide a missing consent even to do this, so long as the other conditions in section 1 are satisfied? It would now seem to be the case that the Scottish court will sanction a complete resettlement. In *Aikman, Petr.*[33] the proposed arrangement contained provision for accumulation of income for 21 years after the date of the interlocutor approving the arrangement. Section 6(1)(*a*) of the Law Reform (Miscellaneous Provisions) (Scotland) Act 1966 permits accumulations for 21 years after the "date of the settlement or other disposition," and the court held that the proposed accumulation was valid since the arrangement was effectively a new settlement, because it "fundamentally and almost completely supersedes the original trust provisions." Lord President Clyde pointed out that not all arrangements will do so, but the decision is authority for the view that the court can resettle, as well as rearrange.

REASONS FOR VARIATION

The trustees or beneficiaries may wish to vary the trust for a number of reasons. There may be considered to be unduly

---

[29] See for example *Colville, Petr., supra* n. 20, *per* Lord President Clyde at p. 51; and in England *Re T's Settlement Trusts* [1964] Ch. 158, and *Mason* v. *Farbrother* [1983] 2 All E.R. 1078.

[30] *Lloyd & Anor., Petrs.*, 1963 S.C. 37.

[31] *Re Seale's Marriage Settlement* [1961] 3 W.L.R. 262.

[32] *Miller's Trs.* v. *Miller* (1890) 18 R. 301.

[33] 1968 S.L.T. 137.

restrictive provisions in the trust deed, such as restrictions on the trustees' right to act in certain ways. If the trustees feel that they can carry out their functions all the better with further powers, a variation may be appropriate. It has been held that in such a petition, the trustees must set out *ad longum* the additional powers they seek.[34] Similarly, if the trust deed contains restrictions on the trustees' power of investment, the trustees may seek the court's approval for an increase in these powers. Any increase approved need not necessarily be limited to the powers of investment envisaged by the Trustee Investments Act 1961.[35]

Alternatively, the provisions in the trust deed may be, in some respect, unfair or undesirable, such as the forfeiture clause directed against Roman Catholics in *Re Remnant*. Such conditions could be removed or altered by petition under the 1961 Act.

However, by far the most common reason why private trusts are varied is in order to minimise the total tax liability from the trust fund, even although this affects the specific proportions and interests being taken by the individual beneficiaries. This was recognised as an entirely proper use of the 1961 Act in the very first petition raised under it.[36]

Tax Point

While an alteration in the beneficial interest under a trust will usually be designed to reduce the ultimate total tax liability, it is necessary to balance the potential saving with the tax charges to which the variation itself may give rise.

For example, if the trust were discretionary and as a result of the variation there was created a liferent or an accumulation and maintenance trust, an Inheritance Tax "exit charge" would be precipitated by the variation (s.65, IHTA 1984).

Again, if the variation brings to an end a liferent, the liferenter is treated as making a transfer of value (s.52). To the extent that the liferenter receives part of the property absolutely, there will be no IHT charge (s.53(2)); but to the extent that it passes to someone else absolutely, it is a "potentially exempt transfer," and will escape IHT charge, but only if the liferenter survives a further seven years. Conversely, if an interest in possession trust is converted into a discretionary one, IHT is immediately payable as if the liferenter had made a lifetime chargeable transfer of the trust fund (IHTA 1984, s.3A), though anti-avoidance provisions (ss.54A and 54B) ensure that in certain circumstances IHT is calculated as if the truster (not the liferenter) had made the transfer.

Where the variation results in a beneficiary becoming absolutely entitled to the trust property as against the trustees, the trustees will be liable to

---

[34] *Nimmo & Anor., Petrs.*, 1972 S.L.T. (Notes) 68.
[35] *Henderson, Petr.*, 1981 S.L.T. (Notes) 40.
[36] *Colville, Petr., supra* n. 20.

CGT as if they had sold the assets at market value (s.54(1), CGTA 1979). In calculating the chargeable gain on such disposals, the trustees are allowed to deduct incidental expenses such as legal fees and outlays (including negotiation charges, counsels' fees, the actuary's fees for actuarial calculations etc.): see *Inland Revenue* v. *Chubb's Tr.*[37] Any unused allowable losses accumulated by the trustees will be transferred to the beneficiaries (s.54(2)).

[37] 47 T.C. 353.

VARIATION OF PUBLIC TRUSTS

CY PRÈS

THE principles discussed in the preceding chapter for the variation of private trusts cannot appropriately be applied to public trusts.[1] The much larger number of beneficiaries and potential beneficiaries would make it wholly impracticable to expect the trustees to obtain consent to the variation from them all. Also, public trusts create public benefits, and it would be inequitable to allow any single beneficiary to veto any necessary change, in the way they could with purely private trusts. However, public trusts, which of their nature tend to last for long periods of time, are for that very reason more likely than private trusts to suffer from the changing circumstances that the passage of time brings. The courts have always looked upon trusts designed to confer public benefits with particular benevolence, and therefore the common law has evolved a system of rules designed to avoid the lapse of public trusts through their becoming impossible or outmoded. The justification for this is that the law will not allow funds perpetually destined to the public good to be diverted back to private use through the medium of a private trust.[2] If a public trust is, for whatever reason, threatened with destruction, or proves impossible to continue (or commence), the trustees may petition the Inner House of the Court of Session, which through its *nobile officium* may sanction what is known as a *cy près* settlement, whereby the trust funds are directed to purposes

---

[1] For a discussion of the distinction between private trusts and public trusts, see Chap. 2.
[2] *Per* Lord Patrick in *Davidson's Trs.* v. *Arnott*, 1951 S.C. 42 at pp. 62–63.

which are different from those for which the trust was set up, but are nevertheless approximate to these purposes. Though a question of *cy près*, or approximation as it is sometimes called, may be raised in the Outer House, for example in an action of multiplepoinding, the matter must always be referred to the Inner House for final approval.[3]

The court's *cy près* jurisdiction over public trusts is very different from the power of the court to approve or authorise variations in private trusts, for it is much narrower and will only be exercisable if the trust purposes are or have become impossible of fulfilment or are particularly inappropriate rather than, as with private trusts, because the trustees or beneficiaries wish the variation. There are numerous different situations in which the *cy près* jurisdiction will be appropriate. For example, the truster may lay down a trust purpose but fail to specify how his wishes are to be carried out. In this case the court will provide the machinery, without varying the purposes. Alternatively, the truster may set up a trust to benefit a particular public institution which no longer exists by the time the gift is to take effect, or which ceases to exist during the running of the trust (*e.g.* a hospital that has been taken into public ownership, or a church that has undergone some doctrinal disruption). In this case the court may sanction the transfer of the funds to another institution with the same general purpose. Or the truster may direct that the trust property is to be used for a particular public purpose, but the funds are insufficient. In this case the court may sanction the funds being used for some similar, but less expensive, purpose. Likewise if the trust funds are excessive for the achievement of the purposes, as may happen with a public subscription fund, say, to deal with some disaster, the court may sanction the surplus being used for some other, but again similar, purpose.[4] The principle of approximation can also be used in limited circumstances to bring outdated trusts into line with today's society,[5] *e.g.* by combining a number of tiny trusts with the same aims into one larger trust. In all cases the purpose of the principle is to ensure the continued and relevant existence of trusts for public purposes.

---

[3] s.26, Trusts (Scotland) Act 1921.

[4] See, *e.g. Gibson & Anor., Petrs.* (1900) 2 F. 1195, in which a fund raised to relieve dependents of sailors lost owing to the sinking of the Dundee ship S.S. Celerity was redirected to the relief of persons from Dundee who might thereafter suffer loss by shipwreck or other perils of the sea.

[5] See Mackenzie Stuart at p. 126; Law Reform (Miscellaneous Provisions) (Scotland) Act 1990, ss.9 & 10.

A *cy près* petition may prove an expensive option, but it is one that might be avoided if drafters bear in mind the long term possibilities of the trust purposes being achieved or becoming impossible of achievement. Without detracting from the main purpose for which the trust was originally set up, it ought to be possible to include other, wider, purposes to which the funds can later be diverted if necessary. For example a trust set up in the wake of some disaster, say on an oil rig or in a factory, may have as a main purpose the relief of hardship of survivors, but may contain longer term purposes in relation to research and development in safety.

EXTENT OF APPLICATION

The principle of approximation may potentially apply in Scotland to any public trust. English law also recognises the concept of *cy près*, though in that system it is restricted to charitable trusts, in the peculiar English sense of that word. In many of the Scottish cases the concept is said to be applied to "charitable" trusts, but it must always be remembered that the word "charitable" in these cases bears the much looser, Scottish, meaning.[6] In *Anderson's Trs.* v. *Scott*[7] Lord Skerrington speaking for the First Division said:

> "There seems to be no reason why we should adopt the English rule that only a charitable trust can be administered *cy près*. The law of charities in England bristles with technicalities for which no analogies exist in our law."[8]

In a later case, Lord President Cooper described the situation as follows:

> "Owing to the plenary jurisdiction enjoyed by the Court of Session over all trusts, there never had been occasion in Scotland to draw distinctions between trusts which were charitable and trusts which were not, the only significant question for the exercise of the *cy près* jurisdiction in Scotland being whether the trust is one in which a section of the public have an interest. This point of view was powerfully reinforced in *Anderson's Trs.* v. *Scott* on the basis of which our *cy près* jurisdiction has consistently been exercised ever since."[9]

---

[6] See Chap. 6.
[7] 1914 S.C. 942.
[8] At p. 956. Only in relation to revenue matters is "charity" defined in the English sense.
[9] *Wink's Trs.* v. *Tallent*, 1947 S.C. 470 at p. 477.

This view was adopted in the case of *Russell's Ex.* v. *Balden*[10] in which it was argued that a bequest to North Berwick Town Council to be used in connection with a named sports centre or "some similar purpose in connection with sport" could not be subject to a *cy près* scheme after the Town Council had ceased to exist consequent to local authority reorganisation, since it was not a charitable gift. Lord Jauncey in the Outer House rejected this argument on the ground that a trust which confers benefit on a section of the public by way of the provision of sporting or recreational facilities satisfied Lord Cooper's test since it was a trust in which a section of the public had an interest. The statutory rules for variation, discussed later, are expressly applicable to "any public trust."[11]

However, a *cy près* scheme will not be available in every case in which a public purpose cannot be given effect to. The jurisdiction can be used neither to validate some defect in the deed, such as a failure by the truster to nominate a person to exercise a discretion, nor to alter a trust purpose that cannot be given effect to because it is uncertain or indeterminate. In *Vollar's Trs.* v. *Boyd & Ors*,[12] Lord Strachan in the Outer House pointed out that such situations were cases not of a failure of a valid purpose, but a failure to lay down a valid purpose: this cannot be rectified by a *cy près* petition, which will only be available if the purpose is legally valid, but for some other reason impossible.[13]

Nor will the *cy près* jurisdiction be available when the trust deed itself envisages the failure of the purposes and makes provision for that event: a valid destination-over, being an elaboration of the truster's wishes, will not be defeated by the principle of approximation,[14] for the principle is only applicable when the truster's wishes cannot be put into practical effect. Likewise the jurisdiction will not normally be used to obtain a retrospective validation of acts of the trustees which are or may be *ultra vires*.[15]

Even when the trust purpose is one that can be altered by the principle of approximation, the jurisdiction will not always be

---

[10] 1989 S.L.T. 177.

[11] Law Reform (Miscellaneous Provisions) (Scotland) Act 1990, s.9(1) and, particularly, s.9(7).

[12] 1952 S.L.T. (Notes) 84.

[13] But *cf.* Mackenzie Stuart at p. 122 to different effect. Variation being a different matter from validation, it is submitted that Lord Strachan's approach is more logical.

[14] *Young's Tr.* v. *Deacons of the Eight Incorporated Trades of Perth* (1893) 20 R. 778.

[15] *East Kilbride District Nursing Association & Ors.*, *Petrs.* 1951 S.L.T. 73.

exercised, for at the end of the day it is a matter within the ultimate discretion of the court. The *cy près* jurisdiction is not to be taken for what Lord President Clyde once called "a sort of cornucopia of judicial favours for distribution as may seem expedient among deserving applicants."[16] In effect the court is sanctioning an alteration of the terms laid down by the truster, so there are a number of conditions that must be fulfilled in order that the court can be satisfied that the alteration is as the truster himself would have wished. It should be emphasised that even if all the necessary conditions are satisfied, the court may exercise its discretion by refusing the petition. However, before discussing the conditions to be satisfied, an important distinction must be made.

INITIAL FAILURE AND SUBSEQUENT FAILURE

In relation to the conditions to be satisfied before a *cy près* settlement will be sanctioned, the law draws a distinction between trusts that have never been effective because they are impossible *ab initio*, and trusts that were originally effective but which have become impossible for some reason subsequent to the trust taking effect.

In relation to the latter, that is subsequent failure, the truster and his heirs are ousted from all interest in the property by the taking effect of the trust, for destinations to public purposes are regarded as perpetual,[17] and the subsequent failure of the purposes cannot therefore involve a resulting trust for the truster, or the truster's heirs. One of the features of public trusts (distinguishing them from private trusts) is that the truster retains little interest once the trust has taken effect, and neither he nor his heirs has any residual right in the trust property. On the subsequent failure of the purposes therefore the question becomes: how can the court retain the trust property in the public domain?

On the other hand, in relation to initial failure, that is when the trust has failed before it has taken effect, the truster and his heirs will not yet have been effectually ousted, and they will, generally speaking, retain an interest in the sense of having a residual right to the property if the trust cannot take effect. In

---

[16] In *Gibson's Trs.* 1933 S.C. 190 at p. 202.
[17] *Per* Lord Patrick in *Davidson's Trs. supra* n. 2 at pp. 62–63; Wilson & Duncan at p. 210.

other words, the trust property can sometimes revert back into private ownership. In order to defeat this result the law requires the satisfaction of an extra condition, which is not required in cases of subsequent impossibility. If it can be established that in setting up the public trust, the truster evinced what is usually called a "general charitable intent," the truster and his heirs will be ousted, for if the bequest is deemed to be to charity in general or to the public in general, with the specific beneficiary being chosen merely as an example of charitable or public intent, it can be taken that the truster intends his heirs never to take and would prefer some other charity to take the bequest.[18]

The distinction between initial failure and subsequent failure can be illustrated by the case of *Davidson's Trs.* v. *Arnott.*[19] Here, a testamentary trust was set up for the benefit of a named hospital in Girvan (which the truster himself had previously founded and endowed by *inter vivos* trust). Some years after the death of the truster the hospital was taken over by the National Health Service, and an action of multiplepoinding was raised in order to determine what should be done with the testamentary trust funds. The truster's heirs on intestacy claimed the capital fund, arguing that the only part of the trust that had taken effect was that relating to the income paid over from time to time to the hospital, but that the capital fund had not yet vested in the hospital. Thus, they argued, a general charitable intent in relation to the capital fund had to be shown, but as this did not exist the funds fell into the truster's intestacy. The Second Division agreed that the bequest evinced no general charitable intention, but merely an intention to benefit one particular hospital; but in addition it held that this was irrelevant since the trust had taken effect when the whole fund vested in the trustees for the purposes of the hospital, which existed at the date of death. Lord Jamieson pointed out that the trustees could be restrained from any attempt to use the unexpended fund for any purpose other than the hospital, and therefore it could not be argued that the trust had not taken effect. This therefore was a case of subsequent, and not initial, failure and consequently a general charitable intention was not one of the conditions that had to be satisfied before the court would sanction a *cy près* settlement.

On the other hand, it was held in *Cuthbert's Trs.* v. *Cuthbert*[20] that the trust purposes were impossible *ab initio* after the trustees

---

[18] See Lord Jauncey in *Russell's Ex* v. *Balden*, 1989 S.L.T. 177 at p. 181.
[19] 1951 S.C. 42.
[20] 1958 S.L.T. 315.

had attempted over a number of years to run a trust as the truster wished, but this had proved unviable.

Just because a beneficiary institution changes its name or amalgamates with another does not mean that it has ceased to exist: there are a number of cases arising from the various schisms and disruptions of the Scottish churches, a common feature of such events being that they are invariably followed by a glut of litigation.[21]

THE CONDITIONS

1. General charitable intention

In cases of initial (but not of subsequent) failure, the court will not grant a *cy près* settlement unless it is clear from the face of the deed that the truster had a general charitable intent, which was defined by Lord Patrick to mean "a general intention that the funds shall be devoted to public purposes."[22] In other words it must be shown that the truster intended to benefit charity or the public in general, rather than simply a particular institution that has charitable or public purposes. It cannot be assumed because a truster leaves his money, for example, to Save the Children, that he intends to benefit needy children rather than a needy organisation: the one does not necessarily presuppose the other. It must be shown that the truster's main aim is to benefit a cause or a purpose, and that the choice of beneficiary is not of the essence of the provision, but is merely the choice of agency for the carrying out of his chosen cause or purpose. Thus with a gift to Save the Children, the court would have to be satisfied that the truster's true aim was to further the cause of child welfare, and that the essence of that aim did not depend upon the named organisation taking the gift.

The distinction between trust purposes that show a general charitable intention and those that do not can be illustrated from a consideration of the following two cases.

In *McRobert's Trs.* v. *Cameron & Ors.*[23] a trust fund was set up for the erection and furnishing of a private ward in a certain

---

[21] For a discussion, see Thomson, "A Question of Identity—The Problem of Bequests to Non-Existent Institutions in Scots Law" 1973 J.R. 281.

[22] *Davidson's Trs.* v. *Arnott supra* n. 2 at p. 60.

[23] 1961 S.L.T. (Notes) 66.

hospital. Before this could be built however, the Board of Management which ran the hospital closed it down. The trustees applied for a *cy près* settlement, but this was refused on the ground that the trust deed contained not a general intention to provide hospital beds, but simply a bequest to a specific institution, which bequest fell since the institution no longer existed. As it could not be said that it was clear that the truster would want another similar purpose to be given effect to in the event of the one he specified failing, the heirs were not effectively disinherited.

This case may usefully be compared with that of *National Bible Society of Scotland* v. *Church of Scotland*,[24] where a fund was bequeathed to the African Lakes Trading Corporation to allow it to carry out Protestant evangelical work in British Southern Africa. The corporation declined the bequest and the court approved a *cy près* settlement whereby the bequest was taken by another institution willing to carry out the truster's aims, on the ground that there was a clear charitable intention in the furtherance of Protestant evangelical work amongst African natives, which could be carried out by agencies other than the corporation. In other words, the bequest was in essence not one to the corporation but one to benefit African natives. The corporation had merely been chosen as an agent to carry out this charitable purpose.

The issue is a matter of determining the intention of the truster from the words used in the trust deed. Each case must therefore be looked at on its own facts, taking account of the particular circumstances, but in all cases there must be shown to be "an intention, going beyond the particular trust arrangements which [the truster] has directed and which have failed, to benefit a class of objects."[25] "The more particular and precise are the donor's directions, the more difficult it will be to find that he had an intention to benefit charity in any wider sense."[26] It would seem that it is easier to deem a general charitable intention if the gift is to a stated purpose rather than to a stated institution (*e.g.* "to save children"[27] rather than "to Save the Children").

There is a clear distinction drawn in English law between gifts to institutions which used to exist but do not do so on the date

[24] 1946 S.L.T. (Notes) 26.
[25] *Per* Lord Maxwell in *Shorthouse's Trs.* v. *Aberdeen Medico-Chirurgical Society*, 1977 S.L.T. 148 at p. 150.
[26] Ockelton at p. 173.
[27] Assuming that such a purpose is sufficiently precise to be given effect: see Chap. 6.

the gift is to take effect, and to institutions which never did exist
in the first place: in the latter situation a general charitable intent
is presumed, while in the former situation specificity of intention
is presumed.[28] This distinction was mentioned obiter with
approval by Lord Dunedin in *Burgess's Trs.* v. *Crawford*,[29] and it
was applied by Lord Sorn in the Outer House in *Tod's Trs.* v.
The Sailors' and Firemen's Orphans' and Widows' Society.[30] Lord
Sorn rationalised this distinction by opining,

> "that, in all cases where the institution cannot be found at the date of death,
> the Court, from favour to charity, leans towards recognising a general
> charitable intention but that, where a named institution actually existed at
> the date of the will, this course is excluded in the view that the testator's
> particularity of intention must be treated as a certainty."[31]

Now this (together with Lord Dunedin's obiter approval) is the
only authority for drawing the distinction in Scots law,[32] and it is
submitted that it is somewhat illogical. It is based on the
assumption that a gift to a specified once existing institution
conclusively shows particularity of intention.[33] Yet that assumption is not made with gifts to a specified and still-existing
institution, when the gift has failed for other reasons. The
National Bible Society case is an example of an institution being
specified, but the court nevertheless holding that there was a
general intention. The assumption not being made in that sort of
case, it is submitted that it is illogical to make it only when the
reason for the failure of the gift is the institution's subsequent
demise. Also, the distinction fails to take account of the possibility that the truster may simply have been mistaken in his
description of the institution. However, as Thomson points out,
"this distinction is only a guide to construction, not a rule of
law."[34] The illogicality of the distinction is shown from the
ludicrous result in the English case of *Re Harwood*.[35] In that case
a trust deed contained, *inter alia*, one provision in favour of "The
Peace Society of Belfast" and another in favour of "The Wisbech

---

[28] See *Re Rymer* [1895] 1 Ch. 19; *Re Spence's Will Trusts* [1978] 3 All E.R. 92.
[29] 1912 S.C. 387 at p. 395.
[30] 1953 S.L.T. (Notes) 72.
[31] *Ibid.*, at p. 72.
[32] Even although Lord Sorn described it as "well recognised" (*supra*, n. 30 at p.
72).
[33] Though the English cases do not talk, as Lord Sorn does, of "certainty": see
Harwell J. in *Re Harwood* [1936] Ch. 285 at p. 287.
[34] *Op. cit.*, n. 21 at p. 282.
[35] *Supra*, n. 33.

Peace Society." The former had never existed, while the latter did once exist but had ceased to exist by the time the trust took effect. It was held that the gift to the Belfast society evinced a general charitable intention, and so could be saved by the *cy près* jurisdiction; but that the gift to the Wisbech society evinced a particularity of intention and therefore could not be saved by the *cy près* jurisdiction. It is suggested that, notwithstanding the high authority of Lord Dunedin's approval, this distinction ought to be resisted in the future by the Scottish courts.

2. Impossibility

In cases both of initial and of subsequent failure there must be a real failure of the public trust purposes: it must be impossible to fulfil the purposes, or at least it must be wholly inappropriate for them to be continued in their present form. It is not sufficient that the trust purposes are or have become more onerous for the trustees than was first thought, or that they can be carried out only to a lesser scope than was envisaged by the truster, or in a lesser degree than happened in the past.[36] Lord President Clyde put the matter thus in *Glasgow Domestic Training School*:

> "I think it necessary to say that the principle of approximation properly applies only to cases in which the object of a charitable foundation can—owing to changed circumstances—no longer be carried into practical effect in the particular form or by the particular means prescribed by the founder . . . But the principle does not apply to cases in which—there being neither failure of object nor obsolescence of method—the changing circumstances of society have made the duties of the trustees and managers of the foundation much more arduous to perform and discouraging in their results. If we opened the door to applications in which the ground for appealing to our jurisdiction was only that, owing to a change of circumstances the achievement of the purpose of the charity has come to make heavy demands on the services and persistence of the trustees and managers, then I am afraid we should be very likely to exceed the powers which we possess."[37]

Fundamentally differently from private trusts, if it remains possible to carry out the original purposes of a public trust the trustees must do so, and the court will not sanction a *cy près* alteration of the truster's stated wishes. In *Scotstown Moor Children's Camp*[38] a trust was set up to provide a summer holiday

---

[36] *Scotstown Moor Children's Camp*, 1948 S.C. 630.
[37] 1923 S.C. 892 at p. 895.
[38] *Supra* n. 36.

camp for "poor and ailing children" from the City of Aberdeen. The trust was run successfully for a number of years, and was assisted by local traders who contributed food parcels for the children. Eventually the tented accommodation was replaced by permanent buildings. However, during the Second World War the land and buildings were requisitioned and food rationing meant that the food parcels could no longer be distributed. After the war ended, the trustees presented a petition for approval of a scheme to transfer the assets to the Aberdeen Battalion of the Boys Brigade. The court rejected the petition on the ground that it had not been established that the objects of the trust had failed completely, or that the method of carrying out these objects was no longer practicable. There was nothing to stop the camp being re-established, though it would require some effort on the part of the trustees, and this was so even if it meant reverting to canvas accommodation instead of the permanent buildings. Reduced activity is quite different from impossibility.

Again, the court refused to sanction a *cy près* scheme in *Grigor Medical Bursary Fund Trs., Petrs.*[39] Here a trust provided bursaries for young men from Nairn to study medicine, and the trustees, finding it difficult to attract suitable male candidates, wanted the purposes altered so that women would be eligible as well as men. The court held that difficulty in finding eligible candidates was not sufficient, and that a *cy près* scheme would only be justified if it could be shown that there never again would be a sufficient number of eligible male candidates.[40]

On the other hand, in finding a real failure of the purposes the court has sometimes been rather more liberal in accepting that purposes are impossible or inappropriate. As was said in *Glasgow Y.M.C.A.*, "to save a charitable trust from wreckage it is not necessary for the Court to hesitate until the trust is actually upon the rocks."[41] Here an association had a large capital fund, but an annual deficit in revenue. The court allowed the trustees to apply the capital fund to pay off the revenue deficit, even although the trust could have continued for a limited period without such an alteration of the trust deed: the work of the association would be "seriously crippled" and that was sufficient to justify the court's

[39] (1903) 5 F. 1143.
[40] Such a variation was sanctioned in *Clark Bursary Fund (Mile-End) Trs.* (1903) 5 F. 433. The difference between these two cases seems to be that in *Grigor* it was found that the truster intended to restrict his benevolence to males, while in *Clark* there was nothing to indicate that the truster would have done so had he known that university education would become available to females.
[41] 1934 S.C. 452 at p. 458, *per* Lord Blackburn.

intervention. An even more liberal interpretation of the doctrine is shown in *Provost and Magistrates of Forfar, Petrs.*[42] in which a scheme was approved whereby a number of trusts with the same basic purposes came under the same administration, as this would be advantageous to them all.[43] The court approved the scheme without delivering opinions, but the reporter to whom the case had been referred for the framing of a suitable scheme (see *infra*) pointed out that the cases suggest that there had to be strong expediency before the court would exercise its power on grounds of expediency rather than impossibility.[44] This sort of situation will now be covered by sections 9 and 10 of the Law Reform (Miscellaneous Provisions) (Scotland) Act 1990 (*infra*).

Likewise impossibility will be held established if the continued running of the trust would be in some way quite ludicrous, or wholly inappropriate in the circumstances that have now arisen. In *University of Aberdeen* v. *Irvine*[45] a trust was set up to provide bursaries for 10 students. The Senatus Academicus of the University of Aberdeen were trustees. Owing to an earlier decision of the House of Lords involving the same trust[46] the revenue available for these bursaries was considerably increased, and the Senate petitioned the Court of Session to allow them to increase the number of bursars. They claimed that the restriction to 10 per year was wholly inappropriate given the size of the funds, and that it would mean that each recipient would be ridiculously wealthy, receiving between £80 and £150 a year. "Experience shews," pleaded the Senate, "that students enjoying allowances much beyond what is required for the payment of their ordinary expenses are apt to fall into habits seriously detrimental both to themselves and their fellow students."[47] The court agreed, and the alteration was sanctioned on the ground that not to do so would render the continued running of the trust quite mischievous to the recipients and to the University as a whole.

An interesting illustration of the same point is found in the English decision of *Re Dominion Student Halls Trust*, in which

[42] 1975 S.L.T. (Notes) 36.

[43] The English courts have always adopted a fairly narrow approach to *cy près* in comparison to the Scottish courts. This is shown by the fact that in England a statutory provision was required before the court there had the power to do as was done in *Provost and Magistrates of Forfar, Petrs.*: Charities Act 1960, s.12(1).

[44] This was stated to be the case in *Gibson's Trs., Petrs.*, 1933 S.C. 190. In *Grant* v. *Macqueen* (1877) 4 R. 734 a scheme was approved for the use of the trust funds only for so long as a foreseeably temporary state of impossibility continued.

[45] (1869) 7 M. 1087.

[46] *University of Aberdeen* v. *Irvine* (1868) 6 M. (H.L.) 29.

[47] (1869) 7 M. at p. 1090.

the judge said that "the word 'impossible' should be given a wide significance . . . It is not necessary to go the length of saying that the original scheme is absolutely impracticable."[48] Here a trust was set up with the aim of furthering community of citizenship throughout the British Empire and Commonwealth, by providing *inter alia*, student halls of residence. The trust deed however restricted its benefits to Commonwealth citizens of European origin: it aimed at community spirit throughout the Commonwealth by excluding the black Commonwealth. The Court of Chancery had no hesitation in sanctioning a *cy près* scheme removing this colour bar. The judge decided that world conditions had changed sufficiently since the trust was set up, particularly as a result of the Second World War, to render a colour bar so inappropriate that a refusal to remove it would frustrate the truster's true intent of fostering community spirit. (This is sophistry of course, as the truster's clear intent was to benefit only white citizens, but the case illustrates the fact that not all sophistry leads to unacceptable results.) The judge in this case also held that the current beneficiaries would not be prejudiced by the variation since various new donors had agreed to contribute to the trust if the colour bar were removed. However, prejudice to current beneficiaries is not normally a relevant consideration, unless that prejudice indicates that the carrying on of the trust has become impossible.

3. Approximation

Again in cases both of initial and of subsequent failure, the scheme suggested must be one that is approximate to the original purposes. The new purposes must be sufficiently close in character to the old ones that they can be regarded as within the ambit of the truster's original intent. A *cy près* settlement is, at the end of the day, an attempt to avoid the denial of the truster's charitable or public intent. It follows that if the truster's intention is unique and a similar purpose cannot be found, a *cy près* scheme should not be available.[49]

The requirement of approximation will be simple to satisfy if the impossibility refers not to the purpose but to the machinery,

---

[48] 1947 Ch. 183 at p. 186.
[49] Mackenzie Stuart at p. 129 suggests that if no similar purpose can be found the court has a free hand. However the only case he cites is a curious and old English decision, and there is no authority in Scots law to suggest that this is the position here.

or is caused by some inappropriate condition, such as the colour bar in *Re Dominion Student Halls Trust*. In these circumstances the court will provide the machinery or remove the condition, and the purpose will not itself be altered. In such cases the court can "encroach upon the letter of the foundation to such an extent as to remove [the] evils, but not one step further."[50]

It is more difficult when it is the purpose that is impossible. In that situation some new purpose must be found, but that new purpose must approximate as closely as may be to the terms of the original deed. The court will not sanction a scheme that it considers to depart too far from the purposes laid down by the truster. In *University of Aberdeen* v. *Irvine*, where the University Senate suggested increasing the number of bursaries from 10 to 48, this was considered by the court to be far too great a departure from the terms of the trust, and the court altered the number to 20. In *Glasgow Royal Infirmary* v. *Magistrates of Glasgow*[51] funds were raised to build a convalescent fever home. Some years later the Town Council established a fever hospital and the trustees presented a petition to divide the funds between the Glasgow Royal Infirmary for the erection of nurses' homes, and a society for fever and smallpox hospitals. The court altered the scheme so that all the funds would go to the society, on the ground that its purposes were more nearly akin to the wishes and intentions of the raisers of the funds than was the building of nurses' homes.

In devising the new scheme, in addition to approximating the new aims to the old as far as possible, the drafter ought also to ensure that whatever limitations the truster placed on the use of the funds are maintained.[52] So a locality clause in the original deed will normally be applied to the new scheme.[53] In *Glasgow S.P.C.A.* v. *National Anti-Vivisection Society*,[54] the court refused to sanction the transfer of funds to an English society from a trust set up to benefit purely Scottish institutions. Any other limitations mentioned by the truster ought also, so far as possible, to be complied with in the new scheme.

It is for the drafter of the scheme to identify an approximate purpose: he will normally be either the trust's law agent, or the

---

[50] *Per* Lord President Inglis in *University of Aberdeen* v. *Inglis* (1869) 7 M. 1087 at p. 1092.
[51] (1888) 15 R. 264.
[52] Unless, of course, the point of the petition is to remove a debilitating limitation.
[53] Wilson & Duncan at p. 214.
[54] 1915 S.C. 757.

reporter appointed by the court, or by the Lord Ordinary in actions of multiplepoinding in which it becomes clear that a *cy près* scheme will be necessary. The Inner House will not itself frame a new scheme *ex proprio motu* (though it may suggest alterations to the one presented for its approval.)[55]

Tax Point
In devising the new scheme it will normally be appropriate to ensure that purposes that were previously "charitable" in the revenue law sense remain so in the new approximated scheme; indeed this is a statutory requirement in relation to statutory variation (considered immediately below).

STATUTORY VARIATION OF PUBLIC TRUSTS

In addition to the Court of Session's *cy près* jurisdiction, section 9 of the Law Reform (Miscellaneous Provisions) (Scotland) Act 1990, now gives both the relevant sheriff court[56] and the Court of Session[57] statutory powers to approve a scheme for the variation or reorganisation of the trust purposes in any public trust. In order to exercise this power, the court must be satisfied either:

(1) that the purposes of the trust have been fulfilled so far as is possible or can no longer be given effect to; or
(2) that the purposes of the trust provide a use for only part of the trust property; or
(3) that the purposes of the trust were expressed by reference to an area which has ceased to have effect for these purposes or by reference to a class of persons or area which has ceased to be suitable or appropriate for the trust; or
(4) that the purposes of the trust have been adequately provided for by other means, or have ceased to be entitled to charitable status for revenue matters[58] or have otherwise ceased to provide a suitable and effective method of using the trust property, having regard to the spirit of the trust deed.[59]

[55] *Per* Lord Salvesen in *Glasgow S.P.C.A.* v. *National Anti-Vivisection Society* 1915 S.C. 757 at p. 763.
[56] Defined in s.9(5) as (a) the sheriff for the place with which the trust has its closest and most real connection, *or* (b) if there is no such place the sheriff for the place where any of the trustees resides, *or* where neither (a) nor (b) applies, the sheriff of Lothian and Borders at Edinburgh: the Secretary of State will by order prescribe the maximum annual income of the trust for an application to the sheriff to be competent.
[57] s.9(4).
[58] See Chap. 2.
[59] s.9(1).

If one of the above conditions is satisfied, the court, on the application of the trustees, can approve the new scheme so long as the court is satisfied, that the trust purposes proposed in the new scheme will enable the resources of the trust to be applied to better effect consistently with the spirit of the trust deed, having regard to changes in social and economic conditions since the time the trust was constituted.[60] The new scheme can include a transfer of assets to another public trust or the amalgamation of the trust with another public trust or other public trusts.[61] The application for a statutory variation must be intimated to the Lord Advocate who is entitled to enter appearance as a party to the proceedings and lead such proof and enter such pleas as he thinks fit.[62]

The court's ability to vary public trusts has been somewhat extended by these provisions, and, where appropriate, will obviate many of the difficulties of the *cy près* jurisdiction, such as in proving impossibility. The provisions do however substantially overlap the common law procedure of *cy près*, which is expressly preserved by the statute,[63] and it would seem that applicants will therefore have a choice of procedure in many cases. It remains to be seen which procedure will prove the more popular.

VARIATION OF SMALL PUBLIC TRUSTS

Section 10 of the Law Reform (Miscellaneous Provisions) (Scotland) Act 1990 introduced new rules in relation to small public trusts, that is public trusts whose annual income does not exceed £5,000.[64] In such trusts, the trustees can either, (a) modify the trust purposes[65] or, (b) wind up the trust by transferring the assets to another trust the purposes of which are not so dissimilar in character to those of the trust to be wound up as to constitute an unreasonable departure from the spirit of the trust deed[66] or, (c) amalgamate the trust with one or more other trusts the purposes of which are likewise not so dissimilar.[67] Such a variation can be effected simply by the trustees passing a resolution that the trust

---

[60] s.9(2).
[61] s.9(3).
[62] s.9(6).
[63] s.9(7).
[64] A figure that can be amended by order by the Secretary of State: s.10(15).
[65] s.10(3).
[66] s.10(8).
[67] s.10(10).

deed be modified or that the trust be wound up or that it be amalgamated. Any such resolution can be passed whenever a majority of the trustees are of the opinion either:

> (1) that the purposes of the trust have been fulfilled as far as is possible or can no longer be given effect to; or
>
> (2) that the purposes of the trust provide a use for only part of the trust property; or
>
> (3) that the purposes of the trust were expressed by reference to an area which has ceased to have effect for these purposes or by reference to a class of persons or area which has ceased to be suitable or appropriate for the trust; or
>
> (4) that the purposes of the trust have been adequately provided for by other means, or have ceased to be entitled to charitable status for revenue matters[68] or have otherwise ceased to provide a suitable and effective method of using the trust property having regard to the spirit of the trust deed.[69]

In passing a resolution either of modification, or of winding up and transfer, or of amalgamation, the trustees must have regard to the circumstances of the locality of the trust if the trust purposes relate to a particular locality[70] and must ensure that the new purposes or the trust to which the assets are being transferred or amalgamated with have the same charitable status as the original provisions.[71] In passing a resolution of modification the trustees must have regard to the extent to which it may be desirable to achieve economy by amalgamating two or more charities.[72] In passing a resolution either of winding up and transfer or of modification, the trustees must ascertain that the trustees of the trust to which the assets are being transferred or amalgamated with actually agree to the proposed transfer or amalgamation.[73]

The variation will be effective two months after the resolution has been properly advertised.[74] The Lord Advocate has the power to intervene and prevent the modification of purposes or transfer of assets, if it appears to him that the proposed variation should not go ahead.[75] The resolution will of course be subject to the common law remedy of reduction.

---

[68] See Chap. 2.
[69] s.10(1).
[70] s.10(5)(a), s.10(9)(a), s.10(11)(a).
[71] s.10(6), s.10(9)(b), s. 10(11)(b).
[72] s.10(5)(b).
[73] s.10(9)(c), s.10(11)(c).
[74] s.10(7), s.10(12).
[75] s.10(14).

CHAPTER 14

REVOCATION AND TERMINATION OF TRUSTS

Introduction

SCOTS lawyers have never had the loathing for perpetuities felt by English lawyers, and as a consequence, in Scotland, there is no necessity for a trust ever to come to an end. Large numbers of public trusts have been run successfully for many centuries and will in all likelihood continue for centuries more. However, with trusts whose purposes are not designed to exist in perpetuity, there will eventually come a time when the trust has to be brought to an end, and the remaining trust property distributed to those entitled to it. A trust can be brought to an end either through its revocation by the truster or by its termination, whether timeously by the trustees or prematurely by the beneficiaries.

REVOCATION BY THE TRUSTER

Sometimes the deed of trust can be revoked by the truster, with the benefits conferred or intended to be conferred by the trust being withdrawn.

Tax Point
Where a trust is revocable (whether at the instance of the truster or of some other person), so that when revoked the trust property reverts to the truster,

or to the truster's spouse, the trust income will be taxed as that of the truster, even although the trust has not yet been revoked (s.672, ICTA 1988). The main exception to this is that where the revocation cannot take place within six years of the trust being set up, the income will be taxed as trustees' income until such time as the power of revocation can be exercised.

Not all trusts can be revoked, and the general rule is that once the trust has taken effect, the truster falls out of the picture and is unable to recover the benefit he has conferred, just as the maker of a gift generally cannot revoke the gift and demand the return of what has been given.

There are certain types of trusts which, of their nature, are never revocable by the truster. For example, a trust which contains a provision for an alimentary liferent cannot be revoked, even with the consent of all the beneficiaries. There has been a qualification to this rule since the passing of the Trusts (Scotland) Act 1961, for section 1(4) of that Act permits the Court of Session to authorise any arrangement varying or revoking an alimentary provision in any trust.[1]

Conversely, there are certain types of trusts which, of their nature, are always revocable by the truster. Trust dispositions and settlements (*i.e.* Wills with ongoing trust purposes other than the mere payment of legacies) are trusts intended to take effect after the death of the truster; in accordance with the general rule that trusts can be revoked before they take effect, a trust disposition and settlement will be revocable before the death of the testator. Another type of trust that is always revocable is a trust for administration.[2] If a trust is set up for purely administrative purposes, with the sole beneficiary being the truster himself, the law will not regard such a trust as divesting the truster of his right in the property: though the legal title will pass to the trustees, the nature of the truster's (beneficial) right is such that he will remain entitled to revoke the trust (as will his creditors). As Lord McLaren put it in *Byre's Trs.* v. *Gemmell*:

"A trust for the administration of the granter's affairs in his lifetime, including the payment of his debts, does not divest the granter. Notwithstanding the execution of such a deed, he retains the radical beneficial interest in his estate. He may revoke the deed at pleasure, or may even without noticing the trust make an effectual destination of his property to heirs or legatees."[3]

[1] See Chap. 12
[2] See Chap. 2.
[3] (1895) 23 R. 332 at p. 337.

However, for any other *inter vivos* trust the question of whether it is irrevocable is determined by the satisfaction of all of the following conditions. Failure to satisfy any of these conditions results in the trust remaining revocable.

1. Property must have passed

A trust will remain revocable until such time as property in the trust estate has passed from the truster to the trustees. The issue of passing property is considered more fully in Chapter 4, but it is appropriate here to quote a warning given by Lord President Clyde in *Scott* v. *Scott*. He said, "the divestiture must be genuine and not simulate. An *ex facie* absolute disposition with a back bond or other reservation behind it will not do."[4]

At the time of the passing of property, it is essential that the truster was solvent, "because if he was not the alienation to his trustees may be reduced at the instance of his creditors."[5] Insolvency of the truster would not entitle the truster himself to revoke the trust, but it would render the trust reducible, and in that sense revocable, at the instance of the creditors.

2. Beneficiaries must exist

Until such time as there are ascertained beneficiaries in the trust, who are different from the truster, the trust is merely one for administration and is, as explained above, revocable by the truster, who may recall the trust as a useless administrative encumbrance whenever he pleases. For example a trust for future children will be revocable until a child is born. In *Watt* v. *Watson*[6] a woman set up a trust with the income from the estate going to herself and her husband, and the fee being held for the children of the marriage. The First Division held that until such time as children were born to the marriage, the woman (with the consent of her husband) could revoke the deed.

It follows that a trust may start out as revocable and then become irrevocable (*e.g.* by the birth of beneficiaries); or it may be irrevocable and then become revocable (*e.g.* by the death of beneficiaries).[7]

---

[4] 1930 S.C. 903 at p. 914.
[5] Enc. 24. 61.
[6] (1897) 24 R. 330.
[7] See Enc. 24. 62.

3. The beneficiaries must have a beneficial interest

A trust is irrevocable only after the beneficiaries have obtained a beneficial interest in the trust property, that is an interest that will give them title to enforce the trust against the trustees and against the granter.[8] This beneficial interest will clearly be conferred when the beneficiaries take a vested right in the trust property; but vesting is by no means essential and beneficiaries may enjoy a beneficial interest even before then. For example the potential beneficiaries in a discretionary trust will not have vested rights to the trust property, but they will have a beneficial interest in the sense of having title to enforce the trust. Similarly if vesting is postponed by a contingency being attached to a legacy (such as, for example, that the beneficiary attains a certain age) the trust may be immediately irrevocable if the contingent beneficiary has acquired a beneficial interest. A beneficial interest is obtained whenever the trustees are obliged to maintain the trust estate for the benefit of the beneficiaries, even though the beneficiaries have no right to demand immediate possession. It will be common for example in accumulation and maintenance trusts for a beneficiary to be entitled to the trust funds only on attaining a specified age. They may have no right to obtain the trust funds before attaining the specified age, but they will have a right to benefit, legally enforceable against the trustees (and thus the trust will be irrevocable). They may acquire a beneficial interest even although the contingency may never occur (*e.g.* they may die before attaining the specified age). However if the contingency is such that it may never occur *and* there is no date on which it must become certain that it will never occur, no beneficial interest will be conferred; otherwise the trustees might be obliged to wait in perpetuity. The beneficiary in such a case would obtain only a *spes successionis*, or hope of succeeding (and thus the trust will remain revocable). For example in *Bulkeley–Gavin's Trs.*[9] a benefit was contingent on the wholesale nationalisation of land in Britain: it was held that this was no more than a revocable trust for administration.

4. The truster must intend the deed to be irrevocable

In a sense this is the most important condition, for all the above must be satisfied compatibly with the intention of the truster

---

[8] *Per* Lord Blackburn in *Scott* v. *Scott*, 1930 S.C. 903 at p. 925.
[9] 1971 S.C. 209.

being that the trust is irrevocable. In order to determine the truster's intention the trust deed itself must be examined carefully, taking account of the language used, any stated motive, the nature of the instructions to the truster, and the nature of the deed itself. If the transfer is of the truster's whole estate, this is an indication (though not a conclusive one) that the truster does not intend the deed to take effect immediately, and that it therefore remains revocable.[10] It is to be borne in mind that if the trust is *inter vivos*, the court is likely to start off with the (rebuttable) presumption that a person will retain control of his own property until death (*i.e* that the trust will remain revocable during life).[11]

A declaration in the deed that it is to be irrevocable is a highly significant circumstance, but it can never be conclusive, for such a declaration may be inconsistent with the nature of the deed. For example, a testamentary deed may contain a declaration that it is irrevocable, but that declaration, like the rest of a testamentary deed, can itself normally[12] be revoked by the testator. According to Lord President Clyde,

> "when . . . the question as to the true intention and character of the investiture . . . is an open question, I cannot regard a declaration of irrevocability otherwise than as strong evidence of intention . . . It seems to me that, when the true intention of the deed . . . is otherwise *in dubio*, a declaration of irrevocability may be enough to tip the balance."[13]

It has been pointed out that, "there appears to have been no case in which a court has held that a provision in favour of existing beneficiaries was revocable where there was such a clause, although the cases show that it has usually not proceeded on this feature alone but has looked for other elements also pointing to irrevocability."[14] In *Dunnett* v. *Dunnett's Trs.*[15] a trust deed contained a clause of irrevocability, and some years later the truster purported to revoke the deed. She then sought declarator from the court that the deed was properly revoked, and Lord Stewart in the Outer House expressed willingness to grant such declarator. However in this case all the beneficiaries

---

[10] See Enc. 24. 64–69.
[11] Enc. 24.63; Mackenzie Stuart at p. 135. This reflects the presumption against donation in Scots law.
[12] This may not be the case in the unusual situation of joint Wills.
[13] In *Scott* v. *Scott*, 1930 S.C. 903 at p. 917.
[14] Enc. 24. 64.
[15] 1985 S.L.T. 382.

appeared to be willing to consent to the revocation of the trust, and the case is probably more properly considered to be one in which the terms of the trust were varied by the consent of all the beneficiaries, rather than being revoked by the truster.

A reserved power of revocation will conclusively show the truster's intention that the deed is to be revocable (except for alimentary provisions, upon which a revocability clause can have no effect).

TERMINATION OF THE TRUST

There are basically two parties who can terminate the trust: the trustees can do so by effectively carrying out the trust purposes and distributing the trust estate; and the beneficiaries may sometimes do so before the trust purposes are fulfilled. In either case, certain tax consequences will ensue.

Tax Point
The termination of a trust invariably has IHT implications, and, where trust assets include stocks and shares or heritage, it also has CGT implications. What these will be will depend upon the type of trust involved (see Chapter 2), whether the fulfilment of the trust purposes occurs by virtue of the death of a liferenter (when there will be a disposal of the trust fund for IHT purposes but an automatic tax-free revaluation of assets for CGT purposes), and who or what will be the recipient of the former trust property (so perhaps giving rise to the IHT "surviving spouse" or "charitable" exemption).

TERMINATION BY THE TRUSTEES: DISTRIBUTION

As a general principle, the trustees may terminate the trust in only one way: by the effectual carrying out of the purposes of the trust. The trustees cannot be compelled to denude office while there are trust purposes remaining unfulfilled, for their duty as protector of the estate requires that they retain control of the estate until the purposes are complete. The final completion of the trust is the distribution of the estate, either through the fulfilment of the purposes, or the passing over of the property to those entitled to it in the event of the purposes not being capable of fulfilment. The duty of distribution is therefore fundamental.

1. Duty to distribute properly

The trustees terminate the trust by distributing the trust property to those who are entitled to it under the terms of the trust deed.

The trust is not terminated by the distribution of the trust property, if that property is given to those who are not entitled to receive it. In that case the trust will continue, and the trustees' obligation remains as before: to pay the beneficiaries that to which they are entitled under the trust. Mackenzie Stuart states the principle thus:

> "Money paid by a trustee to the wrong beneficiary or creditor leaves him still liable to the right one; he is not discharged. He is held in law still to have the money, and he is bound not only to account for it but to do so with interest from the date when it was payable, although he may have acted in the utmost good faith in paying it to another person."[16]

The form that payment is to take is a matter that will be governed by the trust deed; and if there is no direction in the trust deed as to whether the beneficiaries are to take specific items, or cash sums, this is a matter for the discretion of the trustees whether to sell the property or to hand it over intact. The discretion must be exercised reasonably, one important factor to be borne in mind being the potential tax liabilities.

Tax Point
Generally, when trustees sell assets they are assessed to CGT at the appropriate rate on the realised chargeable gains with the deduction of the appropriate annual exemption. If instead they had transferred the same assets to the beneficiaries, they would be assessed to exactly the same amount of CGT, for they are taxed as if they had sold the asset for its market value (CGTA 1979, s.54). However, in some cases it is possible for the gain realised when trustees transfer an asset to a beneficiary to be "held over" until the beneficiary disposes of the asset himself. This can happen for example if the asset is a business asset, or farm land qualifying for the IHT agricultural relief or the trust is a discretionary trust or an accumulation and maintenance trust for children under 25 years (CGTA 1979, ss.126 and 147A).

If the trust is effectively completed and the trustees sell the assets the CGT liability will be calculated as if they had carried out the sale as agent for the beneficiaries, *i.e.* the individual beneficiary's circumstances will determine the rate of tax, availability of annual exemptions etc.[17]

The time of payment is likewise determined by the trust deed, and a failure to distribute the estate at the time directed by the truster will lead to liability on the part of the trustees: either to

---

[16] Mackenzie Stuart at p. 221.
[17] See *Cochrane & Anor.* v. *Inland Revenue* 49 T.C. 299 and *Inland Revenue* v. *Matthew's Exx.* [1984] S.T.C. 386 (a development land tax case where the issue was the same): both cases are discussed more fully by Scobbie & Reid, in "Testamentary Trustees and the Tax Man" (1985) 30 J.L.S. 62.

pay interest from the date the estate should have been distributed, or to make up any depreciation that the estate has suffered since that date.[18] It is to be noted that frequently trustees are given a discretion over when to pay out the trust estate. Like all other matters, this is a discretion that the trustees must exercise reasonably.

Tax Point
Trustees should be careful that they do not pass assets over to beneficiaries before the IHT due from the trust fund has been paid. Liability to IHT can arise for example by way of an "exit charge" from a discretionary trust, or in a trust formerly subject to a liferent where the liferenter has died and the trust fund falls to be aggregated for tax purposes with the liferenter's personal estate. The trustees are themselves primarily liable for any tax due (IHTA 1984, s.201) and they must therefore ensure that they retain sufficient funds to meet any such liability.

2. Liability for improper distribution

If trustees breach their trust by paying the estate to those not entitled to it, they are liable to the correct person for the full amount of their entitlement, whether beneficiary or creditor.[19] It follows that the trustees must interpret the trust deed carefully and must make such enquiries as are necessary in order to discover who is properly entitled to receive the trust estate. This liability to distribute the estate to the correct person is far stricter than the liability trustees are normally under in the administration of the trust. In other situations trustees are bound to exercise the care of the ordinary prudent man of business. For example while ingathering the estate at the commencement of the trust, trustees will be liable for mistakes that cause loss to the estate (and thus to the beneficiaries) only if these mistakes are such that no ordinary prudent man of business would have made them. However, distributing the estate is fundamentally different and the trustees' liability is far stricter: it is determined not by the trustees' fault but by the beneficiaries' entitlement.

Mackenzie Stuart[20] suggests that this strict liability is based on the simple duty to take reasonable care, but that the law recognises no justification in paying the trust estate away to the wrong person, because the trustees can and should always insist

---

[18] *Cross* v. *Cross' Trs.* (1919) 1 S.L.T. 167.
[19] *Lamond's Trs.* v. *Croom* (1871) 9 M. 662.
[20] Mackenzie Stuart at pp. 222/223.

that those who claim to be beneficiaries prove their entitlement. If they are in real doubt as to whom to pay the estate to, it is always open to the trustees to ask the court for directions. It has been held that, while there is doubt about a beneficiary's title, the trustees should withhold payment until the doubt is resolved. In *Corbidge* v. *Fraser*[21] a beneficiary's right to the income from a trust estate depended upon her divorce. To the trustees' knowledge an action for reduction of the divorce had been raised, and it was held that the trustees ought to have stopped paying her any benefit as soon as that action was raised. The doubt over the outcome meant that the rightful beneficiary to whom the trustees would need ultimately to make payment could not be ascertained, and therefore the trustees should have withheld payment until the doubt was resolved.[22]

3. Exceptions to liability for improper distribution

There are some limited circumstances in which the trustees may not be personally liable to pay to the correct beneficiaries if they have already paid away the estate to wrong beneficiaries.[23]

First, the payment may be made through a mistake in foreign law. Foreign law (which of course includes English law) is an issue of fact and it is regarded as not unreasonable for trustees to be ignorant of this fact.

Secondly, the payment may be made to someone who appeared to be directly entitled, but who had in fact assigned their rights to a third party. In this situation the third party is obliged to intimate the assignation to the trustees, and the trustees will not be liable for paying to the original beneficiary if they have received no such intimation. Of course if they have received intimation, they must act upon the assignation.

Thirdly, the person who should have been paid may be personally barred from claiming payment from the trustees. This would be the case if the trustees had made their mistake through the fault of the true beneficiary.

Fourthly, the trustees will not be liable to the correct beneficiaries if they no longer have possession of the estate because it has been stolen or embezzled. Trustees can escape liability in these circumstances only if they have taken reasonable care with the trust estate.

---

[21] (1915) 1 S.L.T. 67.
[22] See further, Mackenzie Stuart at pp. 228/229.
[23] Enc. 24. 209; Mackenzie Stuart at pp. 224–226.

Fifthly, statute[24] now provides that trustees will not be personally liable for distributing trust property without first having ascertained either (1) that no illegitimate person exists who is or may be entitled to benefit, or (2) that no illegitimate person exists, whose existence might affect who is entitled to benefit, or (3) that no paternal relative of an illegitimate person exists who is or may be entitled to benefit. Basically this relieves trustees of having to make enquiries about the existence or otherwise of illegitimate relationships that might affect who is entitled to receive the trust estate. Trustees cannot of course ignore illegitimate relationships of which they are aware, but they will not be personally liable if they distribute the estate in ignorance of them.

Further, under section 32 of the Trusts (Scotland) Act 1921 the court may relieve trustees of personal liability for any breach of trust if it appears to the court that the trustees have acted honestly and reasonably and ought fairly to be excused.[25] The failure to pay the correct beneficiary is a clear breach of trust, and this statutory relief will therefore be available in appropriate circumstances to mitigate the harshness of the trustees' otherwise absolute liability.[26]

4. Recovery of payments after improper distribution

If trustees do pay out the estate to those not entitled to it, they can claim it back under the *condictio indebiti*,[27] so long as the conditions for that action are satisfied[28]: basically the payment must be made through an error in fact and not in law. For example a mistake of identity may found the *condictio indebiti*, but a mistake in interpreting the trust deed will not.[29] Negligence or any fault on the part of the trustees will prevent this action being available.

[24] Section 7 of the Law Reform (Miscellaneous Provisions) (Scotland) Act 1968, as amended by the Law Reform (Parent & Child) (Scotland) Act 1986.

[25] See Chap. 10.

[26] See the English case of *Whittaker* v. *Bamford* [1914] 1 Ch. 1, which was decided under equivalent legislation.

[27] Enc. 24. 211; see also *Armour* v. *Glasgow Royal Infirmary* 1909 S.C. 916.

[28] See Walker, *Principles of Scottish Private Law*, 4th ed., W. Green, Edinburgh 1988, Vol. II, at pp. 507–508. For a discussion of the historical basis of this action and its limitations, see Birks, "Six Questions in Search of a Subject: Unjust Enrichment in a Crisis of Identity" 1985 J.R. 227.

[29] *Rowan's Trs.* v. *Rowan* 1940 S.C. 30.

PREMATURE TERMINATION BY THE BENEFICIARIES

While in the normal case the trust will be brought to an end by the trustees fulfilling the trust purposes and distributing the estate in accordance with the terms of the trust deed, there are some situations in which the trust can be brought to an end by the beneficiaries themselves, even when this would go against the terms and purposes of the trust.

1. Circumstances in which premature termination is possible

There are two major circumstances in which a trust can be prematurely terminated by the beneficiaries. The first is when the remaining purposes of the trust are merely administrative and the beneficiary has already acquired an unqualified vested right in the trust property. This principle is taken from the case of *Miller's Trs.* v. *Miller*.[30] Here, a truster left property in trust for his son, directing the trustees to administer the property until the son reached the age of 25 years. The trust deed however declared that the son was to obtain a vested right in the property on attaining the age of 25, or on his earlier marriage. He married before he was 25, and thereafter demanded that the trustees make over the trust property to him. A Court of Seven Judges held that when a vested, unqualified and indefeasible right of fee is given to a beneficiary of full age, he is entitled to payment of the trust property notwithstanding any direction to the trustees to retain and administer the capital for any longer period.[31] On obtaining the fee the son had acquired as much right to the property as the truster himself had had, and the court refused to maintain a trust that was merely for the management of the property, if this was against the wishes of the person with the full and unqualified right to the fee. Lord McLaren said this:

> "It seems to me to be not only an unsound proposition in law, but a logical impossibility, that a person should have an estate in fee, and that some other person should at the same time have the power of withholding it."[32]

Effectively, such a trust becomes a trust for administration when the vested indefeasible right is acquired (and thus is subject to the tax regime of trusts for administration[33]).

---

[30] (1890) 18 R. 301.
[31] See also *Yuill's Trs.* v. *Thomson* (1902) 4 F. 815.
[32] (1890) 18 R. 301 at pp. 310/311.
[33] See Chap. 2.

The principle in *Miller's Trs.* v. *Miller* can only apply when there is no trust purpose to be fulfilled other than the administration of the estate for the benefit of the fiar. For until such time as the other trust purposes are carried out, the wishes of the beneficiary are subordinate to those of the truster.[34]

The second situation in which a trust can be prematurely terminated by the beneficiaries—and this will apply even where there are trust purposes other than administrative ones to be fulfilled—is when all the beneficiaries and potential beneficiaries consent to it. This is really an application of the principle discussed in Chapter 12, whereby a private trust may be varied if all the beneficiaries and potential beneficiaries consent to that variation. The trustees will be bound to accept the variation, and likewise they will be bound to accept the termination and so be obliged to denude themselves of the trust estate in accordance with the wishes of the beneficiaries. The trustees cannot resist the wishes of the beneficiaries on the ground that termination would be against the terms or purposes of the trust, nor even that it would not be in the best interests of the beneficiaries to terminate on the terms proposed.[35] As with variation, all those who are entitled to consent must have the legal capacity to do so, by which is meant that they must be fully capax adults. Minor beneficiaries cannot terminate a trust one of the purposes of which is their protection. Difficulties arise in relation to contingent rights of unborn issue, who may also have to consent. The court may consent on their behalf under section 1(1) of the Trusts (Scotland) Act 1961[36]; alternatively, if the possibility of issue being born is remote, insurance can be taken out against the possibility of their being able to claim benefit.[37]

2. Exceptions

There are two main exceptions to the principle that beneficiaries may prematurely terminate the trust.[38] First, the termination must not prejudice the trustees in the proper administration of the trust. If it does so, the trustees will be entitled to refuse to denude in favour of the beneficiaries. In *De Robeck* v. *Inland*

---

[34] (1890) 18 R. 301 at p. 305, *per* Lord President Inglis.
[35] Enc. 24. 70.
[36] See Chap. 12.
[37] As for example in *McPherson's Trs.* v. *Hill* (1902) 4 F. 921; see also Mackenzie Stuart at pp. 351/352.
[38] Mackenzie Stuart at p. 346.

Revenue[39] the trustees had arranged to pay estate duty in 16 half-yearly instalments. The House of Lords held that they were entitled to maintain the trust until the estate duty was paid off and they themselves were free of any further liability.[40]

Tax Point

The approach taken by the House of Lords in *De Robeck* would be even more likely to be followed today if trustees were to arrange to pay IHT in 10 yearly instalments. Under estate duty, heritable property was specifically burdened with an estate duty charge for 20 years after death unless clearance from further tax liabilities was obtained from the Inland Revenue. Under IHT there is no equivalent charge on land in Scotland: hence if trustees transferred land to a beneficiary while some instalments of IHT was outstanding, the trustees could be exposed if, for example, the beneficiary went bankrupt.

Similarly, trustees would require to make provision for tax liability where a liferent ceases while the liferenter is alive, for if the ex-liferenter were thereafter to die within seven years he or she would be treated as if he or she had made a lifetime chargeable transfer which could result in the trustees being assessed to IHT.

However it should be noted that if trustees do not wind up the trust only because of a potential IHT liability which could fall on them, any subsequent sale of a trust asset will be treated as if made by the beneficiary entitled thereto (CGTA 1979, s.46(2): see also n.17 above).

Mackenzie Stuart suggests that, "whether administrative arrangements made by trustees will entitle them to refuse to denude when all the beneficiaries concur in making the demand will depend on the circumstances of each case"[41]; and it has further been suggested that "where all the beneficiaries, including those who would suffer prejudice if the adminstrative arrangements were to be disrupted, concur in making the demand, it would seem that the trustees have no right to refuse to give effect to it."[42] It would be a fair position for the law to adopt that trustees may refuse the demands of the beneficiaries to terminate the trust only when this will cause the trustees themselves some detriment: this situation is unlikely to arise often.

The second exception to termination by the beneficiaries is that it must not interfere with the protection of any alimentary rights created by the truster. This is an application of the general principle that alimentary provisions, once created, cannot be renounced by the beneficiary, and this exception, like the general principle, must now be read in the light of the court's power to

---

[39] 1928 S.C. (H.L.) 34.
[40] See, esp. Viscount Dunedin at p. 41.
[41] Mackenzie Stuart at p. 346/347.
[42] Enc. 24. 70.

authorise variation of alimentary provisions under section 1(4) of the Trusts (Scotland) Act 1961.

DISCHARGE

Trustees who carry out their functions under the trust properly and are not in breach of trust are entitled, on their ceasing to be trustees, to be discharged from any future potential liability arising from the trust, and they may refuse to pay out the trust estate or to give up office until such time as a discharge in their favour is granted. Each trustee is individually entitled to a discharge, though a single discharge in favour of all the trustees is competent, indeed common. The effect of a discharge is to protect the trustees in whose favour it is given from any claim that may arise from their previous intromissions with the trust estate and any future or contingent claims that subsequently arise. This could include trust obligations that give rise to personal liability (such as an obligation to pay any benefit to the beneficiaries) as well as liability for breach of trust. "The discharge is primarily a protection to the trustees against personal liability to account to the beneficiaries."[43] The discharge also protects any intromissions it covers from challenge by the beneficiaries. On receiving a discharge covering their own liabilities, trustees will be bound to denude of the trust estate. The discharge is however restricted to those intromissions intended to be covered (*i.e.* known to the party granting the discharge).[44]

It is therefore important for the trustees that they obtain a discharge and the trust cannot truly be considered at an end until such time as the discharge is granted. Trustees are however entitled to be discharged only from liabilities to which they are personally subject, and so they cannot, for example, refuse to denude the trust estate until their predecessors in office have been discharged.[45]

The method of discharge, and who may grant it,[46] may be laid down in the trust deed, but in the absence of any such provision the discharge may generally be granted by any of three different categories of person: the beneficiaries, the co-trustees, and the court.

---

[43] Mackenzie Stuart at p. 343.
[44] *Johnstone* v. *Mackenzie's Trs.*, 1911 S.C. 321.
[45] *Mackenzie's Ex.* v. *Thomson's Trs.*, 1965 S.C. 154.
[46] Anyone, including those who are not beneficiaries, may be given the power to grant a discharge, *e.g.* parents of minor beneficiaries.

The usual situation is that the discharge will be granted by the beneficiaries. A beneficiary of a specific item less than the whole estate need only provide a simple receipt, and that will be sufficient discharge for the payment of his benefit. The receipt need not be probative. A beneficiary of a whole estate, or of the residue of an estate will on the other hand be obliged to grant a much fuller discharge, covering not only the payment of his benefit, but also the ongoing administration for which the trustee is responsible. This distinction is justified on the ground that the payment of a specific legacy is in the nature of a payment of a debt, while transfer of the whole estate involves administration from which the trustees are entitled to be exonerated.[47] A discharge when the trust is being wound up will be far more extensive than a discharge granted during its running. Again, however, it need not be and usually is not probative. There may however be circumstances in which trustees would feel safer with a formal discharge.

On the resignation of a trustee, he may obtain a discharge from the beneficiaries in terms of the above paragraph, but he may also obtain a discharge from the remaining trustees. Section 4(g) of the Trusts (Scotland) Act 1921 provides that unless it is at variance with the terms or purposes of the trust,[48] there will be read into each trust deed a provision allowing co-trustees to grant a discharge to any individual trustee who has resigned, or to his representatives if he has died. Such a discharge will have the same force and effect as one granted by the beneficiaries, though as Mackenzie Stuart points out, "the power given to trustees to discharge resigning trustees and representatives of deceased trustees does not deprive the beneficiaries of their right to challenge any such discharge if it should not have been granted."[49]

Where a trustee has resigned or has died, and he or his representatives cannot obtain a discharge for his acts and intro-missions from the remaining trustees, for whatever reason, and where the beneficiaries refuse or for some reason are unable to grant a discharge, section 18 of the 1921 Act allows the Court of Session to grant a discharge instead. This is a discretionary power of the Court, which will make any such inquiry as may be thought necessary before granting the petition. A petition is competent only when the trustee who resigns or who has died cannot

---

[47] Enc. 24. 215; *Davidson's Trs.* v. *Cooper* (1895) 3 S.L.T. 28.
[48] See further, Chap. 7.
[49] At p. 345.

otherwise obtain a discharge. This section may be used in cases of doubt as to whether the trustees are actually entitled to discharge.[50]

Once the discharge is granted, the trustees are protected from any future liability under the trust, and their intromissions are not open to challenge. However, trustees can be made liable and their intromissions can be challenged if the discharge itself is first reduced.[51] "The beneficiary, when granting a discharge, is only bound by it if he has all the facts before him or deliberately waives all enquiries, and he must know what he is doing."[52] If for example a discharge is granted in ignorance of legal rights, it may be reduced.[53] Likewise, the discharge may be reduced on the ground of fraud, collusion, misrepresentation or essential error.[54] In *Hastie's J.F.* v. *Morham's Exx.*[55] the First Division suggested that a discharge which had been granted by the wrong person could easily be reduced. One wonders whether indeed an action for reduction of such a piece of "waste paper"[56] would be necessary: effectively, there is nothing to reduce. It should be pointed out that, so long as the trustee being discharged takes care to ensure that he is entitled to be discharged, and that the discharge is given by persons entitled to do so, the chances of its being reduced are remote.

The discharge ends the trustees' liabilities under the trust: as such it acts as the true and final termination of the trust. It is only after the trustees have received a full and valid discharge that one can properly say that the trust, like this book, is at an end.

---

[50] Mackenzie Stuart at p. 342.
[51] *Campbell* v. *Montgomery* (1822) 1 S. 484; *Mayne* v. *McKeand* (1835) 13 S. 870; *Macpherson* v. *Macpherson* (1841) 3 D. 1242.
[52] Mackenzie Stuart at p. 345.
[53] *Dickson* v. *Halbert* (1854) 16 D. 586.
[54] Enc. 24. 218.
[55] 1951 S.C. 668.
[56] *Per* Lord President Cooper *ibid.*, at p. 677.

INDEX

207